On Streisand

On Streisand
An Opinionated Guide

Ethan Mordden

OXFORD
UNIVERSITY PRESS

OXFORD
UNIVERSITY PRESS

Oxford University Press is a department of the University of Oxford.
It furthers the University's objective of excellence in research, scholarship,
and education by publishing worldwide. Oxford is a registered trade mark of
Oxford University Press in the UK and certain other countries.

Published in the United States of America by Oxford University Press
198 Madison Avenue, New York, NY 10016, United States of America.

Library of Congress Cataloging-in-Publication Data

Names: Mordden, Ethan, author.
Title: On Streisand : an opinionated guide / Ethan Mordden.
Description: New York City : Oxford University Press, 2019. |
Includes bibliographical references and index.
Identifiers: LCCN 2018033525 (print) | LCCN 2018035027 (ebook) |
ISBN 9780190651787 (epub) | ISBN 9780190651770 (updf) | ISBN 9780190931322
(oso) | ISBN 9780190651763 (cloth : alk. paper)
Subjects: LCSH: Streisand, Barbra—Criticism and interpretation.
Classification: LCC ML420.S915 (ebook) | LCC ML420.S915 M67 2019 (print) |
DDC 782.42164092—dc23
LC record available at https://lccn.loc.gov/2018033525

Illustrations courtesy of the Billy Rose Collection, The New York Public Library for
the Performing Arts, Astor, Lenox, and Tilden Foundations; and private collections.
A few sentences about *On a Clear Day You Can See Forever* first appeared on the
author's blog, Cultural Advantages, on October 30, 2016.

3 5 7 9 8 6 4 2

Printed by Sheridan Books, Inc.
United States of America

CONTENTS

ACKNOWLEDGMENTS

To my sublimely tactful agent, Joe Spieler; to helpful friends Matt Callaway, Jon Cronwell, Ken Mandelbaum, and Erick Neher; at Oxford, to the ever-ready Joellyn Ausanka and to Dominic McHugh; and to my splendid editor, Norman Hirschy.

STREISAND'S CHRONOLOGY

1942 Barbara Joan Streisand born, in Brooklyn, New York, to be educated in public schools through graduation from Erasmus Hall High. Her father dies in her infancy, and her mother, Diana, takes up with Louis Kind, a stepfather out of a crummy fairy tale, verbally abusing BJS when not ignoring her altogether.

1957 and 1960 BJS has a taste of professional acting in upstate New York in summer stock, first interning at the Malden Bridge Playhouse, then turning professional at the Cecilwood Playhouse.

1960 Determined to become an actress, BJS nevertheless takes an informal course in The Great American Songbook, learning repertory from actor Barry Dennen (her first lover) and arranger-accompanist Peter Daniels. Dennen tapes Streisand's vocals—from Harold Arlen to Walt Disney Silly Symphony—and keeps the tapes when the couple breaks up.

1960–1961 BJS introduces her song act in increasingly major New York clubs—the grungy Lion, the spiffy Bon Soir, the prestigious Blue Angel—meanwhile emphasizing the unique in respelling her first name. Barbra: the only one.

1961–1963 BJS enjoys a pride of notable television appearances, from Mike Douglas' afternoon talk show to prime-time slots such as *The Judy Garland Show*, where the two are joined by Broadway's belter-in-chief, Ethel Merman, in a now-fabled belt-off. Overall, the TV exposure reveals not only BJS's talent but also her independence.On *PM East*, empaneled with producer David Susskind, BJS bluntly recalls how, in his agent days, he rudely blew off an appointment with her. In a much-quoted line, virtually a mission statement, she asks—tells—the stupefied Susskind, "I scare you, don't I? I'm so far out, I'm in."[1]

1962 BJS's Broadway debut, in *I Can Get It For You Wholesale*. She becomes personally involved with the leading man, Elliott Gould, though they don't marry till 1963 (and will divorce in 1971).

1962 BJS signs with what is to be her lifelong label, Columbia Records. More independence: the contract gives her complete artistic control.

1963 BJS is *Cue Magazine*'s Entertainer of the Year, a mark of absolute national prominence.

1964 More magazine covers: *Time* and *Newsweek* run BJS on their covers in recognition of her tour de force in *Funny Girl*, her second and final Broadway show. The ideal showcase, *Funny Girl* gives BJS a new-star-in-town triumph almost unprecedented in theatre history, comparable to the excitement created by Jeanne Eagels in the straight play *Rain* (1922), one of the few performances that can truly be termed legendary.

1966– As BJS's recordings and solo television specials appear, she resists catering to the news media in the traditional show-biz manner, provoking a media fury that haunts her from then on. Rex Reed's hit piece in the *New York Times* is typical, calling her "Barbra the terrible—rude, arrogant, anything but a lady."[2] Years later, he apologizes. BJS: "I had more respect for him when he hated me."[3]

1966 Jason Emmanuel Gould, BJS's only child, is born.

1967 *A Happening in Central Park*, a free concert before 135,000 people, expands BJS's popularity on the national scene when most of it is televised a year later. The trash carted away during the four days after the concert takes in a Scrabble game, a Merry Widow corset, a Russian-English dictionary, a sterling-silver ice bucket, and the usual discarded unmentionables without which these events would be incomplete.

1968–1970 BJS's first three movies are musicals, and *Funny Girl* wins her the Best Actress Oscar; Streisand's first words are "Hello, Gorgeous,"[4] her opening line from *Funny Girl* on both stage and screen. Her fourth film is a non-musical, bringing her closer to her determination to act rather than sing. The recordings, however, keep coming.

1969 With Paul Newman and Sidney Poitier (later joined by Steve McQueen and Dustin Hoffman), BJS forms First Artists, to produce movies as she produces her records, with complete artistic control. Again, independence is the key concern. The outfit lasts for some ten years, yielding twenty-three films, three with BJS.

1969–1970 With new folk- and Beatles-influenced pop writing overwhelming the traditional American Songbook, BJS attempts to adopt current styles, first in the unpersuasive *What About Today?*, then in the happily conclusive *Stoney End*. "I don't feel it," BJS says at first. "It isn't me."[5] Me is Rodgers and Hart, Harold Arlen, and—the caption for this upheaval in pop music— "As Time Goes By." Still, the change in repertory, from *What About Today?*'s sometimes stark or gritty numbers to a more lyrical pop sound on *Stoney End*, creates a wedding of singer and song. Suddenly, it's me.

1971–1973 Filming *The Touch* with his usual players and, *als Gast*, Elliott Gould, Ingmar Bergman meets BJS and is struck by a thought: a movie version of *The Merry Widow* starring BJS. Bergman has enjoyed a whopping hit staging the operetta in 1954 in Malmö, Sweden, and now seeks to preserve his vision of the piece, though how BJS will negotiate a role for a classically trained soprano is anyone's guess. Still, here is a rare chance for BJS to appear in a film by a universally acknowledged High Maestro of the art. But she requests script revisions, and Bergman abruptly terminates the project.

1973 BJS makes *The Way We Were*, the ultimate glamour-star film, with Robert Redford. A thorny romance about two strong personalities who must part because of incongruent worldviews, it is sabotaged when its director, panicking after an unappreciated preview, cuts out the movie's political content. Yet it remains one of BJS's great roles, the first to exploit her versatility.

1973–1984 Hair-salon entrepreneur Jon Peters partners BJS. In an apparent surrender of her hard-won independence, she brings Peters into her career as both recording and film producer. This is the time of *ButterFly*, BJS's least impressive disc, and of *A Star Is Born*, a critical fiasco but her highest-grossing movie to this point. The word goes out in Hollywood: "Shoot Streisand singing six numbers and we'll make sixty million,"[6] regardless of the quality of the film itself.

1979–1981 *Barbra Quarterly*, an elaborately produced color magazine, is devoted to the Streisand mythos, a manifestation of the power of show-biz stardom in America.

1983–2012 BJS auteurs and stars in *Yentl*, the most independent—and personal—of all her projects, an obsession she has nurtured for more than ten years. Later, *The Prince Of Tides* and *The Mirror Has Two Faces* affirm BJS's gifts as a director, though establishment Hollywood resists supporting her. Because she's a woman? Because she has never played the flatterbox with the giveme-givemes? You choose. Later movie jobs, except for her excellent performance in the difficult *Nuts*, fail to arouse enthusiasm.

1985 *The Broadway Album* marks Streisand's return to the repertory she started with, featuring songs by Jerome Kern, the Gershwins, Rodgers and Hammerstein, Frank Loesser, and, especially, Stephen Sondheim. He supplies new lyrics to change the autobiographical subtext of "Putting It Together" from his story to hers, to show how BJS's artistic control of her albums doesn't protect her from interference by Columbia's suits.

1986 BJS returns to live performance in *One Voice*, on the grounds of her Malibu estate, with a small band and guest second voice Barry Gibb, as a benefit for political causes. Admission, at $5,000 a couple, is limited to 500 seats, and the program emphasizes BJS's standards, from "People" to "Evergreen." HBO tapes the concert, which then goes to home video.

1986–1996 BJS holds an option on Larry Kramer's AIDS play *The Normal Heart*. This is in effect Kramer's *Yentl*, a highly personal work, and Streisand collaborates with Kramer on the screenplay. But these two highly self-directed egos clash, and after ten years Streisand allows the option to lapse as she prepares to direct and star in the romantic comedy *The Mirror Has Two Faces*. In a *Variety* interview, Kramer complains that "she was all set to make [a film] about a worldwide plague, and … switches to a film about a woman who gets a face-lift."[7] Feeling betrayed, BJS announces that she "will no longer be involved with the project."[8]

1993–1994 BJS makes her first live singing appearance to the general public in twenty-one years, in Las Vegas. She then takes the show on tour, to England, California, and New York. The net is some $60 million, not counting supplemental earnings from an HBO special.

1998 After a career decorated with romantic liaisons, with Pierre Trudeau, Don Johnson, Andre Agassi, ice-cream mogul Richard Baskin, and others, BJS marries for only the second time. The groom is television and movie actor James Brolin.

1999 On the New Year's Eve of the predicted Y2K calamity power glitch, BJS gives the *Timeless* concert, in Las Vegas. Attendees are presented with thin little red-and-white flashlights bearing a silver commemorative seal, just in case.

2003 In a celebrated escapade, BJS appears on Oprah Winfrey's show, a
      gala confrontation (not for the first time, either) of the two most
      powerful women in America. Streisand wins, with a blitz of her
      beloved white. She's dressed in it up to the turtleneck, she sings
      "Smile" backed by stills of her late little white dog, she brings on
      her new little white Coton de Tuléar puppy, and then reveals that
      she had Oprah's staff paint her mic white.

2003 BJS inadvertently gives birth to a concept that becomes a thing:
      the Streisand Effect. This describes an attempt to deflect attention
      (here from an aerial photograph of her Malibu estate, part of a
      series of more than 10,000 such shots of the California coastline)
      that ends only in attracting attention. Few have seen the picture in
      question till Streisand's complaint; it then goes viral.

2012–the present BJS plans a new film adaptation of *Gypsy*, starring as
      Madam Rose. But no studio backs the project; the meme of
      "Streisand singing six numbers" may no longer guarantee a huge
      profit. In 2017, on National Public Radio, when asked about current
      projects, BJS speaks of two subjects, the young Catherine the Great
      of Russia and the *Life* photographer Margaret Bourke-White. Still,
      the mythos of youth and independence yields to the autumn of lost
      time and missed opportunities. Madam Rose, which might have
      been BJS's greatest movie role in something like 1990, is apparently
      never to be.

On Streisand

An Introduction to Streisand's Life and Work

I became a singer," she has famously said, "because I couldn't get a job as an actor."[9]

The two vocations, separately and together, have characterized her career. Streisand started as a singer, but within a short time she was on Broadway, acting and singing, and her movie work (in straight drama, comedy, and musicals) has coexisted with her vocal discs all the way along. On the other hand, none of her movies is thought to stand in the top class of American cinema, while she is arguably the greatest popular singer America has ever produced.

It was a rough childhood, as so often with artists: a father who died in her infancy, an older brother, a mother of too limited cultural background to understand her daughter's talent and drive, a much younger half-sister, and a loathsome stepfather who finally abandoned the family during Streisand's early teens. It was Brooklyn; it was the mid-1950s; it was a working-class world in which young people with a yen to break out of this quotidien normality were discouraged as a rule. On the *Inside the Actors Studio* television show on March 21, 1994, Streisand recalled her mother's insisting that her daughter give up her show-business ambitions and take a steady job as an office typist—the reason, Streisand then joked, she grew her famous fingernails, as long as Turandot's. She couldn't type, so she had to become a performer.

Some parents are like that. It's not because they somehow can't imagine the excitement in embarking on a career in the arts. Nor is it about financial security, though they pretend it is. It's because they don't like you, and your dreams of joining the leadership class of unique individuals irritate them. They say they want you happy, but they don't. They want you under their control.

No amount of success will persuade them that you made the right life's choice, either. When Streisand won the Best Actress Oscar for *Funny Girl* (in a tie with Katharine Hepburn, highly exclusive company), all her mother cared about was her attire. True, Streisand was in an outlandish pantsuit with a vaguely see-through quality. But it's not about a dress, mom. It's about winning the Oscar.

Thus, Streisand had to summon up her self-belief all on her own. It's a challenge many fail to meet, creating instead unstable defenses that impede their ability to succeed. However, Streisand created a defense of simple determination that was leading her forward even in high school. Legend tells us that the teenaged Streisand was already cultivating the highly nonconformist image she became known for, but her biographer Randall Riese tracked down a few of Streisand's classmates and faculty at Erasmus Hall, and they affirm Riese's view of the young Streisand as a more or less typical high-school kid—smart, able, and pleasant.

She was in choral club, not surprisingly. Yet not a single one of the many Streisand books records her as having taken part in any dramatics. This is all but unbelievable considering that Streisand was already determined to get into acting.* But then, Streisand may have avoided school plays because she was already a professional, having interned at fifteen in summer stock and, three years later, played Hortense in *The Boy Friend* at salary. It was just a supporting role, as the maid at the Villa Caprice, a French finishing school for young ladies of rank. But Hortense has the first moments of the show to herself and even gets a song, "It's Nicer In Nice."

So Streisand was, to put it lightly, On Her Way. And she had mentors, first of all actor Barry Dennen, who introduced her to the golden age of popular song, in recordings by Ethel Waters, Libby Holman, Billie Holiday, Mabel Mercer, and even Charles Trenet. A sort of latter-day Maurice Chevalier, Trenet toyed with as much as delivered the music, in a dualistic style that managed to dwell within the song while standing apart from it—a quality Streisand herself would occasionally use, especially in comic

---

* In my long-ago days as a music director on off-Broadway and in the regions, I worked with one actor who had gone to Erasmus Hall with Streisand. He mentioned having appeared in the school's production of the twenties musical *Good News!*, playing Beef (a football ace and bully) opposite Streisand as Babe (a sarcastic man-chaser who lives on the edge, at least as twenties musical comedy knows the edge). This actor was burly and vaguely menacing, Streisand was born to play Babe, and *Good News!* was at this time the most performed musical on the American high-school circuit. It's a persuasive recollection, but one unfortunately without a shred of backup evidence.

numbers. Thus, Streisand doesn't "become" Second Hand Rose, though the piece was written to be sung autobiographically. Instead, Streisand observes Rose at a remove, singing inside scare quotes. It's supposed to be a lament—poor Rose gets nothing but hand-me-downs—yet Streisand makes it merry. However, in more dramatic solos, Streisand does the opposite and personifies the lyrics. In the torch song "Cry Me a River," we hear how she feels about the lover who abandoned her—Dennen himself, according to their friends at the time, for the two had become intimate. This isn't "woe is me" torch; this is revenge torch. As a Dennen-Streisand confidant told Streisand biographer James Spada, "She's not acting in that song, she's *feeling* it."[10]

The singers on Dennen's records were feeling it, too, contradicting the prevailing pop-singing style of the 1950s, which favored an above all smooth delivery—expressive, to be sure, but avoiding extremes. The long-playing discs had replaced the 78 as recently as 1948, so everyone was enjoying the novelty of listening to recorded music without having to get up and change the disc after three or four minutes. So the vocal recital became useful as background music, whether for tête-à-têtes or a bustling party: singing that promised no distraction. Performers thus had to oblige with renditions as even as cream. Think of Doris Day, Jo Stafford, Gordon MacRae: wonderful music-makers but not music-actors. Their torch didn't slash with anger; their comic novelties were lighthearted rather than zany.

So Dennen's discs showed the young Streisand how much she could get out of a song—as long as she broke away from the style of the day and probed a song's meaning. There was something behind the notes, inside the words, and she had to tear the material apart and put it back together *personally*, liberating her feelings as she swept through the melody and the verbal cues. Day, Stafford, and MacRae had a good relationship with their numbers, no more. Streisand, however, created a boundary tension between her songs and herself.

Further, Streisand's first steady accompanist, Peter Daniels, let her adapt each number to her own uses in purely musical terms, to sing not straight off the sheet music but in unique arrangements. And there was an acting coach, Allan Miller, and a manager, Martin Erlichman, who forged Streisand's early career. He got her from humdrum gigs to Columbia Records, from Broadway to Hollywood, and on from there to now (with one long, unhappy break which we will learn about presently). All four men contributed to Streisand's first public manifestations, in what she did and how she did it.

However, Streisand knew how to present herself as a personality without help from others. She preferred—insisted upon—the offbeat. Her dress revived the castoff finery of vanished eras, the kind of thing found on the rack in New York's plentiful line of thrift shops. Bob Schulenberg, an early Streisand associate, told James Spada that the first time Schulenberg met Streisand she was wearing "a new cherry-red velvet skirt...chocolate-brown nylon stockings and gold-lamé and red satin strap 1927 shoes. Her top was a gold, silver, and cherry-red brocade with big square-cut Elizabethan sleeves." The accessories—necklaces, bracelets, and earring—were all glass. Schulenberg concluded with "She looked like a weird *Vogue* illustration from the twenties. I was *fascinated*."[11]

Matching this was Streisand's verbal tone, not the suave and accommodating approach recommended to on-the-rise talent but a jokey, sarcastic, mock-feisty Brooklyn rap. Or there was the drolly fantastical element in Streisand's early biographical blurbs ("Born in Madagascar...") or simply dropping the redundant "a" in her given name. It was all part of the Streisand act, one might say, except it reflected her worldview as it was while her colleagues were trying to fit into the categories that show business tries to impose on newcomers—bewildered maiden, manly sweetheart, cagey sidekick, and so on, going all the way back to the Victorians and their Singing Chambermaid and Heavy Father. Producers (and others with ultimate power) don't like original talent until these originals somehow break through as forces of nature. Then these same producers genuflect before the originals and try to order up imitations.

Defying the norms can sabotage one's advance, but Streisand's singing made her, to some, irresistible—and certain of those autocratic producers found her unpredictable patter engaging. When local television stations started *PM East* (in New York) and *PM West* (in Los Angeles) to rival *The Tonight Show*, then hosted by Jack Paar, in the same time slot, there was no chance they could compete with his model in terms of big-name talent. (It was not a question of money, because Paar paid scale; it was the national exposure he could offer his guests.) However, *PM East*'s host, Mike Wallace, and his team were smart enough to look for out-of-the-way company. "We needed something alive, human,"[12] the show's executive producer, Mert Koplin, told another Streisand biographer, René Jordan. This show wanted to avoid the canned show-biz palaver and go for personalities with tang.

And that, truly, was Streisand, "though," Koplin recalled, "she was wearing a basic burlap bag and looked like a disreputable Judith Anderson."[13] Still, her chat was ingenuous, so far from the practiced schmooze of *The Tonight Show* that it could be called crazy. And her singing was a wonderful shock to those who didn't already know how good she was.

One night, Wallace raised the question of Streisand's purse, which, he said, she had dropped. One of the show's staff had retrieved it, and Wallace was curious about all the keys found inside. There was the sum of thirty cents in it as well:

STREISAND (comically): It *better* have thirty cents in it.[14]

But the keys, she explained, let her into various apartments and offices where she could crash, as she didn't have a fixed abode (except her mother's place in Brooklyn, to which death would be preferable). Yes, she was quite open about it. And then, said Wallace, "They're telling us from the control room...that they'd like another song,"[15] and at the piano Peter Daniels had already started the intro.

To "Moon River." The theme song of the *Breakfast At Tiffany's* movie, a Johnny Mercer lyric on Henry Mancini's melody, it showed Streisand's gifts as what used to be called a "jazz singer," with a free elaboration of the written notes, plenty of back-phrasing, a slight touch of wailing, and an overall sense of improvisation to give the listener the feeling that the vocalist is reformatting his or her interpretation to suit the mood of the moment.*

Streisand was then nineteen years old, and where she derived her technical command is a mystery. (Some of the very greatest opera singers, too, such as Rosa Ponselle and Franco Corelli, did not complete conventional academic vocal study.) Barry Dennen opened up her repertory and Peter Daniels may have revealed to her the musical structure of a number. But this "Moon River"—and all the other specialties of Streisand's early catalogue, from the wistful "A Sleepin' Bee" to her jiving "Lover, Come Back To Me"—give us a vocalist who owes nothing to the many singers Dennen played for her. Streisand's approach is comparable to theirs only in its freedom. This is a style rather than a method, a theorem that can't be proved.

Perhaps it's comparable to the way Streisand avoided the mellow emptiness, the studied flatterbox charm of show-biz chit-chat in her *PM East* talk segments: she didn't know how to converse about nothing. Those keys in her purse were how she was living then, a vagabond toting a folding cot.

---

* Jazz singers of the early-middle 1900s, both black (such as Hazel Scott) and white (such as Ella Logan), should not be confused with the "jazz singer" that Al Jolson played in the eponymous film that launched the sound revolution in Hollywood. In the 1920s, "jazz singer" denoted "a vocalist working in contemporary popular music," as opposed to classical or semi-classical pieces (such as "Trees") or—in the Jolson movie—the religious music of his Jewish cantor father. However, just to make things complicated for us, Jolson's very liberal treatment of melodic lines and their rhythmic underpinning somewhat anticipated the style that Scott and Logan exemplified after him.

So she didn't speak of merry adventures in the world of entertainment. She spoke of how she lived and what she thought.

And that was great for *PM East*'s need to stake out territory in the avant-garde. Still, such unvarnished honesty put many people off, because it was so . . . honest. There was much talk as well about Streisand's looks (including from Streisand herself) as being unsuitable for a major career as a singer, an actress, a movie star. It was even written into her first roles, as with *Funny Girl*: "To tell the truth, it hurt my pride," Streisand sang on returning from her honeymoon, "the groom was prettier than the bride."

Yet I wonder if people were reacting to not her physical appearance but rather her behavior and attire. Wasn't it really Streisand's unique approach to how she wanted to be perceived that was unsuitable? As I've said, people called her "special," some in praise (for her talent) but some in blame for her unruly—or let's say unpredictable—presentation. As photographs attest, Streisand was a perfectly nice-looking kid, and, once she gained stardom, she became the most photographed woman in history, a twentieth-century Cleopatra. The camera would catch her in every conceivable shot—standing on one foot under an umbrella and reading *Sports Illustrated* in a checked sports jacket with the collar turned up; in high fashion (white top, dark jacket and matching dark shorts over high white high-heeled boots) in a London park; sucking a lollipop in pigtails with a Topsy grin; posing with brother Sheldon and half-sister Roslyn or various co-stars and boy friends; making merry; being thoughtful or silly; embracing; insisting; imagining; modeling.

So there was no "looks" problem. There was a "special" problem that got called a "looks" problem because people didn't know how to describe finding Streisand outlandish. "Different" wasn't a genre yet: and Streisand was different. Not only because of the retro attire and flippant attitude, but because a nineteen-year-old isn't supposed to be able to bring the soul and sophistication of maturity to her singing, till even the rustic lilt of "Moon River" becomes worldly wise, a hurt valentine of wonder and regret. For a *New Yorker* piece on singer Mel Tormé by Whitney Balliett, Tormé himself observed, "It's a good idea to allow some small piece of unhappiness from your life to be a part of your work every night. It gives your singing depth."[16]

Yes—but Streisand can as well get playful even in a torch number, so let us consider that aforementioned "Lover, Come Back To Me," by Sigmund Romberg (with a bit of Tchaikofsky in the release) and Oscar Hammerstein, from the operetta *The New Moon* (1928). As Streisand sang it on the old Ed Sullivan variety hour, she explodes the original's sentimentality with a roguishly physical delivery. Romberg marked the refrain as *Più espressivo, ma sempre moderato* (roughly "Expressive yet restrained"), but Streisand takes it at a whirlwind pace, jumping all around the written notes and words and feeling the music through her body.

She's all arms and hands, hips and head, and even shades her eyes at one point to peer into the audience: has lover come back after all? Is he in the house? Now she's leaning her head on her arm, all but throwing a line away; now she's shaking from head to toe, forcing the melody out of her very being. The line "But love was old" turns into "But love...ooooold!," and after the song's final phrase she releases an "*Ow!*" with her head up and arms out. Such exuberance had not been heard since the swing era, for—I repeat—fifties mainstream pop was easygoing, its LP infrastructure used as background music in suburban living rooms.

Most arresting of these early television appearances is the "Happy Days Are Here Again" that Streisand sang in May of 1962 on *The Garry Moore Show*, a variety hour with a stock company (including Durwood Kirby, stuttering Marion Lorne, and a just breaking out Carol Burnett). Moore's show had a regular feature called "That Wonderful Year," saluting bygone tunes, and for Streisand's guest stint the year was 1929, not only reviving "Happy Days" but making it the centerpiece of a seven-and-a-half-minute one-act play. Streisand appeared as a Park Avenue grandee strolling into a bar after hours, with chairs on the tables and all the customers gone. A young waiter reluctantly prepared a place for her, and she launched the number with new vocal material, written by the experts who thronged television in those days, to set up the "Happy Days" chorus. It was champagne that Streisand had come for, we learned in the new intro, to celebrate in expansive irony having lost everything in the Crash.

In her fur cape, her hair in a tasty bun-and-bangs do, Streisand was the very model of elegance, balanced by a democratic bonding with the waiter, whom she addressed (as show-biz tradition demands) as "Joe." With no money left, Streisand offered Joe a diamond earring for a drink, but they pour on the stingy side in this bar; each glass is no more than a swallow. At Streisand's "I'll have another," the waiter pointed to the other earring, and Streisand merrily surrendered it, finally starting "Happy Days" itself. The melody, originally meant as an up-tune, was newly presented as a loving ballad, as if Streisand was singing about a newfound lover. So the song no longer defies the Depression (the original verse began "So long, sad times") but rises above it with aristocratic grace.

More champagne now, in exchange for Streisand's two bracelets, and the cape netted her the whole bottle. As the music mounted, the orchestra sounded a bit of "Auld Lang Syne," Streisand rose to the utmost of the belter's range, an E (a tenth above middle C), and she cradled the bottle as the camera pulled back for the fadeout. To button the number, Moore, looking leftward from stage right, blew her an appreciative kiss.*

In the middle of all this, in the summer of 1962, Streisand had already reached Broadway, in a supporting role in *I Can Get It For You Wholesale*, and had walked away with the reviews (albeit in an ensemble mostly made of what we have to call distinguished has-beens). Clearly, it was time for her to sign a recording contract. Some labels had expressed interest, but Marty Erlichman wanted Columbia, the most prestigious firm after having seized the top spot from Victor by habilitating the long-playing disc to replace the cumbersome, all too destructible 78.**

However, Erlichman and Streisand would have to captivate the snooty head of Columbia's Artists and Repertoire department, Goddard Lieberson. Decca's Jack Kapp pioneered the Broadway cast album, but it was Lieberson, with Columbia's advanced technical savvy backing him up, who made show recordings essential in the ID of the culturally informed middle class. Further, having persuaded the Columbia suits to capitalize *My Fair Lady*'s physical production, Lieberson made two fortunes for his outfit—the profits of the show itself and those of the recording, to that point the biggest seller in the history of music.

So Lieberson, in 1962 (the year *My Fair Lady* closed its Broadway run, after six-and-a-half years, unprecedented for a musical), was in effect his own record label, able to sign any artist at will. And Lieberson was well aware of Streisand, as Columbia had made the *Wholesale* album and also a spinoff, a studio reading of a comparable show, *Pins and Needles* (1937). Both bear music and lyrics by Harold Rome, both deal with labor-management problems in the Depression, and both are heavily Jewish in flavor. There is even one powerful Streisand link between them in that her celebrated solo in *Wholesale*, "Miss Marmelstein," corresponds precisely with *Pins and Needles'* "Nobody Makes a Pass at Me," the comic lament of a lonely office worker who tries every beauty shortcut ("On Ry-Krisp I have thinned . . .") without success. At that, Streisand's performance on Columbia's *Pins and Needles* was even funnier than her "Miss Marmelstein," and it utterly erased the "Nobody" of its creator in the show's original all-union cast, Millie Weitz (Local 22, Dressmakers) on her 78 single. So, to repeat for emphasis,

---

* All three of these cuts can be accessed on YouTube at this writing, the *PM East* (complete with the "thirty cents" dialogue, a rare preservation of Streisand unscripted in a non-interview format) in audio only, "Lover" and "Happy Days" with their visuals.

** It was Victor that introduced the LP, in the early 1930s, but consumers resisted the revolution, and the format was dropped. Suddenly, in the postwar boom of the late 1940s—and, in particular, the appeal of the *Kiss Me, Kate* and *South Pacific* cast albums—Columbia officially authored the relaunching of the LP.

Streisand was a central figure in the view through Goddard Lieberson's windshield.

But there was a snag—typically, one created by Streisand's self-absorption during the recording of the *Wholesale* cast album. James Spada, crediting the account to *Wholesale*'s conductor, Lehman Engel, tells how Streisand broke off in the middle of a take of "Miss Marmelstein" to announce that she didn't like the arrangement and wanted it changed.[17]

This never happens. Not generally never or virtually never. *Never.* Show albums in those days were recorded at white heat all in a single Sunday right after the premiere, using—of course—the charts played in the theatre. Yet here was Streisand, heedless of tradition, the time-is-money aspect of show recording, and the very purpose of the cast album, making diva demands in an ensemble piece of which she was but a part. Lieberson, personally producing the disc, spoke privately to Streisand, and, whatever he said, the taping immediately resumed without incident.

Still, Lieberson would have been intensely unhappy with Streisand's lack of esprit de corps, and that must be why he wanted to make the succeeding *Pins and Needles* album without her. Harold Rome interceded, however, and Lieberson gave in. But now he told Marty Erlichman that, as far as a Columbia contract for solo recitals was concerned, Streisand was—here's that word again—too "special."

What a useless euphemism! It means everything and nothing—and in fact there was another reason Lieberson didn't want Streisand recording for Columbia: he already had a big-selling singer who excelled in the Broadway and Hollywood Golden Age repertory Streisand was highlighting in her club gigs—the Wagnerian soprano Eileen Farrell.

That's not a jest. Farrell was the first great crossover singer, with an instrument capable of adjusting power from opera's "dramatic soprano" down to Schubert, Poulenc, and "Danny Boy." She had her own radio show when still in her early twenties, starting way back in 1941, and her first recording dates took her from Victor Herbert and Sigmund Romberg to the last forty-five minutes of *Siegfried* (Brünnhilde's entire part in that opera). Farrell's operetta is beguiling and her Wagner tremendous, *Siegfried*'s two high C's (a terror for some of the greatest sopranos) casually formidable.* I just do it, she seems to say, and her autobiography is sensibly called *Can't Help Singing.* So by the time Farrell got to Columbia, in the late 1950s, she

---

* Although Farrell sang what we might call opera's "mighty roles" on stage, she never actually appeared in Wagner, limiting herself to excerpts in concert and on disc. In fact, she thought of the Wagner heroines as voice-killers.

was indispensably versatile, taking down Verdi, Puccini, the *Messiah*, and four pop recitals.

Their very titles, such as *I've Got a Right to Sing the Blues!* and *Here I Go Again*, suggest taking on a dare, not merely singing classic pop but styling it. Thus, these discs anticipate some of what Streisand would be doing when Columbia finally signed her, and doing so in comparable numbers— "The Man I Love" and "Old Devil Moon" (from the stage), "A Foggy Day" and "I'm Old Fashioned" (from the screen), Bart Howard's "In Other Words" (which everyone thinks is called "Fly Me To the Moon"). It's everything from torch to up-tunes, and even boasts a number created for Farrell by Luther Henderson (one of her arranger-conductors) and Charles Burr (Columbia's liner-notes editor), "Solitaire," a kind of hommage to the lazy-ballad style of Duke Ellington with a period feeling in both words and music.

Streisand, too, would sing numbers written just for her (though much later on), and Farrell further points toward Streisand in the creative or-chestral settings she works in, Henderson's in particular. And note that, partnered by arranger-conductor André Previn in *Together With Love*, Farrell ends the Gershwins' "Love Is Here To Stay" by repeating the first four notes of the A strain, leaving the music hanging on an unresolved su-pertonic $\frac{9}{2}$ chord. The effect is offbeat and exotic, two words commonly used to describe Streisand at the time. And while diva Farrell does slip in an op-eratic high note here and there (which Streisand does in "Who's Afraid of the Big, Bad Wolf?"), she is unquestionably at home in the pop style.

She even gets playful with the text, interrupting the flow of "Ev'ry Time" (from Hugh Martin and Ralph Blane's *Best Foot Forward*), after a lyric about her boat's not being "yare" (meaning "easy to handle"), to ask, "What's *yare*?" Streisand would soon after do exactly the same thing on her first solo LP in "My Honey's Loving Arms," when she has to sing about "a morris chair." Anticipating a "Huh?" from the listener, just as Farrell had done with "yare," Streisand sings, instead of the succeeding written lyric (and in an almost plaintive tone), "What kind of chair is a morris chair?"

In other words, Lieberson didn't "need" Streisand while he had Farrell, and his personal take on vocal style inclined him away from Streisand in the first place. "Special" meant "intense," and Lieberson preferred placid, suave, the velvety wishfulness of the singer soaring in fantasy. Farrell's torch found beauty in woe. Streisand's torch was the charge of a Viking warrior, as in that "Cry Me a River," in which we hear less sorrow, more fury. She isn't going down: he is.

All right, then. What *did* Lieberson want? He liked what everyone liked before Streisand showed them the alternative, a sweet sound largely free of intense vocal or psychological inflection, very evenly presented and with an attractive personal flavor. The Frank Sinatra sound, the Rosemary Clooney sound. It would be impossible to conceive of Sinatra or Clooney singing "Cry Me a River" with Streisand's bite. Indeed, it would be impossible to conceive of anyone's trying to launch a career in about 1960 with so much audacity of tone, so much variety. Singers of the day turned each number into *their* number, in *their* way of being; Streisand turned *herself* into each number. Too special.

Let's imagine a different kind of Streisand whom Lieberson might have signed—and in fact we don't have to. It was Shirley Bassey, the Welsh singer who rose up at the very start of the stereo era in the mid-1950s. Unlike Streisand, Bassey had a fondness for big-band arrangements featuring swinging brass choirs, lots of strings, and even the occasional oohing chorus. A huge asset for EMI Records, Bassey was the key artist who broke with the standard fifties smooth style to enliven the scene with very outgoing delivery, perhaps most famously in the soundtrack theme song to the James Bond film *Goldfinger*. A belter, Bassey owned a very bright high range that centered her melody with arresting climaxes. Further, she had great *espressività* and a unique youthful loveliness in her timbre.

She fielded a wide repertory, getting into classic Broadway, from "Somebody Loves Me" to "April In Paris," while concentrating on ephemeral pop. Yet she approached each number with the same easy care, never condescending to the pop or getting arty with the show tunes. Music is music.

Thus, there are few moments in a Bassey interpretation that one singles out. Streisand, by contrast, plays all kinds of tricks, on a phrase-by-phrase basis; Bassey runs on an all-purpose effervescence. So she can revive "The Song Is You," a passionate ballad from the Jerome Kern and Oscar Hammerstein operetta *Music In the Air* (1932), as if unveiling the latest pop hit, in an uptempo arrangement and with an inspiring reading of the number's climactic line, "Why can't I let you know the song my heart would sing?," capping it with a splendid high note on the last word.

Once more, this turns out to be no more than the C above middle C, yet Bassey makes it a cry of love, youth to youth. This is not a nuanced aesthetic but rather a forward-charging presentation based on a response to the music above all. Bassey would never question a lyric with "What's *yare*?," and *her* "Cry Me a River" is slow and sad, hardly acted at all. Still, whether "interpreting" or direct, the best singers fall under the music's spell, like—to add more names to our short list—Judy Garland or Sammy Davis Jr. They're not just singing: they're *being sung by the music*, with a dense emotional range and plenty of tone.

But aren't there great singers who don't fall into this category? Singers who seem totally in control of the music rather than controlled by it? Here's one: Ella Fitzgerald. In her classic Verve series of Songbooks by Rodgers and Hart, Cole Porter, the Gershwins, Duke Ellington, and others such, Fitzgerald avoids the portrayals that many singers find irresistibly embedded in the material. Nor does the music lure her into expanding her customary approach. In her very early days, in the late 1930s with the Chick Webb Band, Fitzgerald could cut loose, as in her jiving rendition of "A-Tisket, A-Tasket (a brown and yellow basket)." The number swings with such invitation that the band members have to get in on it. "Was it green?" they cry, to Ella's "No, no, *no*, no!" and "Was it red?" Oh, "No, no, *no*, no!"

She was full of the dickens then. But in 1956, in attacking the Cole Porter assignment—and such it was, rather than a labor of love—Fitzgerald is, we might say, even-tempered. Hers is not the sound usually associated with Porter, whose favorite Broadway exponent was the trumpeting Ethel Merman and who later attracted cabaret sophisticates such as Lena Horne and Bobby Short.

Fitzgerald, however, never quite "got" Porter. The memorial website of her arranger-conductor, Buddy Bregman, recalls Fitzgerald's slighting of the words to perform entirely on the melody and her distaste for set-up verses. "Why do I have to do this?" she would say, for instance of the all-important introduction to "Just One Of Those Things." Nor could she place most of its soigné cultural allusions (to Abelard and Heloise, Dorothy Parker, and so on). "It's as if she's reading words off the paper," Bregman observes.

Even so, through some mysterious alchemy—a kind of delicacy of strength, relaxed and confident, and generously dipping into the *chalumeau* of her lower range—Fitzgerald takes the music for her own. She doesn't seize it or toy with it (except in some jazzy inflections on the second choruses), and the whole affair is almost free of interpretation of any kind. Yet the two-LP Cole Porter album became (along with *My Fair Lady* in the same year) an instant classic, vital infrastructure of the American pop style. To repeat: Fitzgerald is in control of the music. Shirley Bassey, in comparable material, is excited, taken by the music.

Streisand, however, pulls all this to the next level: in control yet possessed as well. There was nothing mysterious about how she bonded with her songs. Hers was conviction art. Ah—was *that* what Goddard Lieberson meant by "too special"? Was Streisand getting too *inside* the music for his somewhat fastidious taste? Or was it her all too candid way of communicating, as we've mentioned? Her odd attire? Her self-absorption?

Streisand marked a break with tradition in many ways, but it was her singing style in particular that marked her as unique, and no doubt Lieberson finally realized that she wasn't a curiosity but the next Original. So he not only signed her but let her go her way, though the Columbia suits must have been eager to stuff Streisand into one of their categories. As I've said, her contract gave her artistic control—but the label retained commercial control. So Streisand could choose her repertory and present it in her nonconformist Streisand fashion. That's the artistic side of things. But all decisions on manufacturing, promoting, and shipping were Columbia's—the business side of things, whereby anyone in power at the label who didn't like Streisand could sabotage sales, especially in the crucial matter of the release of 45 singles, essential for radio airplay and counting the tiniest window of marketing opportunity before they are deemed hit or failure.*

It is amusing to contemplate the intrusion of sheer blind luck here. Timing isn't everything in show business; talent is. But timing is very influential, and while Streisand and her mentors created the singing opportunities that gave her her berth at Columbia Records, the key event in her rise from ambitious kid to movie star was the show *Funny Girl*, which led to the movie *Funny Girl* and the rest of Streisand's charmed life.

But what if the *Funny Girl* project, which bounced around in various forms from the early 1950s, had materialized before 1964? It was to have been a film first, then, instead, a stage show, so let us imagine the outcome if *My Man* (as they were to have called it) had reached Broadway in the late 1950s, next to *The Music Man* and *Flower Drum Song*, before Streisand had had a chance to establish herself.

My Man might well have failed—a show with a comparable storyline called *Sophie*, on the life of Sophie Tucker, with Libi Staiger and Art Lund singing a score by Steve Allen, flopped miserably just a year before *Funny Girl* in the same theatre, the Winter Garden. Or *My Man* might have succeeded and gone Hollywood but with, for instance, Shirley MacLaine in the lead. What would have happened to Streisand if she and *My Man/Funny Girl* had not crossed paths just when each was ready for the other?

At that, before Streisand's skyrocket of a rise, there already was a perfect Fanny Brice all set to go: Kaye Ballard, who auditioned for the role with an MGM LP, *The Fanny Brice Story in Song*. Here Ballard revived "Second Hand Rose," "I'm an Indian," "Rose Of Washington Square," and such little-known Brice specialties as "Ain't That the Way," "Lovie Joe," and "When You Know You're Not Forgotten (By the Girl You Can't Forget)," all delivered strictly in

---

* We should quietly note that amid Streisand's triumphant conquest of Lieberson and his hesitations, Eileen Farrell became no longer useful to Columbia. When it was time for the label to review its agreement with Farrell, Lieberson offered her an insulting drop in terms, as if inviting her to leave. And she did.

Brice's style and even following her inflections in the numbers she had re-corded herself.*

Ballard would have been fine in *Funny Girl*, as she was not only a sharp comedienne but a wonderful singer with a tone that grew radiant in its upper register. And isn't that Fanny: a *funny* (and very musical) yet not (she thinks) romantic girl? But now we encounter a show-biz game of thrones, as the stage *Funny Girl* had at first two producers, David Merrick and Ray Stark. Merrick, of course, was one of Broadway's canniest showmen while Stark had put on only two shows, one a fast flop. So he deferred to Merrick … except when he didn't. Their main task lay in finding the perfect Fanny. Headliner? Discovery? Ballard?

Merrick was the producer of *Carnival* (1961), in which Ballard in fact played someone not unlike Fanny Brice: funny rather than romantic and involved with an unreliable guy. Merrick might well have recommended the flavorsome Ballard as their Fanny, but her style, however invigorating, was loud and crazy, whereas Stark—who happened to be Fanny Brice's son-in-law—was looking for someone more genteel, to flatter his wife's memory of the offstage Fanny, a saloniste intimate with everyone who mattered right up to the Prince of Wales when he was the most "exclusive" bachelor in the Western world.

So there was some tension between the two ruling houses. But Merrick and Stark did agree that their Fanny had to be a star of the first division, and while Ballard wasn't big enough, the skyrocketing Streisand was almost surely going to be. Merrick had not only produced a show with Ballard: he had also produced one with Streisand, the aforementioned *I Can Get It For You Wholesale*. He had hated Streisand then, but he was coming around, and Stark (though we sometimes hear otherwise) was very taken with this youngster who sang with the confidence of a seasoned pro.

It would be easy to say that Streisand simply squeezed Ballard out. But in fact the signing of Fanny was extremely complex, especially because, for some time, the show's director was Jerome Robbins, who could be exasper-atingly deliberate yet wildly expansive in his casting. Streisand biographer William J. Mann discovered in the archives Robbins' list of potential Fannys. Ballard isn't on it, but Chita Rivera, Judy Holliday, Tammy Grimes, and Eydie Gormé are among those present, as is a certain "Barbara Streisman."[18]

What combination of talent and luck does one need in this business? Big stars and little stars had been coming and going, including Mary Martin (apparently Mrs. Stark's choice) and Carol Burnett, who famously said, in the understatement of the century, "You need a Jewish girl for this."[19]

---

* The CD reissue was retitled *Kaye Ballard Sings … Fanny Brice*.

Robbins, however, wanted Anne Bancroft, who was not Jewish. Nor would she be able to sing the score Jule Styne and Bob Merrill were writing. But she was a semi-Heavy Name with a quality that, Robbins believed, would be entrancingly intimate amid the hurly-burly of musical comedy. (Robbins was also directing Bancroft in Brecht's *Mother Courage* at the time.)

It had been something like twenty-five years since most people had had any contact with Brice's show-biz persona as mischievous Baby Snooks or Brice's trademark numbers as Jewish girls bewildered by ballet, courtship rituals, modern dance, and other checkpoints in the travels of the emancipated woman. The name of "Fanny Brice" was still very famous, but the experience of seeing her perform was gone, and her few movies were not generally available then.

So Anne Bancroft might have been a valid choice for the role—in the non-musical version. With songs—real Broadway power numbers like "Don't Rain On My Parade"—Fanny had to be a singer, perhaps even a most unusual singer who, like the real Fanny, could carve a place for herself in the arts *that had not existed before*. And then Robbins, the main creative who was blind to Streisand's powers, dropped out of the production. Sheer blind luck.

Nonetheless, there was a last holdout, though this one wasn't a creative. It was Ray Stark's wife (Fanny's daughter, remember), who hated Streisand on sight. Oh, she may seem like a Fanny to you, in those silly onstage numbers. But that is *not* my mother in the real-life scenes. Elegant! Dressy! Saloniste! Prince of Wales!

So here was another case of mistaking Streisand's unapologetic originality for a failure of refinement: an inability to see that this was not wrong art but new art, corrected art. Brice as Streisand was Brice, whether Fran Stark liked it or not.

The thrones in alignment, Merrick and Stark signed Streisand. Rehearsals began. And then, living up to his reputation as the Peck's Bad Boy of Broadway, Merrick suddenly decided—after all this—that he couldn't stand Ray Stark, and sold to Stark Merrick's interest in the production. Now Streisand was on her way, in the long view of things, to one of the biggest careers in Hollywood history.

Sheer blind luck—because it happened *just* when Jule Styne was able to catch Streisand in one of her club dates (he went almost every night), bringing the others to see for themselves what Streisand was able to do in front of an audience. Though he is not famous for it, Styne was a generous character who loved giving young talent a break. And, as it happens, Bob Merrill supposedly had had an affair with Anne Bancroft, and the parting was something other than sweet sorrow. In fact, they kind of hated each other.

If this were one of Aesop's Fables, I might end with "And that's how the fox got his tail." For Streisand was now to be a star on Big Broadway—the "Stop the presses!" sector of American theatre, wherein everybody knows about you. Of course, from the start, Streisand intended to work not live on stage but on film. Yes, she sang in stage musicals: but her need was to act, in cinema, and especially in what we might call "movie-star movies," the ones that exist not out of a wish to enlighten the intellectual in us or to stir us with artistic vision but simply to pleasure us with the company of wonderful people—*It Happened One Night* or *The Awful Truth*, to keep to classic inventory.

True, by Streisand's day they weren't writing them as well as they used to. In the studio age, even the fribbles could count on a pungent use of the language, because if the producers were dumb, at least they hired smart. By the 1970s, however, movie-star movies were often written by well-intentioned hacks, denuding the stories of wit. And without that Certain Something Extra in their way of expressing themselves, the characters are handicapped—as obtains, in Streisand's canon, in such items as *A Star Is Born* and *The Main Event*.

There is this as well: what *kind* of movie star did Streisand intend to be?—because, unlike many, she had a choice. Limiting our discussion to the way Hollywood used its marquee names in the decades leading up to Streisand's transfer from the playhouse to the sound stage, in the late 1960s (and omitting the hardcore low comics like Bert Lahr, mainly a male preserve anyway), there were three varieties of star:

> The Glamour Star: a compelling looks-and-personality package who may or may not be truly gifted, such as Jeanne Crain or Elizabeth Taylor.
>
> The Acting Star: noted primarily for dramatic power, for example George Arliss (in the early days of the talkie, a grandfatherly presence useful in historical pageants such as *Disraeli*, *Alexander Hamilton*, and *Voltaire*), Katharine Hepburn, or Bette Davis.
>
> The Talent Star: who builds the career on a skill, as with Fred Astaire's dancing or Jeanette MacDonald's singing.

Note, however, that there is some movement among these categories and a fair amount of buts and excepts. For one instance, Sterling Hayden turned up in the late 1930s on his looks alone, for he was a limited actor who didn't even move naturally. At six feet five inches, however, with a blond topping that seemed far more "locks" than hair and a superb physique in a day when romantic male leads were trim but not extrapolated, Hayden was irresistible. Then he went off to war and returned as a wholly different person, dark and menacing rather than pretty and in roles that called for four-day stubble. Incredibly, Hayden was now an excellent actor—as long as the script gave him something to bite into. The distance between Hayden's sleepwalking beach boy in *Bahama Passage* (1941) and his intensely sinister Brigadier General Jack D. Ripper in *Dr. Strangelove* (1964)— shot from below as if to awe us with a monster, obsessing over Communist interference with "our precious bodily fluids" and biting out his lines over a cigar that looks like a hard-on—demonstrates how much wiggle room the movie star had in developing his or her character type.

Consider the case of Marilyn Monroe, arguably the most beautiful woman in the world: which is why some people have trouble accepting her as an actress. Her intellectual sorties—involvement with Method gurus Lee and Paula Strasberg and marriage to the socially conscious playwright Arthur Miller—seem to Monroe's critics the affectations of a dilettante. Yet an unbiased view of her screen work, especially in *Bus Stop* (1956), reveals a genuine talent: a character player, not just a looker. Monroe's pathetically feckless "singer," Cherie, is so sharply observed that one wonders where the actress logged all the experience to comprehend the world of the loser who is nevertheless steeped in charisma. Cherie is simple, while Monroe's portrayal is a doctoral dissertation on human nature.

Further, while Monroe seemed cast inevitably as "herself" (unlike Streisand, who has played a Communist agitator, a cross-dressing rabbinical student, a homicidal prostitute, and a fancy psychiatrist ordering dinner for two in impeccable French), Monroe still found something new to discover every time.

True, Monroe was always perceived as a glamour star and nothing else. But many stars map around the possibilities. Doris Day moved from talent star (as a singer in musicals) to a kind of personality icon, such good company that she stole scenes from Rock Hudson and Frank Sinatra—and Mike Nichols originally offered Day the role of Mrs. Robinson in *The Graduate* precisely to match her sunny mien with a dark character for a macabre twist on suburban adultery culture. Yet for all her charm, Day wasn't a glamour star in the usual sense, because her appeal was basic and classless yet somehow idealized. She made the ordinary special, even unique, like someone from the neighborhood who is actually a corporation head in disguise. It's how she moves and sounds more than anything else.

And there is this: the most captivating stars tend to hold us with an essential quality that "speaks" in their every characterization. Humphrey Bogart's cynicism is an example, or Rosalind Russell's gallantry or Clark Gable's brutal honesty. Or Katharine Hepburn's self-assurance, so casual, so lofty, as secure as a detective who just figured out who the murderer is.

Does Streisand have an essential quality? In one of her rare interviews, with *Life* magazine in 1966, Streisand called herself "a cross between a washwoman and a princess...a bit coarse, a bit low, a bit vulgar, and a bit ignorant."[20] Yet also "sophisticated, elegant, and controlled." It was a paradox she would toy with regularly in her career, most obviously in her dual role of Regency temptress and modern-day kook in *On a Clear Day You Can See Forever*, but, really, in many moments in almost all her roles, when the energy softens or the humor gets aggressive. Or even when, on *PM East*, her banter would turn bluntly edgy (as with David Susskind) and then the music would start and, just before she began singing, a little smile suggested that she had instantly turned into someone else, one driven by art rather than by ambition.

So, yes, she was an Original, and many people dislike Originals—at first. Breakaway talent is confusing and therefore threatening, and we've seen this as a theme endemic in the arts: in the early rejection of composers from Hector Berlioz to Stephen Sondheim; in the struggle to establish schools of modern painting in the late nineteenth and early twentieth centuries; in the fear of James Joyce's honesty (the first printer hired for *Dubliners* refused to set the type for some of the stories, and the second printer withheld and then destroyed the pages); and, so obviously, the Parisian first-night audience's enraged sabotage of *The Rite of Spring*, hating Stravinsky's music and especially Nizhinsky's choreography, thinking it deliberately aimed at taunting a passéiste public.

Typically, all the breakaway talent listed above became accepted in time, but the first to do the accepting are always the nonconformists. One reason Streisand's first fans in her very early days at the Lion and the Beau Soir entertainment clubs were gay men is that gays, in the 1960s, were living breakaway lives. They didn't need to acclimatize themselves to Streisand's style, because (and I may be getting overly metaphorical here) they were in effect living on the edge just as she was singing on the edge. It's the conformists who like conformist art; nonconformists like—or at least understand—Originals.

"Damn it," says a character in Philip Barry's play *Holiday* (1928), "there's no life any good but the one you make for yourself." It's a theme that runs through American art, perhaps because our outstanding artists are less like, for instance, such formal conservatives as Brahms, Dickens, or Ingrès and more like revolutionaries such as Orson Welles. Virtually every choice in life becomes a defiance of society's cautions and pieties, even a refusal to flatter one's supposed superiors—the already-made-its, the "royalty" of the professions. "I don't know what to say to these people,"[21] Streisand complained, of the countless celebrities who filled her dressing room when

Funny Girl opened. The famous do love to be around others like themselves, especially the brand-new ones; it makes them feel so young. "All the hugging in this business!" Streisand cries. "And by people who don't even know me! I *hate* it—it's so fucking phony!"[22]

With so many people—from the puffed-up know-it-alls to genuine experts—constantly saying, "But you can't do that," the Original learns that freedom of expression lies precisely in doing that. How else are you to see the world, when they know only what has already happened while you are the next thing to happen, the as yet unknown? You ignore your mother, correct your critical friends, defy the authorities. Because you have absorbed the salient lesson in getting the world to appreciate you:

EVERYBODY ELSE IS WRONG.

Unfortunately, this did lead Streisand to assault even sensible protocols, when she was still on the rise and thus vulnerable. We've seen how she tried to change the orchestration of *I Can Get It For You Wholesale* in the middle of a one-day-only recording session, and she was back-seat driving the director of her first film (William Wyler on *Funny Girl*) despite his stature as a very successful Hollywood veteran who led his stars to Oscar nominations.

Streisand's defenders call it a forgivable perfectionism, but while some questioning of interpretation or a camera angle or a lighting setup may be useful, when it's chronic it enervates company morale and wastes money. There are apologists who claim that this essentially power-driven behavior looks good on a man and questionable on a woman, but in fact no one in the movie business likes any actor's ceaseless attempts to take over a set, and gender has nothing to do with it. Again, it creates tension, and every extra minute of shooting time adds to a film's negative cost, making it harder for the picture to bank. And bank, after all, makes everyone look good. So everyone wants bank—another reason the Hollywood establishment has long resented Streisand and may have withheld from her certain Oscar nominations she arguably deserved. As screenwriter Jerome Kass told Michael Bennett biographer Kevin Kelly, "You just don't make a movie with Barbra Streisand: *she makes a movie with Barbra Streisand!*"[23]

Oddly, Streisand's plan to become a glamour star rather than a talent star led her to favor popcorn films over more ambitious projects. Again, to keep to golden-age paradigms, are there many *important works*—*Of Human Bondage* or *Alice Adams*, say—in Streisand's calendar of titles: cinema gorging on extraordinary women leads against a background of intense social inquiry? In the former, Bette Davis dared play a character so hateful that her home studio thought it might kill her career. (She did it on a loan-out.) In the latter, Katharine Hepburn is the despised wallflower taking on a townful of scorn and disappointments. And in both films, the background (respectively, London and village America) is very strongly dramatized.

True, Streisand made *Yentl*, which suits my definition of an important title—and this was the one in her oeuvre that she was most committed to, in a virtual crusade to discuss women's rights amid an environment of religious fundamentalism and, as well, as a valentine to the real-life father she had lost in her infancy. Further, despite *The Way We Were*'s high-gloss finish and soap-opera romance, the original pre-release print actually bore significant cultural witness to the plight of a social agitator too absolute to thrive in a compromised society. All the same, Streisand has too often favored schlock, at times terrible schlock at that.

We note as well that the movies Streisand turned down—*Klute, Cabaret, The Devils, Alice Doesn't Live Here Anymore, Evita*—may have threatened her with strong directors who would have refused to flatter her sense of self (respectively, Alan J. Pakula, Bob Fosse, Ken Russell, Martin Scorsese, and Alan Parker). True, Streisand turned down also *They Shoot Horses, Don't They?*, directed by Sydney Pollack, who later was in charge of *The Way We Were*. But the latter was the ultimate glamour-star picture, a project Streisand couldn't have turned down under any circumstances. (Then, too, the High Maestro directors of Streisand's era, like Fosse and Russell, didn't tend to take on glamour-star movies, if only because they lack not only artistic challenge but intellectual prestige.)

No, the general run of the Streisand movie director gives us a group of not iconoclasts but propitiators, willing to accommodate rather than control the star. Was it simply arrogance that led Streisand to offend Ingmar Bergman by asking for script revisions on *The Merry Widow*, or a cunning way of resisting the prospect of being overwhelmed?

In an entirely different concern, we note that, despite those many romances with men both in and out of show business, Streisand kept them out of her career. She did this even with Elliott Gould when they were married and he was starving for work. Taking *Funny Girl* to London after the New York run, Streisand surely could have insisted on Gould's being cast opposite her; Nick Arnstein was a good fit for him. True, British Equity might have raised an objection, but such matters can always be negotiated, and Gould was coming over to England with Streisand in any case.

And of course there is one glaring exception to all this, in Streisand's affair with Jon Peters, the hair-salon entrepreneur whom Streisand brought into her professional life in every capacity, though he had no experience whatsoever in the making of recordings or movies, even no knowledge of music or cinema, period. Surely, if so self-directed and seasoned a performer took in a partner, it would have to be one as expert as she is. Peters wasn't. Worse, his ideas were cockeyed. Screenwriter Kevin Smith has a wonderful routine he once brought out at a comic con, detailing his first meeting with Peters in Peters' post-Streisand years, when he had taken over the *Superman* movie franchise. As Smith tells it, Peters' plan for the man of steel's next adventure ran thus:

> One, I don't want to see him in those tights.
> Two, I don't want to see him fly.
> Three, he has to fight a giant spider in the third act.[24]

Topping this was Peters' idea for the actor to play Superman himself: the glowering, notoriously tyrant-loving Sean Penn, a cognitive-dissonance casting notion of spectacular proportions.

Or we can consider the proposal sent to New York book publishers for Peters' autobiography, *Studio Head*, styled as "Charles Dickens meets Jackie Collins" and promising a ton of salacious gossip as Peters "play[s] love guru" to a harem of partners, "from muff-dyed hookers to Prada-clad studio chiefs."[25]

Leaked online, the proposal—prepared with a writing ghost—was a study in crass narcissism, yet a prominent house made an offer in the high six figures (which Peters had to turn down after his subjects threatened to litigate his fantasies in court). The ghost, William Stadiem, then reported on his working relationship with Peters in *Vanity Fair*, only adding to the picture of an uncultured man with a violent temper.

Of all the men Streisand had become involved with, why was Peters the one to whom she opened her professional life? It's a puzzle, because Streisand is not a creature of impulse. She makes considered—even excruciatingly interrogated—judgment calls, because her work is her identity. Here is no Warholian figure, known for what she represents rather than for what she actually does. On the contrary, we know Streisand for her singing and acting—that is, her credits—along with her political activism, on the left.

The Warholian celebrity, such as Marilyn Monroe or (and, yes, this is a real stretch) John Fitzgerald Kennedy, becomes a mythical version of him- or herself, symbolic rather than actual. And when the facts contradict the myth, the myth prevails. "Print the legend," as someone says in John Ford's *The Man Who Shot Liberty Valance*. Thus, to comprehend the Warholian type, one doesn't even need to know what the life is like. People who've never seen a Monroe film or who know nothing of Camelot's politics understand "who" Monroe and Kennedy were, however vaguely. But if you haven't heard Streisand sing or seen her films, you do not really know who she is.

Defined by her career, Streisand makes choices that steer her art—why she started off singing Old Broadway and Hollywood, for example, then moved into contemporary pop and later reclaimed Old Broadway with an infusion of Sondheim, younger than springtime. She makes appointments, nags directors, edits scripts, sometimes interminably. Everything is planned. The Warholian figure, on the other hand, dwells in a kind of karma: destiny does the choosing, and all the appointments are in Samarra.

So this long-term allegiance with Peters, who would have known Monroe and Kennedy but reportedly hadn't heard of Streisand before they met, is baffling. Nor did Streisand's music-and-film output at this time mark an advance of any kind. *ButterFly*, which Streisand let Peters produce, might be her worst album (she herself now regrets having made it), and *A Star Is Born*, something of a Streisand-Peters valentine to themselves, was commercially a huge hit but held up to scorn by the opinion class.

After Streisand disentangled Peters from her career, she pursued her goals as before, save that *Yentl* stands well outside the general run of her film work. Unlike *The Way We Were*, *A Star Is Born*, and even such piffle as *The Owl and the Pussycat* (whose stage original at least helped pioneer race-blind casting, an effect lost in the movie), *Yentl* is not a movie-star project. For one thing, it has a powerful religious flavor—always a risky program, in commercial terms—and for another, it's neither a musical in the usual sense nor a straight film. One could say that it's a musical except when it isn't, but it isn't really a musical even when it is, giving every one of its vocals to Streisand's character as psychological yearnings, which creates a score made of nothing but Heroine's Wanting Songs.

This approach to the film's musical ID is so subdued that some writers recall the songs as voiceovers. In fact, Streisand's character can be seen singing most of the vocal lines: but she's singing to herself, even in the somewhat grand finale, on a ship carrying the very independent young heroine to America and freedom. Yes, even as she paces the deck, surrounded by people who seem to see her and not see her at the same time (a visual metaphor for the way all the movie's characters have been treating her, as she has been masquerading as a male). Thus, *Yentl*'s other principals are locked out of the lift that music bestows on a story. But then, there are scarcely more than two other principals in the first place.

All this independence, this freedom! Again, we comprehend Streisand from what she *does*—yet a few personal bits have jumped out at us through her wall of privacy. One is the "Streisand Effect" mentioned in the

Chronology chapter, which we can restate as "When famous people complain about something, they tend to make it famous, too."

Thus, everyone now knows what Streisand's estate on the southern California coastline looks like. At that, Streisand published *My Passion For Design: A Private Tour*, a coffee-table book filled with views of her place, inside and out. And lo, one of the stops on the tour is a little mall that she had built in the basement of the main house, as a way to maintain her collection of knickknacks, including an assortment of one-of-a-kind antique dolls.

It sounds eccentric, perhaps, though it could be seen simply as a sensible way of setting out one's collectibles, as opposed to Andy Warhol's habit of leaving the loot from his antiquing trips in shopping bags despite having a townhouse's extensive area to display them in. *That*, surely, is eccentric.

Streisand's little underground mall would have been no more than a few photographs in her book till playwright Jonathan Tolins got an idea for a counterfactual: what if Streisand hired some smart young out-of-work actor to run the doll shop, and what if Streisand came down to shop? What if she asked for the backstory on a doll and tried to bargain with the quoted price?

Of course, he'd have to be a gay guy, because who else could keep up with all the memes—the show-biz meme, the Streisand-as-singer-but-also-actress-especially-movie-star meme, the Broadway meme, the pop-music meme, the collecto meme, with its worshipers of the rare and unique and their dread deity Demento, who knows nothing yet tells all. Tolins' play, entitled *Buyer & Cellar*, could easily have been a traditional full-cast comedy, as there are a number of characters besides the protagonist and Streisand. But Tolins instead laid it out for a single player doing all the roles, and its creator, Michael Urie, gave a performance of such effervescent charm that *Buyer & Cellar* was successfully launched as a work ideal for national exposure.

So here is a different Streisand, imagined as listening avidly while the "shopkeeper" rattles off an extemporized legend of the doll and jousting with him over the price. Of course, she could simply *take* the doll, because it belongs to her, along with the shop, the mall, the estate entire. But that would dispel the fantasy, and Brigadoon would vanish forever. Instead, she retreats and then returns... with a coupon she has run up for herself on her computer.

This is an intriguing Streisand, normalized from stardom even as she is made manifest as landed gentry with her very own shopping mall—complete, by the way, with a frozen-yogurt machine. The shopkeeper is totally fictional, invented for the play, and even Streisand is only a possible Streisand, another invention, as Tolins had never met her when writing.

Yet here the idea of an achieving being, an artist, an American, collides with what the theatre calls truth. And, for a few minutes, Streisand's privacy evaporates and we can try to discern in the invented character the reality of her extraordinary career as singer and actress, the independence and the choices of a life created—as so often in the American arts—out of an originality so persuasive that it gives orders to destiny.

And that's how the fox got his tail.

Streisand's Theatre

The variety bill—an evening of song, dance, and comedy—used to be one of the musical's central genres. The minstrel show, one of its earliest forms as a revue in three acts, was extremely popular for much of the nineteenth century. Then, in the 1910s and 1920s, the glamorous annuals like the *Ziegfeld Follies* and *George White's Scandals* were big draws and major talking points among those who talked of Broadway. In the 1930s and 1940s came the "theme" revues—a world tour, newspaper features, army life staged and performed by soldiers, and so on.

By the 1960s, however, television had absorbed the variety show, and only off-Broadway maintained the form, using very small casts on a virtually bare stage and favoring a zany tone. Needless to say, the early Streisand of the offbeat approach to performing was ideal for the form, and with little stage experience beyond her several supporting roles in summer stock and the like, Streisand made her New York musical-theatre debut* in *Another Evening With Harry Stoones* (1961), a revue written entirely by Jeff Harris.

Typically for this offbeat outing, there was no Harry Stoones in the show. The first act was called "The Civil War" and the second act "The Roaring Twenties," both irrelevantly, while the opening number, called "Carnival in Capri," consisted of the eight-person cast coming out to greet the public, abruptly say goodbye and thanks, and tear off in a fast exit.

---

* This was not Streisand's first time on a New York stage. In 1959, aged sixteen, she took part in a semi-amateur production of a play called *Driftwood*, produced in the apartment of the playwright, Maurice Tei Dunn. A year later, Streisand appeared in several small roles in Karel and Josef Čapek's *The Insect Comedy* at the Jan Hus Playhouse, where the young actress met her first serious amour, Barry Dennen.

The show did nothing for Streisand, but, looking back, we can see how quickly theatre people responded to her unusual qualities. Author Harris at first typed her simply as a ballad singer rather than the comic he needed, but soon enough he realized that the crazy way she behaved at her audition—her ability to locate logic in the absurd—was exactly what he wanted from her as a performer. So he hired her, setting out to write comic numbers to bring out her inner Topsy.

One of these was "Value," in which she considered the relative merits—family wealth, a car—of a possible husband and, just maybe, a few other boys. She really loves this one boy, you see, and yet...well, what do you want, love or a car? Only two minutes long, the number is charming and silly, more arioso than outright song, and its kooky combination of decisiveness and ambivalence made it ideal for the whimsy that Streisand exploited in her early years (though rather less often afterward). Further, she had an instinct for sketch comedy as well.

Unfortunately, these bitty little revues without marquee names (even if, besides Streisand, Dom DeLuise and Diana Sands would go on to major careers) couldn't survive without raves from the first-night stringers, and those assigned to these esoteric addresses in the neighborhoods were a gang of killjoys, too sour to enjoy a piece as wacky as *Stoones*. Once they got through with it ("Not exactly unbearable"...the *New York Times*),[26] the show was over after opening night and vanished without a trace, save a single photo in the 1961–62 *Theatre World* and Streisand's use of "Value" in her club act.

Then came *I Can Get It For You Wholesale* (1962), Streisand's Broadway debut. Her audition was a stunner, the talk of The Street, and it affirms my theory that some thought her unpretty because of her eccentric dress and behavior—that confusion of the logical with the absurd. Based on Jerome Weidman's 1937 novel about the rise of a young man without scruples or ethics in the New York garment business, *Wholesale* was going to revel in the local Jewish tone in both words and music. So Streisand decided to stage her audition to make the most of the jokey Jewish inflections she could put on at will, along with her signature goofy style.

Dressed in her thrift-shop chic, Streisand started on the gala side, letting loose a hail of sheet music at the piano and perhaps crying out, "Oh, dear!" in an endearing little wail that she might have rehearsed a dozen times in the mirror. (You can hear it on her subsequent recording of the thirties labor show *Pins and Needles*, at the very end of "Nobody Makes a Pass At Me.") Characterization: vulnerable.

Okay, time to sing, for Weidman (who wrote the musical's script), Harold Rome (the show's songwriter), and the director, Arthur Laurents. As Weidman later recalled in *Holiday* magazine, Laurents asked if she could sing, and Streisand replied, "If I couldn't sing, would I have the nerve to come out here in a thing like this coat?"[27] Delivery: lovably cynical.

"Okay, then," Laurents told her. "Sing!"

But Streisand wasn't done with her skit. "Even a jukebox you don't just say, 'Sing!' You gotta first punch a button with the name of a song on it!"[28]

They left it up to her, and, sitting in a secretary's chair on casters, Streisand appeared to take her chewing gum out and stick it below the seat. Effect: raw but game. She then sang "Value," while sliding about the stage on the chair wheels. Image: the reckless madcap. But what a voice!

The three men asked for more, and more after that, no doubt already planning how they were going to regale their thespian friends with the story; Harold Rome, who wrote *Pins and Needles* as well, must have been struck by how perfect Streisand would be for a new cover of "Nobody Makes a Pass At Me." Rome whispered, "Isn't she something?"[29] to Laurents, and he agreed. So Streisand got a callback, to sing for the show's producer, David Merrick. He hated her. In Merrick's view, audiences came to the theatre to see lovely blondes with a mystique of Aryan confidence, not someone they could have gone to high school with.[30]

Eventually Merrick gave in, grumbling all the way. Still, with five woman leads in an ensemble show (and some parts already cast), Streisand was wrong for all of them: too comic for the sweetheart (played by Marilyn Cooper), too young for the wife and mother roles (given to Bambi Linn, who dated back to the original *Oklahoma!* cast, nineteen years before; and to Lillian Roth, so veteran that Hollywood had already filmed her biography), and just wrong for the showgirl (Sheree North, in the David Merrick Aryan blonde slot). There was as well a spinster secretary, written as an older woman, though there was no reason it couldn't go to anyone with talent. This was Miss Marmelstein, one of the best-known character names in the musical's history, because it's also the title of what became Streisand's show-stopping solo, the cri de coeur of a girl who can't get on a first-name basis with the boys.

So much emphasis has been placed on "Miss Marmelstein" as Streisand's breakout musical spot that we tend to overlook how much Streisand had to do in *Wholesale* generally, especially given that with the four lead males there were nine principals. In fact, after a mimed prologue showing labor unrest on the streets, it was Streisand who launched the first dialogue, started the first number, "[He's not a] Well Man," and got the biggest laugh in the scene:

MISS MARMELSTEIN (pointing an unwanted character toward the door): Out!

HER BOSS: Miss Marmelstein.

MISS MARMELSTEIN (surprised): Me?

HER BOSS: You.

MISS MARMELSTEIN (now pointing herself toward the door, defeated): Out.

Streisand went to and fro in the action all night, besides taking part in three numbers beyond her solo. In her climactic number, she led the chorus in "What Are They Doing To Us Now?," a scathing workers' complaint in the unsettling meter of $\frac{6}{4}$ and unusually pointed even for a serious musical like *Wholesale*, virtually a Hebraic carmagnole.

Rome clearly understood what he was unleashing in Streisand's ability to drive home such furious music, giving her a long-held "Hey!" over the pounding accompaniment to launch the line "Hey, there, do yourself a favor, don't get born!" Goddard Lieberson, though still ambivalent about Streisand as an all-purpose vocalist, was so impressed by what she made of this song that he placed it on the cast album not in story order as the penultimate number but at the very end of the disc. It was too conclusive *musically* to fit anywhere else.

At 300 performances, *Wholesale* did not last long enough to pay off. Nor did the show ever catch on as a cult favorite. It did, if nothing else, give Streisand her first taste of doing the same thing over and over, an experience she found all but intolerable. She hated not being able to extemporize, though changing blocking and line readings throws the other actors off. A star in his or her own vehicle can demand that the production accommodate personal eccentricities, as Al Jolson, Gertrude Lawrence, and Zero Mostel were known to do. But even after Streisand took center stage in *Wholesale*'s reviews, she was nevertheless only one-ninth of the principal crew.

At least, though, she felt entitled to experiment with "Miss Marmelstein," as she had the stage to herself for the entire number. By coincidence, it was rather the sort of thing Fanny Brice used to sing, as in "Second Hand Rose" or "Rose Of Washington Square," the confessions of a girl who is cut off from the standard joys of life. *Funny Girl* was already in the works, too (and David Merrick was at the time its co-producer), but all Streisand knew was that with this particular number she had a good chance of being on the way to the rest of an important life, and she needed to play with the piece, not adhere to a doctrinaire staging plan.

The song's cue was a stream of insistent demands from co-workers— "Miss Marmelstein! What happened to the shoulder straps on 807?"—till

Streisand, "at the end of her tether," as the stage directions put it, "collapses into a chair at her switchboard."[31]

That chair was on casters, and Streisand wanted to use that feature to glide around the stage during the song as she had done in her audition. Director Laurents, however, was adamant on letting the lyrics and Streisand's idiomatic Noo Yawkese do all the work. Let's imagine:

LAURENTS: Stay in that spot and don't move.
STREISAND: But what if I—
LAURENTS: Don't. Move. Just. Sing.

During the show's run, Streisand kept begging the show's conductor, Lehman Engel, to let her try the number in her own way. Just once? she wheedled. Just for one teeny little matinee? As Engel once told his BMI workshop in writing for the musical, her personal vision for the number was so wrong that, for the first time ever, the song failed to land.

So Streisand was still on the raw side, in need of coaching. Yet in certain scenes she knew exactly what she was doing all on her own. Thus, when Laurents checked the chair she sang her first audition in, there was no chewing gum under the seat. It had been part of the act.

The following year, 1963, saw the release of Streisand's first two albums, as well as a number of notable television guest spots. And then came the break-out year, 1964, with *Life* and *Time* covers following Streisand's smash second Broadway appearance, in **Funny Girl**. But, as I've already said, this show ran into terrible trouble during its tryout. There were a number of problems, but mainly three: the scriptwriter, the director, and Streisand herself.

The writer was Isobel Lennart, a Hollywood but not Broadway regular, whom producer Ray Stark hired when *My Man* (again, the working title for a long time) was going to be a film. Lennart had written movie musicals, mostly light fare such as *Anchors Aweigh* and *It Happened In Brooklyn*. However, she did co-write the more serious *Love Me Or Leave Me*, on Ruth Etting's relationship with an outlaw and vaguely similar to what happens in *Funny Girl*.

However, Lennart belonged to a world wherein the story material lies in the script, not in the score (with the obvious exception of dance musicals and operettas). A film musical tends to do everything important in the dialogue, while a stage musical does everything important in the songs. Though *Funny Girl*'s very seasoned songwriters, Jule Styne and Bob Merrill, knew that, Lennart never got the hang of it, and she had to be assisted by an unbilled John Patrick (whom Stark knew from a play he had recently produced, *Everybody Loves Opal*, though Patrick's script didn't save that piece from folding almost overnight).

As for *Funny Girl*'s director, Garson Kanin, here was a real disaster, helpless in mastering the intricate machinery and character interplay of a big show. A playwright who got into directing simply because it used to be routine for writers to stage their own works, he had directed only one musical, *Do Re Mi* (1960), and there he was protected by the show's stars, Phil Silvers and Nancy Walker, old pros who didn't need any guidance. *Do Re Mi* was a David Merrick production, and Merrick, again, was Stark's co-producer on *Funny Girl* during its preparation period. But Merrick, who could be a one-man *Our Gang* comedy when he was feeling frisky, must have decided he was going to pull out of the project, because first he twitted the very sensitive Bob Fosse, *My Man*'s director for a time, into quitting, and then he (I surmise) brought in Kanin with every intention of selling his share in the game to Stark, to sit in the bleachers and watch the fun as the direly overparted Kanin failed to put a big—indeed, sprawling—and only half-written musical together. It may be that Merrick continued to believe that Streisand was a born supporting player, unable to carry a show—and we do know that he hated Ray Stark. And when Merrick hated, he was capable of anything, even sabotaging a production.

Now Streisand: it turned out that she was not ready to delineate the conflicted Fanny, confident of her abilities (as a performer) but not of her personal appeal (as a woman). Thus, she's the *funny* girl—good, she fears, for a laugh but not for romance. And this despite Nick Arnstein's being attracted to her right from the start and Eddie, her sidekick (and the only other man in her life besides her producer, Florenz Ziegfeld), revealing in his big number, "I'd Be Good For Her," that he was in love with her, too.*

Streisand was fine in delivering her numbers, of course, and though she was already cultivating her lifelong habit of keeping everybody waiting for her to arrive for work, she never balked at the constant changes in script and score. On the contrary, she found the transitory nature of the extended tryout exhilarating—it was like playing a different show every night. She was, however, hindered by the confused script, which started as a show-biz saga and then, after the intermission, turned into a soap opera about a failing marriage.

Worse yet for Streisand was the hopeless Kanin, whose idea of directing was to let the actors get on with it while he and his wife, Ruth Gordon, sat

---

* *Funny Girl* opened out of town in such sloppy shape that at least nine numbers listed in the Boston and Philadelphia playbills were cut before New York. (Most musicals lose two or three at most.) "I'd Be Good For Her," which Eddie sang while standing on a chair in a dress that was being fitted for Fanny, was dropped because the show was juggling too many "other people" in what was essentially a one-person story.

in the orchestra murmuring to each other about who knows what. To many of the cast and crew and even to various theatricals who looked in on rehearsals, it was clear that *Funny Girl* was a mess and Kanin wasn't even trying to straighten it up. Some ten days in, he was blithely holding run-throughs when individual scenes were in a shambles.

Why was Streisand so at sea? It would appear that she could not negotiate Fanny's psychology, as well as bonding the character who sang with the character speaking the lines, without expert guidance. *Wholesale's* Miss Marmelstein had been a cinch, because there was no psychology to delve into: the secretary was a stick figure with one moment of personal revelation. Fanny—so grand yet so intimate, flamboyant and demanding and vulnerable by turns—was a challenge. It called for more than gimmicks and charisma. It required technique, the sheer physics of working through a role to find the soul hidden within it and to marry the songs to the dialogue. In musicals, the audience must understand what is happening in a scene's spoken lines before it can enjoy the lyrical expansion of the scene's emotions when the music slips in. And with *Funny Girl's* dialogue scenes gurgling in mystery, important numbers—even "People"—weren't working properly.

Isn't that shocking? "People" is not only one of the last truly big standards the American Songbook produced: it is as well one of Streisand's signature numbers. Yet the *Funny Girl* powers that be kept trying to eliminate it. The first of these was Bob Fosse, who merrily explained to Jule Styne why the song just didn't belong in the show, whereupon Styne did his own explaining. "People" belonged in *Funny Girl* because

STYNE: It's going to be fucking Number One on the hit parade![32]

Yet "People" really was dying on stage out of town, mainly because Streisand didn't know how to handle the ramp-up dialogue and how to "play" the song while she was singing it. And of course Garson Kanin was giving her no assistance.

Only one man, it seemed, could help Streisand find her way into the soul of Fanny Brice—Allan Miller, her former acting coach. Streisand wanted Miller to join the *Funny Girl* company (disguised as her cousin, to gull Kanin) and guide her work, line by line and scene by scene. As Miller recalled to Streisand biographer Randall Riese, Miller slipped into a rehearsal, then spent the evening with Streisand and her manager, Marty Erlichman, "going over detail after detail [about what] needed to be done with the show.[33] Barbra was saying, 'Oh, yes! Yes, right!'"[34] So Streisand hired Miller as her coach, offering him "the worst deal I could possibly imagine." Miller held out for what he believed he was worth, and Streisand, he says, "*hated* what I asked for."[35]

But she was lucky she had him, for a personal disaster in *Funny Girl* would have blasted Streisand's career as an actress, and the show really was *Barbra Streisand's Funny Girl*. She had a co-star, Sydney Chaplin, and he was the matinee idol of the day in light theatre. But it wasn't their story: it was hers. She got the star entrance, for example—walking across the near-empty Winter Garden stage from house right in a smashing white coat to enter a little dressing room setup to look into the outline of a mirror and say ("with self-derision,"[36] according to the script), "Hello, gorgeous!" Only it was less derision than a triumphant jest, because so many were so sure that Streisand—Barbra, the performer herself—couldn't make it this far.

Then, as a wagon bearing the poker-playing ladies of Fanny's mother's social loop rode onstage out of the past and Fanny dialogued with them to cue in "If a Girl Isn't Pretty," we understood that the scene was juxtaposing two time zones. One was Fanny's past, in the poker game, when she was just starting out. The other was Fanny's present, when she was a Ziegfeld star. "The whole world will look at me!"[37] Streisand cried, pulling off the chic coat to travel back in time in middy skirt and bloomers to join the line of dancing girls at a third-division music hall. And get fired: because "You don't look like the others!"[38]

No one ever gives praise to *Funny Girl*'s script, but in fact its first act tells a good story and gave Streisand major opportunities, especially after Jerome Robbins—the show's original director, way back when—rejoined the team in Philadelphia to cut and clarify. The show's poster billed Streisand and Chaplin together above the title (in that order), but she had eleven numbers to his two, both duets with her, and his own tiny reprise of "Don't Rain On My Parade." And by the time all his other songs had been dropped, he had no ballad to define his side of the "feelings" plot. And in a musical, a leading man without a ballad is a supporting player. Even Henry Higgins and Harold Hill have ballads.

And, to repeat, the entire work turned on Fanny's needing to see that she was not only funny but lovable, and, even after all the tinkering, the show never quite stated that clearly enough. Just for instance, the all-important final dressing-room scene, for Fanny and her shining love, Nick, appears to conclude this funny-lovable question. But then Nick leaves, someone offstage calls out, "Onstage, Miss Brice!," and she brings the curtain down with a reprise of the intensely ambitious "Don't Rain On My Parade," which throws us back into the professional world of the *funny* girl when we just thought we heard her redeemed as *lovable*. (The movie concludes more logically, letting Fanny sing her trademark torcher, "My Man," which does relate, if ambivalently, to the lovable theme.)

Indeed, isn't the "Don't Rain On My Parade" finale simply the climax of an evening of Streisand vocal spots? It suited the star more than the character she was playing. But then, *Funny Girl* was under construction right up to the day of the New York opening, when Streisand and Chaplin were rehearsing the last rewrite of the final dressing-room scene minutes before the curtain went up.

All those revisions affirmed Fanny while simply tolerating Nick, because in the end *Funny Girl* didn't care about the romance or even the funny-lovable theme: it cared about Fanny as a life force, a natural phenomenon, because that's how all the creatives viewed Streisand herself. Act One played well because it was obsessed with the unstoppable Fanny, while Act Two meandered because it had to deal with a Fanny in need, and it didn't believe there was such a thing. This is why *Funny Girl* is a difficult show to revive. It isn't really about Fanny Brice. It's about Barbra Streisand.

It certainly isn't about Nick in even the slightest way. Back before he started evaporating as Jerome Robbins cut away everything that distracted from the audience's engagement with Streisand, Nick had identifying numbers. One was in fact rather sharply observed, "A Temporary Arrangement [is the only permanent thing in life]," which warns us how unstable Nick's relationships are.

In all, Styne and Merrill supposedly wrote some fifty different songs for the show, including a title tune in the swinging Styne style. It does touch on the funny-lovable paradigm—"When his lips feel softer than bunnies," it advises, "show him that you do more than make funnies." But it was apparently meant only for Streisand to release as a single (backed by "Absent Minded Me," dropped during *Funny Girl*'s rehearsals) to create PR talkabout.* Rather a lot of Fanny's songs were dropped, including a repellent onstage number, "Something About Me," in which Streisand (costumed as a baby boy) and the chorus women (dressed as baby girls) discovered the difference between male and female genitalia. We're sometimes told that this piece went in and out on the same night, but it went in in Boston and was still listed in the playbill in Philadelphia.[39]

One number seemed to sum up the show's stagey sparkle so neatly—despite a smutty title—that it inspired the logo illustration of an upside-down heroine on wheels, "I Did It On Roller Skates." A flavorsome Bowery waltz, it was rehearsed (Streisand had to undergo skating lessons, duly photographed for PR purposes) but never made it onstage. Quixotically, it nevertheless

---

* Styne and Merrill wrote another "Funny Girl" for use in the film version, this one slow and reflective and very suited to Fanny's ID problem. With the addition of this number, the work's title, which on Broadway reads as a celebration, becomes on the screen a cross to bear.

remained on the show's poster art, and that of the film as well, though at least the movie featured a skating sequence, which Fanny comically wrecks.

Sydney Chaplin wasn't happy at his role's being whittled down, but he and Streisand had become intimate (or so the cast thought). Then the relationship soured, and Chaplin began to revile Streisand in an undertone during their scenes together.[40] This led Streisand to try to get through their dialogues at a certain remove, giving her a reputation as something other than a devoted thespian. A friend of mine in the show (heard as "Private O'Brien from Texas" on the cast album) thought Streisand was pacing herself to carry a big role eight times a week—and almost never missing a performance—by taking the book scenes at 4 or 5 and the songs at 7 or 8.[41] Too, she sometimes cut the ballad "Who Are You Now?," an awkward omission because it rounded off an important scene late in Fanny and Nick's relationship. George Reeder, a member of the ensemble who understudied Sydney Chaplin (and replaced him between Chaplin's departure and the arrival of a new Nick, Johnny Desmond), told James Spada that there were three tracks the *Funny Girl* company could play, at Streisand's command: "There was the full version, then a shorter version where she wouldn't do one or two of the reprises. In the shortest version [presumably the one without "Who Are You Now?"] we'd eliminate entire scenes."[42]

All this, combined with, again, Streisand's chronic and unapologetic lateness, may have led Tony voters to deny her an award for the second time. On *Wholesale*, Streisand's Best Supporting nomination set her against Phyllis Newman of *Subways Are For Sleeping* in a role with one outstanding exhibition number, "I Was a Shoo-In," the confessions of a beauty-contest entrant and as funny as "Miss Marmelstein" with more variety. (At one point, Newman recreated her talent-spot Civil War vignette in which a southern belle helps her Yankee lover to evade mean Cousin Willis.) Newman won.

Then, in *Funny Girl*'s season, in the highly competitive Best Actress category that included the beloved veteran Beatrice Lillie for *High Spirits* and a superb acting-singing tour de force from Inga Swenson in *110 in the Shade*, Carol Channing won for *Hello, Dolly!*. Nevertheless, *Funny Girl* truly expanded Streisand's abilities, once Allan Miller and Jerome Robbins joined the proceedings. Certainly, Streisand could not have gone directly from *I Can Get It For You Wholesale* to Hollywood: too much of the sheer physics of acting was missing.

Streisand looked upon her long run in *Funny Girl* in New York and then London as something she had to endure to begin her "real" life as a movie star, but the experience was a great deal more: a college of seminars in how to move, how to think, how to listen. No matter how independent a talent you may be, sooner or later somebody else has a line that changes your character's life. And you'd better be ready to hear it.

Streisand's Television

The old game show *What's My Line?* always featured a final segment in which the four VIP panelists, in masks, had to identify after a round of yes-or-no questions a guest celebrity, who might be anyone from Eleanor Roosevelt to Noël Coward. The big moment came at the very start, when the subject entered and signed his or her name on a chalkboard as the studio audience reacted with varying levels of hubbub and applause.

Streisand was the guest on April 12, 1964, just after *Funny Girl* had opened, and the public's response as she signed in was just polite. (There was more excitement when overconfident panelist Gore Vidal guessed Streisand was Joanne Woodward and removed his blindfold, which led to his immediate disqualification.)

Almost exactly one year later, Streisand was again the show's celebrity guest, this time to plug her first television special, **My Name Is Barbra** (which four words she used when she signed in), and when she first appeared on this occasion the audience erupted with an ovation. After all of her scattered broadcast guest shots, several bestselling solo albums, her *Time* and *Newsweek* covers, and the nearly block-long marquee of the Winter Garden overlooking Broadway with the girl, the roller skates, and Streisand's name above the title of *Funny Girl*, Streisand (who had just turned twenty-three the day before) was suddenly a full-fledged *national* star.

As with her discs, Streisand had artistic control of her "specials" (as they were called then), so she could dispense with the guests and the fake banter that invariably accompanied those television star turns—Dean Martin fielding jokes about his drinking, or Andy Griffith's rustic shtick. Instead, Streisand encouraged co-director Joe Layton to devise one of the unique evenings to that point in television history, not just because of the lack of guests but because of the way it juxtaposed disparate concepts into a unified whole.

One of those concepts repeated something Layton had tried when directing the Richard Rodgers musical *No Strings* (1962), bringing the musicians right onstage to dress the set and even take part in the action. Thus, after setups involving five violinists, then 'cellos and flutes, then—getting trendy—electric guitars, Streisand faced off with a tympanist (Layton himself, stone-faced and distant) for "How Does the Wine Taste?," given here as a subtle tango punctuated by another percussionist playing the "bones," lending the music a slinky eros.

Another concept involved the theme of the child versus the adult. The show began with a photograph of the very young Streisand wearing a paradox of a smile, obedient yet insecure, the photo slowly moving toward the viewer as, in voiceover, Streisand sang another kid's song, this one "My Name Is Barbara" [*sic*], by Leonard Bernstein. Then Streisand herself appeared, concluding the short passage at the title words. This led into "Much More" (from *The Fantasticks*), a young girl's ruminations about her maturity. Will she be sophisticated? Free?

It's an arresting number for Streisand to use as her point of contact with the public on her first national event, because it's such a *personal* portrait, especially as Streisand sings it. *Is* she sophisticated: that is, not just a regional talent, from Noo Yawk? *Is* she free: of show-biz cant, not to mention Guest Stars Doing Phony Banter?

And all this prepares for, eventually, an entire childhood sequence, using "I'm Late" (from the Walt Disney *Alice in Wonderland*) in reprises to transition from visual to visual, at first in a little house with five boys playing reed instruments and a toy piano for Streisand to try out. Slipping outside, she sang a group of kid's songs, including a Danny Kaye specialty, the rebellious "I'm Five," that brought out Streisand's zany side.

My Name Is Barbra put its star through plenty of costume changes, from sheer couture to a black turtleneck over white slacks for a real oddity, "I Got the Blues," rescued from *Another Evening With Harry Stoones*. This segment unfortunately involved an interminable story about an antique clothes button. Though the studio audience seems to find it uproarious, it's the very model of witless droning, perhaps the one flaw in an otherwise impeccable execution. (We should note an instrumental flub in "Second Hand Rose," in the "Jake the plumber" section: on the word "man," you can hear the percussionist come in too early and immediately cut out.)

In all, there is an energy of contradiction—first the grown-up child, later the moneyed pauper. So when Streisand arrives *en grande fête* at Bonwit

Teller, she wantons through the empty store trying on elaborate outfits even as she sings of poverty (in "Nobody Knows You When You're Down and Out" and "The Best Things In Life Are Free"). The show's most obvious innovation was the very simplicity of the agenda, An Hour With Barbra Streisand and No One Else. But the touches of now harmony and now dis-union made the presentation unique.

Finally, referring back to the musicians we saw helping things along ear-lier, Streisand got into concert dress in a vast room filled with orchestra players to close out the show with a simple song concert. We note the violin-ists tapping their bows (their way of contributing to the artist's applause, familiar to classical buffs but seldom seen on television), and now comes an epilogue: Streisand launches the verse of "Happy Days Are Here Again" (the published introduction, not the special one devised for her spot on *The Garry Moore Show*), and, as she reaches the chorus, the credits begin to roll.

In all, *My Name Is Barbra* was a mixture of long-established show tunes (such as "Make Believe," nearly forty years old then) and objets trouvés new and bygone ("How Does the Wine Taste?" came from *We Take the Town*, a Robert Preston musical that had closed in tryout just two years before), of Streisand's standbys and songs new to her. Her singing style reflected the different modes she had been using, from the liberty of jazz singing (in a "Lover, Come Back To Me" different from yet comparable to the one we've already encountered, on *The Ed Sullivan Show*) to the power-ballad style epit-omized in her "People," along with her comic voice for the children's numbers.

On this first view of Streisand by the nation at large—not just *Time* and *Newsweek* readers or theatregoers but the great mass of Americans "out there in Televisionland" (as airwave folk used to put it)—her most impres-sive quality was versatility. No other singing star could move from "People" to "I'm Five" or to ritual concert dress from "character" costuming with such carefree aplomb. Here was Streisand at her best but, as well, here was all of Streisand at once.

The critics were *very* impressed. But the best blurb came from "a young fan" whom Streisand quoted when she accepted the Emmy for Outstanding Individual Achievement: "Of all the people on your show," the praise ran, "I liked you the best."

Odd as it may seem now, *My Name Is Barbra* was taped in black and white. The first color show, telecast in 1951, was a variety hour called *Premiere*, featuring famous television hosts Faye Emerson and Ed Sullivan with some of the cast of the Broadway show *Guys and Dolls*. It apparently went over well to the five or six people who could actually watch it. (Black-and-white receivers couldn't pick up color broadcasting.) But then, the technology discouraged swift habilitation, and when *My Name Is Barbra* aired, most new television sets sold were still the old non-color models. However, CBS, which held not only Streisand's recording contract but her television agreement, too, thought a second Streisand special had to marry the new format.

It became the theme of the show, ***Color Me Barbra*** (1966). Right from the start, as Streisand, in voiceover, sang, "Draw me a circle..." while a silly-happy face appeared in crayon-style pastels, the show seemed conceived to exploit color, especially in its first segment, taped in the Philadelphia Museum of Art. Wandering alone through the rooms, Streisand let the works on view instruct her repertory. She sang Jerome Kern's "Yesterdays" (a natural choice in the presence of Old Masters) and then Sigmund Romberg's "One Kiss [one man to save it for]," after sitting in contemplation of a painting of a dreamy woman in pink. For the number itself, Streisand was transformed into the woman to tell us what her dream was about.

Next, gowned and bewigged as Marie Antoinette, Streisand added a dab of color into an antique black-and-white print, looking down from a balcony on the French Revolution in full swing, with the guillotine on hand. Aware that her time with us was limited, the queen rushed through a vocal version of Chopin's "Minute" Waltz (complete with some nutty Brooklyn intonations and a high G), finishing just before being dragged away by a black-gloved hand.

Modern art, next on the tour, demanded a wildly colorful "modern" dress, for "Gotta Move," written by Streisand's most constant arranger in these years, Peter Matz, and an Egyptian gallery led to Rodgers and Hart's "Where Or When" (because it's about déjà vu and reincarnation), with Streisand now done up as Nefertiti and the "Color Me Barbra" face reproduced as a hieroglyph.

It was an ingeniously thematic sequence, succeeded by one with live animals in a circus ring, adored by Streisand in clown attire, this to be followed, as in *My Name Is Barbra*, by a closing concert with an overwrought audience. The circus sequence emphasized the natural world after the rarified creative world of art, especially when Streisand got into a cage with a tiger or when a little penguin crew tried to jump out of its containment ring, and, as if soothing the public after so much adventure, the concert was somewhat conservative in both the choice of songs and Streisand's vocalism.

In all, there were three very distinct acts, each with its own guiding idea:

The Museum	curiosity
The Circus	whimsy
The Concert	glamour

and each reminding us that a Streisand special was a *Streisand* special, hers in every detail, working with the same team as on *My Name Is Barbra*. And this second show, too, was a smash in both ratings and critical opinion.

But the third special, *The Belle Of Fourteenth Street* (1967), co-directed by a returning Joe Layton, proved an outstanding misfire, so dire that Columbia declined to release the expected complementary album. The central problem was the overall concept: a revival of the kinds of acts normally seen in vaudeville in its heyday, before and after the turn into the twentieth century. Obviously, Streisand couldn't represent the sheer variety of vaudeville singlehanded, and, for the first time, she brought on guests. The central one was Jason Robards, then known for straight acting (in Eugene O'Neill especially) and not at all for musicals. It was a prestigious but inexpedient choice, for while Robards could sort of get through a song, his dancing was so primitive that he generally just stood there, clapping his hands, waving his hat, and trying to look at one with the thrill of the number despite being sidelined.

Furthermore, by 1967, very few Americans had even a remote knowledge of vaudeville, which had died out in the early 1930s. As *The Belle Of Fourteenth Street* attempted to bring back vaudeville more or less as it was rather than through the filter of modernistic retouching, the acts it presented came off as esoteric and even bizarre. Then, too, the constant views of the audience, the ladies in vast wedding-cake headgear and finery as foreign to 1967 as a costume parade for *The Vagabond King*, added to the confusion. Was this a spoof or a serious resuscitation?

For instance, the opening number introduced Robards and the usual beauty chorus in "You're the Apple Of My Eye," and already we were in trouble, because there was nothing usual about the chorus. Its six women were specifically chosen to revive the so-called "beef trust" of not vaudeville but early (that is, pre-stripper) burlesque, so called because the true beauties appeared on Broadway while the neighborhood burlesque houses took what they could get.

Thus, the show's primary director, Joe Layton again, advertised in the trades for women "under 45 (years) and over 45 (bust)" who could "fracture the scale at 200 or more."[43] But wouldn't Streisand's television viewers be baffled by a chorus line so unlike the ones of their experience? They knew nothing of the field expedients of ancient burlesque, and the "apple" number left them possibly more than baffled—uncomfortable. Because it looked as though the staging was mocking women.

Streisand then appeared to sing one of the oldest show tunes she ever took on, "Alice Blue Gown," from *Irene* (1919). During the vocal, slightly invisible wires pulled off bits of her outfit, then her gown, then even the top of her parasol, leaving her in tights and high-button shoes while an outraged mother dragged her leering young son out of the theatre.

This created another mystery: did vaudeville really undress its women?

In fact, no. Vaudeville was downright prudish in what could be seen or heard on its platform, with a censorship that forbade even jokes about divorce and an implacable blacklist to threaten any rebels. On the other hand, burlesque (in its later format such as we see in the musical *Gypsy*) did feature stripping, though ecdysis by concealed wires would have been technically rather advanced for any burlesque house short of the industry's Palace, Minsky's Republic, on New York's Forty-Second Street. Not that the television audience would have cared, but *The Belle Of Fourteenth Street* was confusing vaudeville with burlesque, though they were in effect contradictory forms playing to wildly different audiences. Why did Layton and company think that the rather grand public at their little vaudeville house would tolerate the "Alice Blue Gown" striptease? Yes, we know a mother is offended, but in real life the house would have emptied with shouts of outrage.

At least the following act was more forthrightly archival, though still bizarrely offbeat to modern eyes. This bit offered John W. Bubbles (the original Sporting Life in *Porgy and Bess*, thirty-two years before). Joe Layton must have seen that old photograph of Bert Williams spoofing Edmond Rostand's play *Chantecler* in *Follies of* 1910* and decided to animate it: so Bubbles now sang and danced "I'm Goin' South" in the costume Layton saw in the Williams photograph, against a backdrop of barn and haystacks. (In another anachronistic error, the scenery looks exactly like something from the original *Oklahoma!*, which came along more than thirty years after Williams performed the *Chantecler* parody.) Worse, where Jason Robards wasn't musically gifted, Bubbles—who was—never really takes stage.

It says a lot that "The Dancing Duncans," the following act, is the least terrible on the entire bill yet still isn't good. It, too, revives an old vaudeville trope, the family "patriotic" number, such as The Four Cohans used to perform when George M. was still working with his parents and sister. Streisand and Robards are the dad and mom, of son Lee Allen (who had taken over the sidekick role in the stage *Funny Girl* and would play it in the film), a little girl, and, at the very end, a baby. Everyone's dressed in red,

---

* This new work by the author of *Cyrano de Bergerac* was announced for Broadway for 1911, in a Charles Frohman production starring Maude Adams. The combination of the witty Rostand, the classy Frohman, and Adams—the most farouche and seductive of the women stars—made the show such big news that Ziegfeld could program a take-off skit fully half a year before *Chantecler*'s New York premiere. Everyone in the play is a barnyard animal, and Williams appeared in the spoof as a rooster.

white, and blue, proclaiming love for America and, as the genre demands, adding that they're originally from somewhere else, Robards a Scot and Streisand Irish, complete with a brogue.

A salute to vaudeville wouldn't be complete without a recollection of the quick-change playlet, in which one or two actors took on a host of characters through ingenious two-second costume alterations. Robards and a flying (for Ariel) Streisand give us a taste of *The Tempest*, with backstage shots so we can See How It's Done—yet, again, who among us actually knows why these two are performing Shakespeare in this manner? The last time I saw a sketch of this type (on television) was so long ago that numbers don't go back that far, and even then it was incomprehensible: so much trouble yet for what purpose? Why not hire the extra actors? And why is Robards taking a fast drink out of a liquor bottle? Why is Streisand slapping away her dresser?

At that, why do we keep getting views of Streisand as a boy in the audience, attired in a bottle-green suit and reacting to all this? Eventually, this gets cleared up: the real Streisand, as a classical prima donna on stage, encourages him to sing the old Irish title "Mother Machree." And here the word "jejune" becomes irresistible. What could be less appealing than "Mother Machree"? A chorus in Grecian robes hymning "Trees"? A *This Is Your Life* segment devoted to Ethelbert Nevin?

As on the two earlier specials, Streisand closes with a concert, on a curtained stage with an accompanist at the grand, the diva now in ceremonial black with elaborate white fluffernutter trim and bearing a Tosca walking stick. So at least we get Streisand simply making her music, which is what we came for.

Keeping to the period theme, Streisand sings titles from the 1910s and 1920s, opening with "Everybody Loves My Baby." This treats us to a tech fail when Streisand moves downstage on the song's second A: for a few seconds, a microphone can be seen dangling above her. Amusingly, Streisand sings the number's second chorus changing vocal style every few phrases—a Mae West imitation, a rapid-fire delivery, a grandiose "operatic" version, and so on.

The other titles in this segment are done straight, but each one creates a shift in atmosphere. So if "Everybody Loves My Baby" is fun, "I'm Always Chasing Rainbows" is romantic and a medley of "My Buddy" and "How About Me?" is sad. Now Streisand speaks, to reaffirm the period flavor in crediting "How About Me?" to a "new young composer named Berlin, Irving Berlin. Remember that name—he's a good man."

This cues in "A Good Man Is Hard To Find," followed by the finale, one of Sophie Tucker's specialties, "Some Of These Days," capped by the ritual presenting of red roses to the artiste and the falling of the curtain. And note a witty touch in "I'm Always Chasing Rainbows": its main strain was lifted from the *Più Lento* middle section of Chopin's keyboard piece the "Fantaisie-Impromptu," and Streisand's pianist, David Shire, pointedly accompanies "Rainbows" with Chopinesque filigree. Further to pursue this in-joke for classical-music buffs, Shire quotes very precisely from the "Fantaisie"'s *Allegretto Agitato* theme at the close.

The Belle's terrible write-ups discouraged the Streisand cohort from pursuing the television format for a while, and after the broadcast of Streisand's open-air concert as *A Happening in Central Park* (1968), there was one more created-for-television variety special, *Barbra Streisand... And Other Musical Instruments* (1973). Previously, her shows had two directors, one (usually Joe Layton) for creative development and the other (usually Dwight Hemion) to know where to put the cameras. On *Musical Instruments*, Hemion worked alone, and Streisand, after the disastrous use of interlopers on *The Belle*, did, too...almost. She allowed one guest star, Ray Charles, for a self-contained segment with Streisand and five backup gospel women, the numbers including Charles' "Crying Time" with a disarming, murmured "Sing, baby" to Streisand when she gets a solo section.

There is, however, a huge orchestra of somewhat multicultural assortment, taking in a koto player (who arrives in a ricksha drawn by a Kabuki performer), a barrel-organ operator with a parrot, a musical saw, an Indian sitar, Streisand's temple-dancer finger cymbals and pitchpipe, and, in a grand finale, choirs of juice squeezers (complete with oranges), a coffee pot and tea kettle, sewing machine, toasters, and so on.

Most important, Streisand's own numbers adhere to the Broadway masters with whom she debuted, from Kern and Rodgers to Arlen and Burton Lane (for a spectacularly radiant "On a Clear Day [You Can See Forever]"). There is even a taste of Franz Schubert, though on disc Streisand had already moved on to contemporary pop, tentatively in *What About Today?* and conclusively in *Stoney End* and *Barbara Joan Streisand*. Further, she had launched the career she had wanted from the first, not that of the singer but the movie star—not a talent star, vocalizing her way through her parts, but a glamour star, setting music aside to provoke the iconolatry centered on charismatic figures who don't have to sing for supper.

Then came Streisand's aforementioned return to live concertizing after the passing of a generation; this gave us the *Live at the Arrowhead Pond, Anaheim* (1994) broadcast. Streisand's staff for the production was drawn from her "family," for while she staged the concert herself, Dwight Hemion co-produced (with Streisand) and mapped out the camera geography; Alan and Marilyn Bergman, lyricists on many a Streisand outing, wrote the script; and Marvin Hamlisch, who had worked on and off with Streisand since his job as the stage *Funny Girl*'s rehearsal pianist, arranged and conducted.

We get a lot of reality footage first, from various venues of the tour map, filled with encomiums from the fans and celebrity sightings. The only point of comparison in all of show business would be Judy Garland's live concerts in the 1950s, though there was always a touch of hysteria on both sides of the footlights when Garland sang.

Oddly, Streisand had decided to perform on a set suggesting an elongated living room. It was all in the white that Streisand loves, and backed by huge windows through which the large orchestra could be seen. Most impressive is the size of the Anaheim arena. While the usual big screen (seen but once in the broadcast, as if by accident) relays the action to those in the farther regions, the venue is so colossal that those in the balconies might as well be watching at home. At a certain distance, it just isn't "live" anymore.

"I don't know why I'm frightened," she begins, the first line of "As If We Never Said Goodbye," from Andrew Lloyd Webber's *Sunset Boulevard*. It's a very pertinent choice, its subject the return of the diva (who in fact suffers from stage fright) to once familiar but now alien precincts. And when Streisand gets to "I've come home at last," the audience responds with a standing ovation. They already gave her one when she entered, and we wonder if they're going to do this all night. So much affirmation of the diva would make the event grander than it needs to be, because the living-room set and Streisand's little ad libs on top of the rehearsal script create an intimate feeling, as if Streisand were entertaining a few friends. Of course, the Streisand crowd are all on hand, including mother Diana Kind, who is given a close-up during one of the many ovations.

"Mom, you stood up!" Streisand cries, along with "I'm glad you're here." It's a moment of reconciliation, after Kind's deflation of Streisand's youthful aspirations. Or was it so simple, after all? She did let her daughter try a season of summer stock when she was barely fifteen. True, Kind was adamantly opposed to the idea, but Streisand was adamantly in favor of it—and, in the adamant contest, Barbra always wins. One might call it stubbornness or fixity of purpose, but without it the Original ends up a sidelined eccentric rather than a pathbreaker.

Meanwhile, as Anaheim's welcoming ovation subsides, Streisand pursues the first half of the concert. She's in black with a lavish necklace, and, as the numbers parade before us, we realize that she's come home at last in more than one way: we're in a late period of Streisand's music career, when she had rehabilitated her Broadway repertory after a long time in contemporary pop, and the air is filled with Sondheim, Kern, Loesser, Styne, Bock and Harnick, and Arlen. But note that the audience responds most warmly to the Streisand standbys—"People," "Evergreen," "On a Clear Day [You Can See Forever]," "The Way We Were," "My Man."

Streisand, in charge of everything as always in this era, has clearly put some thought into the look of the show, especially in the use of projections. For *Guys and Dolls'* "I'll Know," she first recalls how impressed she was with Marlon Brando in the film version, then projects footage of Brando in the number and duets with him in descant. She even "enters" the footage with a shot of herself as the iconic bobbysoxer crushing on a movie star. Later, a segment with Prince Charles of England shows us Streisand bantering with him backstage somewhere, leading to a much-quoted joke:

> STREISAND: If I had been really nice to him, I could have been the first *real* Jewish princess![44]

Her singing throughout the program is very inflected, often different from her recorded versions, reminding us of Streisand the jazz singer, musicianly and extemporaneous in her dilations. She even improvises with her son, Jason. At the end of "Not While I'm Around," the camera picks up Jason and his father, Elliott Gould, in the audience. First Streisand was the dutiful daughter; now she's the protective mother, mouthing, "I love you" to Jason, who responds with "I love you, too."

There's interaction with others as well, when a *Yentl* medley inspires someone in the house to shout, "You should have won the Oscar!" And "You play so pretty, Randy," she tells the orchestra pianist, Randy Waldman, who is giving the keyboard an expertly light-fingered busybody of an accompaniment during "For All We Know." At the Las Vegas New Year's stand that spurred Streisand to take the show on tour in the spring of 1994, Streisand even programmed a sketch of sorts with Mike Meyers, in his *Saturday Night Live* ID as suburban yenta Linda Richman, in which Streisand and Myers traded quips in Yiddish. (Meyers did not take part in the tour and is thus not on the telecast.)

The Anaheim concert presents a personable and carefree Streisand, despite an almost political delivery of *West Side Story's* "Somewhere," which becomes a drums-and-trumpets war anthem ill-suited to the song's wistful nature. Clearly, she enjoyed the live experience despite her qualms, and in 2006 she produced another such show for television, making an exuberant entrance as if by magic, in a lighting trick, to materialize on the last chord of the original *Funny Girl* overture (in a new symphonic orchestration).

The crowd goes wild, and we're all in Fort Lauderdale for ***Live in Concert 2006,*** gazing at a set very different from the one in Anaheim. In fact, there isn't a set as such. Instead, Streisand moves around on a series of interconnected catwalks, the central span halving the orchestra with the conductor, William Ross, on the left; he's fun to watch. Other than a chair and table with a simple glass vase of flowers (and another table and vase way "upstage," so to say), the only visual on the "set" is Streisand herself.

Clearly, she wanted this television concert altogether different from the previous one, though, as always, she emphasizes white with a black supplement. The only color in view belongs to the two sets of flowers. And here's something new: tonight, the diva accepts vocal assistance, from Il Divo (Italian for "the god," most usually in the operatic sense of a Pavarotti or Villazón). Despite the singular billing, Il Divo is four opera-trained men who sing pop—a Frenchman, a Spaniard, a Swiss, and an American. Here's another innovation: Streisand plays the piano, albeit with rudimentary technique. "So I'll never be [Vladimir] Horowitz," she admits, and, as she is playing "Ma Première Chanson" from the *Je M'Appelle Barbra* album, she lets out a "Merde" when she hits a clinker. We also get to meet Streisand's bichon frise, Samantha, obviously uncomfortable onstage. Sammy "doesn't like show business," Streisand explains; and the dog takes the first chance to run to the exit.

By this time in Streisand's recording output, all three of the Songbook "comeback" discs—two devoted to Broadway and one to Hollywood—had appeared, and 2006 focuses even more than 1994 on the Arlen to Sondheim canon. True, a "short version" (as she calls it) of "Stoney End" reminds us of how influential Streisand was in separating contemporary American pop from the Broadway masters. Ironically, one of her old standbys, "(I Stayed) Too Long At the Fair," pure pop by the sound of it and which she revives here for the first time in forty years, is actually a show tune, from *The Billy Barnes Revue* (1959).

Naturally, the audience welcomes its favorite numbers at the first few bars, but these Fort Lauderdale folk are less familiar with Streisand's repertory than the people at Anaheim; the Floridians are a bit tentative here and there. In a *Funny Girl* medley, few of them recognize "The Music That Makes Me Dance" (from the stage show only) but respond strongly to "My Man," the old Fanny Brice number that replaced "Music" in the film.

It should be noted that, by 2006, Streisand's vocal abilities were unmistakably in slight decline. She is sixty-four years old now; her tone has thinned and her technique doesn't "speak" as brilliantly as of old. Singing "Somewhere" with Il Divo, she inflects the last word of the lyric, the title word, till she gets a melisma of eight notes out of the two syllables, an exciting conclusion but not as freely delivered as it wants to be. Singing is physical: the voice ages along with its owner.

Streisand's fans greatly enjoy media souvenirs of the **Back To Brooklyn** tour (2012), presented with the Italian male vocal trio Il Volo (Flight) and even family—Jason Gould and Streisand's younger sister, Roslyn Kind. Some actually prefer this concert to earlier ones, though one has the feeling that Streisand is husbanding her resources more prudently than ever.

Still, Streisand eventually planned another telecast, this one, in the modern style, for streaming on Netflix, **Barbra: The Music . . . The Mem'ries . . . The Magic!** (2017). A modest venture by comparison with 1994 and 2006, it offers no set in any real sense and uses a small band with, besides Randy Waldman at the piano, the metallic squeal of three synthesizers. Guests Jamie Foxx, Patrick Wilson, and (posthumously, on tape) Anthony Newley repeat their duets with Barbra from her CD *Encore*, and the difference between them and their hostess in vocal production is notable. The show was taped (in Miami) in 2016, when Streisand was seventy-four, and the slight difficulties apparent in 2006 are now unfortunately in the calamity stage. Streisand said at the time that she felt this would be her last tour.

In closing this chapter, we should note that while Streisand's television specials were pioneers in widening the parameters of the form, there is much less one can do in the strict concert genre, which is why we needn't discuss all of them individually. Streisand's fans are so eager to hear her singing to them live that the less "creativity" the better. They are great occasions, yes, but there is no way they can rival the imaginative variety of, for instance, *Color Me Barbra* without losing the essence of the concert: you, Streisand, music.

Streisand's Recordings

Streisand's establishing LP was to have been a live performance taken down at the Bon Soir, if only because her larger-than-life interpretations seemed to need the personability and audience hubbub that club dates emphasize. But there were problems with the sound, and the proposed title, *Barbra Streisand At the Bon Soir*, sounded too niche, with its reference to a venue known only to some New Yorkers. So, on January 23, 1963, Streisand began a three-day studio taping of *Sweet and Saucy Streisand*.

At least, that was Columbia's proposed title; she herself, as CEO of the artistic side of the project, called it **The Barbra Streisand Album** (1963). She chose also the cover art, her photograph, taken (by Hank Parker) during her stand at the Bon Soir and intended for the canceled live album: Streisand half-emerged from nightclub darkness, in a brown herringbone vest over a white shirt, collared with a big bow and sealed with a black necktie, all of her own design. It's an arresting shot, as Parker caught her in mid-note, looking winsome and contented.

The program on this first Streisand recital disc is devoted to the singer's versatility, theatrics, bravado, humor, and unpredictability. Yes, winsome is in there as well, but so is Streisand's vengeful "Cry Me a River" and her sophisticated take on "Happy Days Are Here Again." Then, too, Peter Matz scored the music (working, perhaps, off of Peter Daniels' arrangements that Streisand used in her club act) to emphasize a *concertante* approach, using a great deal of solo lines for the players.

Of course, as some of Columbia's executives were skeptical of Streisand's reach, every expense was spared, and Matz had to use a smaller orchestra than was usual. So, instead of the string or brass choirs expected of pop recitals, Matz spotlit specific instruments. A walking string bass introduces the first cut, "Cry Me a River," much too histrionic for the opening song, if you're going for normal. Tradition requires the singer to *usher* the listener in. Easily, casually, gently.

Streisand does that, in fact. But she's fooling you. She starts on the sweet side over that plucked bass fiddle, and Matz brings in sustained strings and then the brass in the second A. As Streisand highlights certain words, the anger starts to break through, so she deliberately fudges composer-lyricist Arthur Hamilton's cute rhyme of "Love was too ple*beian*" with "You were through with *me an'* [for "and"]." Streisand thinks it's too clever, a distraction from her "bust the dam" intensity. She is so in command of being out of control that it's not about the words or the music: it's about telling a story. "Come on!" she almost shouts, then repeats it. She isn't just singing; she's *taunting* her ex, with a fierce blend of short and long notes, mounting to a steady blast on the belter's high D (that is, the ninth above middle C). Streisand grasps that note, throttling the miscreant, while the band plays a finish as if trying to make her stop. They must have angry ex-girl friends, too.

But now the second cut, "My Honey's Loving Arms," strolls in, with a bright, jazzy vamp and a lot of brass and xylophone. This is the number in which Streisand gets whimsical about the reference to a morris chair, omitting the following line ("Oh, what a happy pair") to ask the listener what a morris chair is.* Though Streisand sounds totally at one with the merry romance, she phrases the last word of the lyrics ("arms") as a question: just kidding, after all.

The third number is neither intense nor merry but rather an even-tempered cavatina made mostly of chains of smoothly moving half- and quarter-notes, lending it an air of sublime stability. The piece is "I'll Tell the Man In the Street," from Rodgers and Hart's *I Married an Angel* (1938), and we now sense that Streisand's debut album has been designed not only to show off her versatility but to reaffirm her engagement with us on every single band, creating a disc with nothing but very striking opening numbers.

Thus, the fourth song, "A Taste Of Honey," is notable in just that way, as a slow and tender version of a number generally given a livelier rendition. Bobby Scott composed it as an incidental theme for the 1960 Broadway production of Shelagh Delaney's play of the same title, and Ric Marlow gave it lyrics in a vaguely romantic context. There are instrumental versions (most famously by Herb Alpert's Tijuana Brass) and vocals (including

---

* Webster 3: "An easy chair with an adjustable back and removable cushions." In other words: a make-out seat.

one from the Beatles), but none as atmospheric as Streisand's here. The guitar and viola (later joined by flute) suggest a folk song, in stark contrast with the album's earlier cuts, as if the orchestrations are displaying their versatility, too.

The fifth number is the most contrasting of all—"Who's Afraid Of the Big Bad Wolf," from the 1933 Walt Disney Silly Symphony *Three Little Pigs*. Again, we first hear a solo from the band, a perky melody in the clarinet— but the first eight notes are the Cat Theme from Prokofyef's *Peter and the Wolf*, just as we hear it in the original. As a little inside joke, it is another reminder that Barbra Streisand Inc. was, in a certain way, an outfit drawing on the expertise of knowledgeable musicians.

"Big Bad Wolf" was the selection that most distressed Columbia's suits, so Streisand knew it was the right choice. Suits know only three things: money, convention, and doing what everybody else is already doing. One might even suggest that the history of art—from the ancient Greeks to the present—has been a war between Originals and suits. In fact, "Big Bad Wolf" is a hoot, with an arrangement pitched partway between affectionate and spoofy, and Streisand twice jumps up to a mock-soprano high note. As used in the Disney cartoon, the number is an eight-minute opera, with solo lines for the three pigs and the wolf; for general use, Disney published a narrated version, and this is what Streisand sings.*

No doubt her unapologetic sense of fun puts some people off; most singers would "manage" the fun instead of openly enjoying it (if they sang this crazy piece at all). However, *The Barbra Streisand Album* was meant to free Streisand from the constraints of the book musical. She made the disc after *Wholesale* and before *Funny Girl*, story shows that obviously did not give her the artistic control she wielded in the recording studio. On *The Barbra Streisand Album*, finally, she isn't concerned with the problems of Miss Marmelstein or Fanny Brice: she's creating her own world.

After "Big Bad Wolf," in "Soon It's Gonna Rain"; in the ecstatic "Happy Days Are Here Again" (this time with the published verse, as on her first television special and thus without the special material used on *The Garry Moore Show*); in the jaunty "Keepin' Out Of Mischief Now" (with the band coming in on two "Oh, yeah!"s); and in a "Much More" fondled by the harp, Streisand finds something new in everything she sings. Yes, it's true of

---

* "At the Codfish Ball," a Shirley Temple tune from *Captain January* (1936), was the other kid's number Streisand maintained in her club act. But this one she delivered in a lazy "after hours" manner quite unlike Temple's prancing version. "Codfish" was included on the aborted Beau Soir live LP; Streisand never recorded it again, though she did include *Pinocchio*'s "I've Got No Strings" on the *My Name Is Barbra* disc.

many other vocalists—but Streisand introduces the quixotic or mysterious as well, as if her numbers had been sleeping beauties, waiting to be awakened by talent.

There is one mishap, in the succeeding selection, "Come To the Supermarket (In Old Peking)," from Cole Porter's last score, for the television musical *Aladdin* (1958). If "Big Bad Wolf" comes off as camp, "Supermarket" is a straight comedy number, a list song on the store's inventory, unfortunately without a single clever phrase. The citations run from "a teapot early Ming" to "a bee without a sting," which is Porter not even trying. (Think, for comparison, of Porter's "You're the Top," with its cornucopia of saucy similes, such as "You're the moon over Mae West's shoulder.")

Streisand sails breathlessly through the piece in hopes of giving it some absurd presence, to no avail. If the album needed a sophisticated comedy number to balance the infantile "Big Bad Wolf," why not Porter's "Always True To You In My Fashion" or "The Physician," a list song with a point? (It turns out the good doctor lusts but does not love.)

Now comes the last cut, a Streisand staple from her earliest days as a singer, the exquisite "A Sleepin' Bee," from Harold Arlen and Truman Capote's *House Of Flowers* (1954). Here, too, is a dramatic notion: if you catch one of those Cole Porter bees without a sting, to hold painlessly in your hand, you will be blessed with romance.

It's worth comparing Streisand's reading with that of Diahann Carroll on *House Of Flowers'* original-cast disc, for the two versions highlight for us not only the difference between the Broadway and pop styles but also between prevailing manners in interpretation Before Streisand and After. Carroll has the advantage of the full theatre kit, with some dialogue ramp-up and three facetious friends to assist in her bee test, based on the advice of the local voodoo mage. "What you give the Houngan for this information?" one of the girls asks suspiciously, sensing the usual scam (Carroll had to give up her gold bracelet), and the immediacy of the exchange brings us right into the Alvin Theatre during *House Of Flowers'* original run.

And of course there's Carroll herself, hired for the part because she was young and cute and sang in an odd kind of low-range soprano that gave her a girlish contrast with all the belters in the cast, which included Pearl Bailey and Juanita Hall. Carroll's "Sleepin' Bee" is smooth and rather uninflected till an emphasis on "one true love" in the final phrase.

With no theatrical trappings to play with, and skipping the explanatory verse attached to the published sheet music, Streisand nevertheless creates a sense of innocent wonder from the first note, in a very slow and free rendition, broad and beseeching; one sees why this number in particular alerted her first listeners that she wasn't just a new talent but an insurgent one. "Sleep on, bee" (because of course it didn't sting her) is nearly whispered, and when Streisand gets to that last phrase she takes an unwritten high note in very light head voice on an F, holding it out and then dropping down from it in an all but strangled gasp.

Thus Streisand pushes the interpreter's dramatization to its limits. Any more and the music would implode—but any less, from any other singer, will now feel undersung. *The Barbra Streisand Album* was very influential, but only in the long run, for sales started off slowly (to the smug delight of at least a few of the suits). Yet the album eventually charted in the Top 40 for seventy-eight weeks and won the Grammy as Album Of the Year.

The Second Barbra Streisand Album (1963), released six months later, marked a certain slight departure, though the arrangements were again by Peter Matz and (now credited) Peter Daniels. Gone were the comedy numbers, the campy bits, the goofy *Lucia di Lammermoor* high notes, the band coming in on the smartypants "Oh, yeah!"s. Most commentators prefer this disc to its predecessor for its sheer consistency, though it does hide an essential Streisand characteristic, her disarmingly self-deprecating sense of humor. Perhaps we can say the first recital is about exploration and discovery. This second recital is about colonizing and settling.

Even the overall structure is tightly conceived, opening and closing with "Any Place I Hang My Hat Is Home"; giving almost half the program to Harold Arlen; and alternating strong interpretations with soft ones. Strong leads off, though this first "Any Place" begins with only strings and harp in support. Then a crashing tutti brings the rhythm in, and by the release ("Birds roostin' in the tree...") Streisand and the players are flying through the air toward a *big* last A. One has the feeling of having listened to an impulsive vagabond—exactly the personality that Arlen and his lyricist, Johnny Mercer, were limning in this heroine's number from *St. Louis Woman* (1946). It's akin to Rodgers and Hart's "The Lady Is a Tramp," telling of a young girl with no address but freedom. And that's exactly what Streisand sings to us.

This is why Jule Styne's liner notes for the album likened Streisand to "a great *actress*" who turns a song into "a well-written three-act play."[45] Harold Arlen himself had contributed the first disc's liner notes, a thin little puff piece. Styne, however, analyzes Streisand's ability to build a number on the grand scale by turning it into a kind of characterological sonata-allegro movement, with an exposition, a development, and then (instead of a recapitulation) a "tremendous conclusion,"[46] as Styne phrases it.

Of course, not every Streisand number is a little three-act play. The second cut, "Right As the Rain," is soft, starting out with the cool, placid sound of the flute and never building the tension. But then comes the third Arlen in a row, "Down With Love," this one soft and *then* strong. It starts with the voice a cappella, brings in another of those walking bass fiddles on the second A, and lets the brass compete while Streisand indulges in one wacky touch, rendering "birds" as "boids." We've heard from the orchestra's soloists throughout the first chorus; now the entire band swoops in with maximum prejudice.

"Down With Love" originated in the show *Hooray For What?* (1937) as a merry goof on torch songs, put over in Kay Thompson close harmony by the show's singing leads, Jack Whiting, June Clyde, and Vivian Vance.* Streisand, however, makes the number a burning issue. Even: a dire "Where do I go from here?" cascade of lyric clichés that she raps out over bongo drums. Love gone sour isn't grim: it's hysteria. We hear chance quotations of Kern, Rodgers and Hart, Lerner and Loewe, the Gershwins, Arlen-within-Arlen, and, at the number's end, that soigné Cole Porter. Deliriously, radiantly angry, Streisand asks—no, demands—of us, "What is this thi-hing called love?"

But next we go soft, on *Oliver!*'s "Who Will Buy?" In the show itself, the song began with an introduction of London street vendors' cries, then interspersed them within the lines of the refrain, which eventually became a production number. Yet Streisand scales everything back for her version, not only soft but intimate, in a chamber scoring. As always, she points up the words as no one else does, picturesquely, whimsically, as in an indescribably engaged pronunciation of "wonderful feeling" in the last A. You don't just hear her: you see her.

And then we go very strong, in "When the Sun Comes Out." It's more Arlen, premiered in 1941 by the Jimmy Dorsey Band, so Peter Matz scored it to emphasize forties swing-band brass. The original vocalist, Helen O'Connell, would have given the tune a sweet sound, but Streisand pulls it apart and then puts it back together in a fierce reading capped by the jazz singer's typical final high note.

Thus the album continues, from strong to soft and back, with many arresting touches—a solo violin for Kander and Ebb's pop tune "My Coloring Book"; an accordion for their "I Don't Care Much" to honor its European derivation (it was written for *Cabaret*); a high F sharp in head voice for

---

* Famed as the non-musical Ethel Mertz on *I Love Lucy*, Vance sang on Broadway throughout the 1930s with a belt secure enough to let her understudy Ethel Merman in *Anything Goes*.

"(I Stayed) Too Long At the Fair"; and, as I've said, the return of "Any Place I Hang My Hat Is Home" at the end of "Like a Straw In the Wind," to close the concert with unifying punctuation.

Between these first two releases, Streisand appeared at San Francisco's Hungry i, long established as a showcase for innovative talent. (Typically, Streisand's opening act was an unknown comic named Woody Allen.) An indie label, Bel Canto, brought out an unauthorized LP of one of Streisand's sets as *Streisand Live—1963*, with a cover shot of the singer in the sailor blouse and fluffy tie she favored in those days, and the program entirely duplicates songs heard on the first two Columbia discs (except for "Bewitched," recorded for the first disc but not published till *The Third Album*, discussed below).*

Accompanied by San Franciscans on guitar, bass, and drums and her own indispensable Peter Daniels on piano, Streisand treats her Hungry i audience to the same arrangements heard on her commercial releases, albeit without Peter Matz's superb orchestrations. There are little changes here and there as Streisand improvises, and she is not in her best voice in her upper range; she omits the high note at the end of "Happy Days Are Here Again." But we get a rare impression of early Streisand shmoozing with the audience, as when she credits her players. "At the left side here," she jokingly tells us of the drummer, "at 183 [pounds]...wearing black trunks...,"[47] and when one lone fan tries to applaud after a little taste of Leonard Bernstein's song cycle *I Hate Music*, Streisand explains, "That's not a song. That's a thing."[48] She even indulges in a bit of the "flatter the public" shtick, with "Oh, you're a good group"[49]—but only after they go all out in cheering "Down With Love."

With most singers, a live performance before an attentive audience is artisanal music-making, more vital than the canned studio product. Streisand, however, is one performer who is vivacious in the studio, so this bootleg is not as essential as one might think. In an odd side note, however, the voice heard introducing Streisand at the start of Side One belongs to a historical personage: Alvah Bessie, one of the Hollywood Ten. Blacklisted out of screenwriting, he made his way to northern California and ended up running sound and lights for the Hungry i. Bessie creates a link with *The Way We Were*, as Streisand's Katie Morosky Gardiner travels to New York to support the Ten, dramatizing the reason her marriage breaks apart: politics beats love. Sub-side note: Bessie mispronounces the singer's surname, with a z instead of an s.[50]

---

* This live performance should not be confused with the live Bon Soir concert that was to have been Streisand's first Columbia LP.

The Third Album and *People* (both in 1964), Streisand's immediately succeeding Columbia recitals, adhered to the model created in *The Second Barbra Streisand Album*: a preponderance of old and new Broadway but without the zany touches of the first album. Matz and Daniels were still on the arranging team (now joined by Sid Ramin and Ray Ellis on *The Third Album* and only Ellis on *People*), in the same very varied scoring charts and lots of solo work—a lone violin at the end of "Bewitched" on *The Third Album*; a jazz xylophone rampaging through "I'm All Smiles" or driving bongos in "Love Is a Bore" on *People*.

To repeat, the gags are notable in their absence, though Streisand ends *People*'s "When In Rome (I Do As the Romans Do)," a Cy Coleman-Carolyn Leigh hit for Peggy Lee, with the spoken interpolation of Julius Caesar's "Veni...vidi...vici," with the indicated little pauses that suggest a touch of lampoon. Of course, "I came...I saw...I conquered" not only sounds a classy archival note but also sums up Streisand's intrepid rise to power. In 1961, she was nobody in an off-Broadway revue that closed in a night. Now, three years later, she was the cover-girl star without whose acquaintance all the established stars' hold on fame would be incomplete. *Funny Girl* opened, and they came...they saw...they paid hommage in her dressing room—where, as she has told us, she didn't know what to say to them. Why did famous people have to "know" other famous people?

Streisand's interpretations on *The Third Album* and *People* are a bit freer than on the first two recitals, with lyric changes and more variations on the written notes. As always, there are certain lines she emphasizes for dramatic reasons—a very grand and conclusive "The world will always welcome lovers" on *The Third Album*'s "As Time Goes By"; or, on *People*'s "Love Is a Bore," a great crashing boldface delivery of the last line, when your ex-lover will show up again "to be the *bore* that he was *before!*" It catches the song's aperçu that need, not wisdom, is what drives us.

Oddly, for recitals with unhackneyed material in such smartly crafted arrangements, each of these two discs has a failure. On *The Third Album*, the mishap is "Never Will I Marry," a resoundingly defiant combination of credo and lament written for Frank Loesser's *Greenwillow* (1960), about a young man cursed with wanderlust. The song has a folkish tinge, conjuring up the fantastical world of a village located somewhere between Brigadoon and J. R. R. Tolkien's weekend getaway cottage. Anthony Perkins introduced the number in a ringing cry of pain, but Streisand's setting, by Peter Matz, is too pushy and modern—sophisticated, really, which wrecks the rustic purity of the piece.

People's mistake is *The King and I*'s "My Lord and Master"—another song written for a specific dramatic situation that loses its meaning when performed on its own. Worse, Peter Matz gives us an incorrect setting, as a foxtrot, where the original arrangement has a pseudo-Asian stillness about it. It's a very rangy piece, too, taking its stage interpreters to a high A sharp. Streisand sings the number down two-and-a-half steps, robbing it of the agonized brilliance of the last measures and making the high note (which is now an F natural) too forced and demanding.

We should note a ridiculous controversy over *People*'s album-cover art. Streisand's early recitals naturally bore a photo of the diva, each completely different in style from the others. After the aforementioned winsome neophyte caught in the shadows of High Cabaret (on *The Barbra Streisand Album*), the next cover was a bright black-and-white bust shot of Streisand in a sultry mood, all hair and skin to just below the neckline. For *The Third Album*, Roddy McDowall caught the singer in the nautical top we noted on the Hungry i pirate disc, here in color and quite small on a black background, Streisand herself rhapsodic, deep in the music.

Where do you go from there? How about to a beach on a cloudy day, where Streisand, hands on hips in summer attire, faces upstage (so to say), looking out at the sky, the world, the possibilities. It's a great photograph (by Don Bronstein), but the Columbia executives were horror-struck. Because, as everyone knows, if you don't show your face on the cover—even with a "Barbra Streisand" (in red) and a "People" (in blue) printed on the top right of the picture—*no one will know who is singing*!

It's that reflexively doctrinaire worldview that the Original must fight at every checkpoint of his or her life's itinerary. Suits, by their very nature, have no sense of theatricality, so they never understand that a star knows how to make an entrance. It recalls actress Eva Le Gallienne rehearsing Chekhof when the lighting designer got very busy with her gels and zircons for a moment when Le Gallienne was to appear, though she was an unmistakable presence in any lighting. As her biographer, Helen Sheehy, tells the tale, Le Gallienne dispenses with all this lighting fantasia. She'll come on and strike a match for her cigarette in her typically assertive way. Says Le Gallienne, "They'll know who it is."[51]

It was the same thing here—and the beach photo would have been clear to read even without the lettering. At a certain point, the word *star* suggests more than mere prominence. It's about that unmistakable presence.*

* Naturally, Streisand sings "People" the song on *People* the album, but the cut was first released as a single almost a year before the rest of the recital. This is because Capitol Records had the contract to record the *Funny Girl* original-cast disc, impelling Columbia to bring out its own "People" even as the show was still in rehearsal. Columbia's 45 was backed by another number from *Funny Girl*, a version of "You Are Woman" tailored for Streisand's gender as "I Am Woman." Onstage, it was almost

By now, moving past 1964, we reach the time of Streisand's television specials, so we'll skip past the accompanying discs (even though they have material not on the telecasts) to assess Streisand's first departure in her album format, *Je M'Appelle Barbra* (1966). This is French for "My Name Is Barbra," and all the material is French popular song as well as one new item, "Ma Première Chanson" [My First Song], with music credited to Streisand herself, all sung bilingually and featuring on all but one track an arranger new to Streisand, the Parisian composer Michel Legrand.

Exactly how French should this album be, now, as French popular singing is much spicier than the American style? For one thing, to French listeners the lyrics are at least as important as the music. In America, the reverse is true. In fact, French vocalists are often termed *diseurs* or *diseuses* (the feminine form), literally meaning "speakers," which explains why so many historical French cabaret singers—Aristide Bruant or Yvette Guilbert, for instance—have no singing voice to speak of: they recite. It also partly explains the "whispering" style in French pop, as exemplified by Lucienne Boyer and Jean Sablon in the 1930s. Further, there is the division between the *fantaisiste*, who toys with the material, staying outside its emotional content (such as Maurice Chevalier or Charles Trenet) and the *réaliste*, who treats each number as drastic autobiography (most obviously, Édith Piaf).

A natural-born *réaliste* herself (as in, especially, her Madame Defarge version of "Cry Me a River"), Streisand cultivated a *fantaisiste* side as well (most obviously in her merrily high-strung rendition of "Who's Afraid Of the Big Bad Wolf"). Yet we hear little of that more outgoing Streisand here, as if she were observing diplomatic protocols to avoid an international incident. And why is there nothing by Jacques Brel, whose zesty storytelling would have aligned with Streisand's sense of drama (though she did get to him later on)?

Her French, apparently learned by rote, is good; she often gives the verse in the original, switching to English for the refrain. Still, the program is curiously inauthentic, French yet not French in style. The second cut, "Les Feuilles Mortes" (Dead Leaves, known here in Johnny Mercer's translation

---

entirely a solo for Sydney Chaplin, because the tick-tock patter section for Streisand ("Isn't this the height of nonchalance . . ."), as she takes stock of the elaborate dinner-with-a-happy ending layout of the chambre séparée, wasn't written till the Philadelphia tryout. Thus, "I Am Woman" boasted a second chorus of lyrics never used in the show, and, further, gave Streisand an "extra" *Funny Girl* melody to sing. Better yet, it's a snazzy reading, with a lot of jazz-singer inflections, drawn-out emphasis of specific words (she crowds so many mmmms into the word "much" that it's almost copulating with itself), and a slambang final A. Unfortunately, when Columbia slipped the "People" single onto the *People* album, it left off the B side, and "I Am Woman" never got onto CD except as a bonus track on a 2002 remastering of *People* to be sold only in foreign countries, never in North America.

as "Autumn Leaves") is at least properly haunting, with an ingenious arrangement. It begins with a solo violin playing hurried scales *arco* (with the bow), changing to *pizzicato* (plucked by hand) when Streisand starts singing. She is simple, precise, engaged, reminding us that this once ubiquitous pop tune is the sweetest of all torch songs, as Mercer emphasizes the image of withered greenery as emblems of lost love.

That was Streisand soft. However, the seventh track, Charles Trenet's "Que Reste-t-il De Nos Amours" (What Remains Of Our Love), known in English as "I Wish You Love," is Streisand strong, too much so. Trenet wrote it as playful. It's not a drama. It's fun, with that very French view of sex/love as life's great sly joke. Trenet doesn't get strong in the number: he amuses himself. Streisand tears the fabric of the piece.

Then, directly after this, Streisand tries Lucienne Boyer's old hit "Parlez-moi d'Amour" (Speak To Me Of Love). Boyer's own version sounds like a toy ballerina cooing inside a music box; Streisand gives the song more body, turning it into something less delicate and almost ordinary, erroneous, even when she slips into French at the close. True, no rule demands that Streisand be as wispy as Boyer. But when sung full out, as here, the number isn't very French anymore—so what, really, is the point of this Gallic adventure?

Simply Streisand (1967) returned the singer to her standard format, with six of ten tracks all from Broadway and one from the movies; classics predominated, even from the 1920s. This was a less showy recital than usual, however, even given Streisand's stylistic quirks—her dramatic use of a song's verse to make the ensuing chorus a continuation of a narrative; her starting a number soft, then building to strong; her pointing up of specific words, as when "laughable" in "My Funny Valentine" is more chortled than sung; her use of melisma for dramatic sharpening, as in the last phrase of "I'll Know," when she gives the monosyllable "Yes" as three notes, intensifying the line. Above all, there is the overriding imagination that renders the familiar as delightfully alien, in "All the Things You Are," when Streisand sings the last word of the verse ("...you") as the first word of the refrain ("You..."), a touch at once logical and surprising.

Came then another departure—*Barbra Streisand: A Christmas Album* (1967). Though urban sophisticates go through life without ever hearing one, the Yuletide disc has been a staple since the dawn of the LP era. Everyone made them, not just the corny figures such as Donny Osmond or Kate Smith: Frank Sinatra, the Beach Boys, Louis Armstrong, Diana Krall, the rock band Chicago, Julie Andrews, the Everly Brothers, Elvis, Bing, and the Chipmunks. Now it was Streisand's turn.

And she is, for the first time in her album history, on the subdued side, dramatizing less and musicalizing more. A discreet choral backing and the ocasional tolling church bell add to the respectful atmosphere, but then the very nature of Christmas recitals—especially those that, like this one, include "Silent Night" and "O Little Town Of Bethlehem" and even the Lord's Prayer and Charles Gounod's setting of the Ave Maria—do call for a certain reverent attitude. This is a commemoration of the most momentous birthday in Western Civilization, and while Streisand opens with a headlong "Jingle Bells" and gets to such non-spiritual items as "The Christmas Song" (the one known as "Chestnuts Roasting On an Open Fire") and "My Favorite Things" (a show tune, no less), she is for the most part celebrating a religious more than secular holiday.

So everything is gentled down somewhat. Despite a *continuo* harpsichord on "White Christmas," we hear little of the arrangements in which Streisand sang against a *concertante* palette of soloists, and there is much less inflecting of the vocal line than before. "Silent Night"'s first chorus is sweet and pure and its second chorus a bit varied, yet we still sense a reluctance to take the music out of its traditional place. While *Je M'Appelle Barbra* abducted French chanson from its traditions, *A Christmas Album* is very much in style.

A year later, the *Funny Girl* movie appeared, and, in an apparent tie-in with its release, another celebrated pop singer, Diana Ross, released her own *Funny Girl* album, on the Motown label, giving us an interesting comparison with Streisand. For one thing, Ross isn't playing Fanny Brice: she's simply singing songs written for the character. Still, aided of course by Mary and Cindy, the Supremes, Ross clearly knows what *Funny Girl* is about, even if "Sadie, Sadie" perforce loses the sarcastic Jewish inflections that drove the number onstage. As Ross presents it, this is a hymn to marriage rather than a satire on the folkways of wedded life.

Interestingly, Ross includes "The Music That Makes Me Dance" and "Cornet Man," which are not in the film. And she omits the old Fanny Brice numbers that we hear onscreen, such as "My Man" (though Ross does render the film's title song). Thus, this tie-in actually adheres more to the stage *Funny Girl* score than that of the movie. Further, Ross takes a few liberties with words and even notes (that is, aside from her usual inflecting of the vocal line, in the Motown idiom) and adds a new spoken sermonette to the middle of "People" ("God's children...born to be free..."),[52] typical of black performing style at the time.

The album is terrible because of its coarse orchestrations, but Ross is good. What we do notice is a lack of characterization. One could say that Ross is soft and Streisand is strong in this music, Ross on the sweet side because music is a form of lovemaking while to Streisand it's a form of information. It reminds us yet again of Jule Styne's view of a Streisand song as a three-act play—and Styne, who wrote the liner notes for Ross, too, calls the Ross *Funny Girl* "a great concert [with] a relaxed feeling of fun."

That is a key phrase, because there is nothing relaxed about Streisand's approach to her art. You notice this particularly when listening to the original-cast *Funny Girl* after Ross' version, in all the colors Streisand brings to "I'm the Greatest Star," in the goofy ethnic strutting of "Rat-Tat-Tat-Tat" (so terminally loony that Ross avoids it), and especially the intensity of "The Music That Makes Me Dance." In Streisand's reading, you hear the hunger. Ross is simply spinning a dream. But the song isn't a dream: it's about hunger.

We should note, all the same, that—as Private O'Brien from Texas informed me—Streisand didn't quite sing what we hear on the Capitol disc on all eight performances a week in the theatre. Indeed, no one could have done that while keeping up the energy for the book scenes and the costume changes. You have to adjust from 10 to an 8 or 7 here and there along the way, and what we hear on the cast album reflects how Streisand sounded during the New York previews, on opening night, at certain other performances, and on her final Fanny in New York, when, after the calls, she sang "My Man" and everyone joined in for "Auld Lang Syne."

But how long could Streisand continue to concentrate on the Songbook? A vast revolution in popular music had just occurred with the release of the Beatles' *Revolver* (1966), and, especially, *Sgt. Pepper's Lonely Hearts Club Band* (1967), revealing how much potential lay untapped in "rock music." Indeed, the Beatles demonstrated that rock wasn't simply "rock" anymore, as in the dramatic melodizing of *Revolver's* "Eleanor Rigby," accompanied by four violins, two violas, and two 'cellos.

Streisand could hardly continue to dwell within what had come to seem an ivory tower; further, her recent albums weren't selling as well as the early recordings had done. The agent of change was Clive Davis, whom Goddard Lieberson brought into Columbia to update its sales appeal. And Davis duly moved the label out of the Songbook, signing Janis Joplin, Bruce Springsteen, Chicago, Kenny Loggins and Jim Messina, and Pink Floyd among many others. Streisand had no choice but to enter the lists.

Her first entry, in 1968, was a single—just a toe in the water—of "Our Corner Of the Night," rockish pop composed by George Goehring, a veteran songwriter with at least one classic in his résumé, "Lipstick On Your Collar [told a tale on you]," from back when rock was the more limited rock and roll and spent much of its energy detailing the ins and outs of teenaged dating. "Our Corner Of the Night"'s lyricist was identified only as S. Rhodes, and his work is hard to judge through the hazy sonics. There was certainly a beat to the music, announced at the start by an electric keyboard sounding the same chord over and over, but the number as a whole was tuneless twaddle.

Ironically, the single's B side, "He Could Show Me [things I've dreamed of]," was yet another of Streisand's Broadway helpings, this one from Nancy Ford and Gretchen Cryer's *Now Is the Time For All Good Men* (1967), actually an *off*-Broadway offering, on a nonconformist and even pacifist schoolteacher defying the rule of fathers in Indiana. As ingenue Sally Niven sang it in the show, the number was at first a ballad and then, in the more earnest second chorus, a typical stage-show character piece with the added life of Niven's soprano.

But Streisand, over a lightly Latin beat, makes it a wondering delight, and one can imagine her relief at encountering a real song on this "audition" for her sortie into rock. "Our Corner Of the Night," a bit of nothing set in the land of nowhere, gives her no outlet. In "He Could Show Me," when she gets to the phrase "I've never been there" at the start of the release, she lets the first syllable of "never" hang in the air for a moment, relishing this opening up of a character she can introduce us to. Backup singers get in the way on the second chorus—don't you people have a session of Carpenters covers to get to?—but at the end Streisand shows us the rhapsodic sensitivity of a the Girl realizing that the Boy can not only love but enlighten her, and that is what Streisand needs when she sings: a role to play. This "vocation," so to say, is her most significant break with the pop style that prevailed before her emergence—that "easy does it," non-dramatic approach epitomized by (just for example) Frank Sinatra. Maria Callas used to say, deprecating her own intense powers of musical acting, "It's all there in the score"—meaning that she was simply the handmaiden of Bellini's or Verdi's notes and markings.

Balderdash. Callas, like Streisand, was first of all an imaginative recreator of what lay in the scores. Also like Streisand, Callas wiped away certain predecessors in her music, the so-called canary Lucias and Violettas, who sang the notes but not the person inside the words and music.

However, this would become problematic when Streisand pursued, at Clive Davis' insistence, a relationship with the new sounds of popular music. She would have to find material whose style spoke to her, songs she could fit inside as comfortably as she did "A Sleepin' Bee" and her jazzed-up "Lover, Come Back To Me." And rock, even as opened up by the Beatles' experiments, did not necessarily complement the characterological content of the Songbook numbers Streisand had founded her art upon.

Her first full-length album in the new-to-her format was ***What About Today?*** (1969), whose cover art heralds a revised Streisand, with a curly hairdo and a somewhat insecure look on her face in her Richard Avedon photograph. Peter Matz is still with her, but the songwriters on offer are Paul Simon, Buffy Sainte-Marie, Jimmy Webb—and three numbers are Beatles covers. There are as well a (new) Harold Arlen tune and something by Michel Legrand and the Bergmans, but the rock element predominates, and Streisand is not yet in tune with it.

The Beatles' "Honey Pie," for instance, tricks Streisand with its faux-twenties sound. She camps it up with laughter and odd noises and ends with a goofy question (as on "My Honey's Loving Arms," on the first album). All this is wrong for the composition. Another failure is "A Little Help From My Friends," from *Sgt. Pepper*, designed as an exhibition piece for Ringo, the least exhibitionistic of the Beatles. Fans fondly saw it as, subtextually, suggesting that the other three were carrying the apparently artless Ringo, and it's a loving piece with a gentle swing. Streisand's reading ignores all of this, as she is trying to make dramatic sense out of a drama-less bit of whimsy.

Even Jimmy Webb's "Little Tin Soldier" feels stylistically incorrect, though in an interview with Lisa Torem for the British website *Penny Black Music*, Webb says, "I wrote ["Little Tin Soldier"] with Barbra Streisand."[53] Really *with* her? She collaborated? The piece is anti-war, as Streisand would have been, but Webb comes from "a very democratic, left-leaning family" in the first place. So what singer's input would he have needed? In any case, Streisand's delivery of the number gets bombastic just where the lyrics are plaintive, a strange note to sound in a pacifist song.

When Streisand gets to "Alfie," the theme song of the Michael Caine movie, she is on more certain ground. It's not a very pungent event—few Hollywood theme songs are, as they're meant mainly to attract PR and award-show attention—but she knows how this music goes. Michel Legrand's arrangement assists her stylishly, with high, wondering strings overlooking the voice at the close. And the final "Goodnight," John Lennon's lullaby for his son Sean, makes a suitable finale, with its spoken "Good night, everybody, everywhere" and a last sung "Goodnight."

All the same, we face the problem of a Broadway-oriented artist sampling contemporary pop without understanding that pop is often *atmospheric* where Broadway is *dramatic*. True, the Beatles themselves habilitated drama in pop, as in the aforementioned "Eleanor Rigby." But one can sum up "Goodnight" in its title word. Nothing else happens.

THE SECOND PERIOD

What About Today? got a mixed reception. But Clive Davis, determined to succeed with Operation Streisand and retool her appeal to the public that wasn't as sympathetic to Arlen and Styne as she was, brought in Richard Perry to produce the next album, **Stoney End** (1971). And here begins a new era for Streisand, because Perry found contemporary pop that was capable of bridging the distance between what Streisand felt comfortable singing and what was currently being written—to introduce her to, for example, the imaginative intimacy of Randy Newman and Harry Nilsson. If Broadway gives us situation songs that describe activity, pop takes a snapshot of a moment.

So *Stoney End*'s first track, Joni Mitchell's "I Don't Know Where I Stand," shows us a simple picture: a woman uncertain about her relationship with a man wonders what her next move should be. "Funny day, looking for laughter," she begins, and we know that Mitchell, originally Canadian, is telling us of another of her archetypal California women, her "ladies of the canyon." It's an interesting note for Streisand to start on, because Broadway was New York but Streisand is now in pop, and pop is Los Angeles. In effect, she has moved her art—and the cover photograh displays a western vista with two fancy red chairs simply hanging out while Streisand sits on a matching fancy red couch in the back of a pickup. Who took this picture, Sam Shepard? (Actually, Tom Wilkes designed the jacket and Barry Feinstein made the actual shot.)

From Joni Mitchell's ballad, Streisand moves to the up-tune, in "Hands Off the Man (Flim Flam Man)," a swinging Laura Nyro tune somewhat reminiscent of Jule Styne. With brass, piano, and backup singers moving the piece along, it's nothing but catchy, an amusing turnabout after Joni Mitchell's poetry. The album's arrangements, by Gene Page, Perry Botkin Jr., and Claus Ogerman, are wholly unlike what we've heard in Streisand's First Period; one wonders what Broadway would sound like if one of these gentlemen had orchestrated a musical at the time.*

From a showy humoresque, we drop back to a medium-quick ballad sort of thing in the third track, Gordon Lightfoot's "If You Could Read My Mind." Guitars and strings dominate what sounds like a big orchestra, and the lyrics give Streisand something to bite into, though they deal heavily in bemusingly unconnected images (as in "an old-time movie 'bout a ghost from a wishing well"). Rather than tell stories, these songs often collect pieces of a larger narrative left unstated, so the singer has to substantiate it with his or her personal engagement with the material. Not to get too highfalutin about it, we might quote Edmund Burke (with my italics): "I must *see* the things, I must *see* the men." This is one reason Streisand's fans were so keen when she finally started concertizing again. Not every singer

---

* In fact, each of the three was to have some connection to a Broadway production (however slight), though only Page actually helped score a show: *They're Playing Our Song* (1979), whose music splits the difference between Broadway and pop.

gets more out of a personal appearance than on recordings, of course, in how much he or she adds to a song's meaning. Ella Fitzgerald was as complete an artist on disc as live; her concerts were events but not, in terms of dramatic presentation, eventful.

The sixth track, Laura Nyro's "Stoney End," obviously holds the very center of the album as not only the title cut but the essence of the new sound Streisand needed to claim as her own. Still in her "movie musicals based on Broadway shows" period (*The Owl and the Pussycat*, her first non-musical film, came out one month after *Stoney End*), Streisand clearly feels exhilarated to happen upon contemporary pop music that suits her need for meaning in lyrics. "Cradle me, Mama," they cry, but Nyro calls up "the good book Jesus" as well, warning us that something lies subtextually behind the words we hear. Everything has gone wrong for the singer, including "his" love. Does she mean the boy in her life or Jesus?

The message lacks the conclusive precision of "A Sleepin' Bee" or "Lover, Come Back To Me." But Streisand eagerly responds to Nyro's shifting assertions, as when, on "Match my raging soul," she lets out a cry of crazy, joyous pain. The lyrics sound worried yet the music is jubilant. Later on, at the 2006 Fort Lauderdale concert, Streisand sang the piece quite merrily—at the suggestion of the audience, in fact, who seemed to mark it as a feel-good item. Yes, let's all rejoice in the song—but what if this Stoney End place isn't Loveland? Maybe Laura Nyro saw the phrase on a street sign pointing toward a beach, as legend tells. Maybe. But there's a persistent belief that the singer of these lyrics is a sinner who betrayed that good book Jesus and is headed for the ancient method of punishment for social outliers (Nyro was bisexual; is this what she means?), still in use in backward corners of the world: literally a "stoney" end.

As we move through the recital, we notice Streisand using few of the quixotic interpretive touches with which she has teased us in the past, as if she wants to get this unfamiliar repertory into her voice before she starts toying with it. There is an odd little laugh to launch the ninth track, Harry Nilsson's "Maybe,"* but otherwise Streisand lets the eccentricities of the material itself supply the fizz. The only problem with this richly pleasurable disc is the sound balance during orchestral tuttis. Given Streisand's meticulous management style, it seems odd that she let pass playbacks wherein the scoring muffles the singing.

Stoney End proved not only pleasurable but historical: Streisand, as the foremost adept of the Songbook, was hereby signaling her personal

---

* The first *Stoney End* CD release incorrectly programmed the laugh at the end of track eight; apparently, the engineer thought it more a caption than a foundation.

concession to rock's overwhelming of the Broadway-Hollywood inventory as America's national music. Here was a Streisand album with no Kern or Rodgers, no Loesser or Arlen, stating, in synecdoche, that the Songbook would now be, to an extent, marginalized.

It was a catastrophe for the legacy of the Broadway masters, but it was going to happen with or without Streisand; she was simply bowing to a cultural force majeure. For her own part, she grew artistically in learning to work with the somewhat ghostly lyrics of pop after Broadway-Hollywood writing, which is on the contrary explicit and character-based.

True, *What About Today?* found Streisand uncertain in the new style. *Stoney End*, however, was a triumph. And we can see how revitalized, how renovated, her repertory became by comparing the content of *Stoney End* with that of *The Second Barbra Streisand Album*, which formed the matrix of most of her First Period releases:

THE SECOND BARBRA STREISAND ALBUM

Five songs by Harold Arlen.
Two by Kander and Ebb, though one, "My Coloring Book," is
    non-theatrical in origin.
One by Romberg and Hammerstein.
One from *Oliver!*.
One pop-sounding show number, "(I Stayed) Too Long At the Fair."
And just one pop tune, albeit by her main Songbook arranger, Peter Matz.

STONEY END

Three songs by Laura Nyro
Two by Randy Newman
One by Joni Mitchell
One by Harry Nilsson
One by Carole King and Gerry Goffin
One by Barbara Keith
One by Gordon Lightfoot
One by Barry Mann and Cynthia Weil

It's all contemporary pop.*

---

* More songs were recorded and not used, a few to be published on later releases. However, some have never been available commercially, and these, too, are contemporary pop: Nyro's "He's a Runner," Newman's "Living Without You," and Lightfoot's "[Listen to them talk about] Your Love's Return."

Barbra Joan Streisand (1971) was very much *Stoney End*'s successor, with the same producer, Richard Perry. This disc includes two numbers by John Lennon, as if redeeming the unsatisfying Lennons on *What About Today?*. But there's also one cut by Michel Legrand and the Bergmans, whose sentimentalistic clichés sit oddly with Carole King and Laura Nyro, also on hand. In the following *The Way We Were* (1974), Streisand becomes something of a Legrand-Bergman propagandist, taking down three tracks. One, the sappy "Summer Me, Winter Me," had actually been sung by Frank Sinatra, who fails to match Streisand's commitment when she is all but helplessly singing past the instant poetry into the rhapsodic music itself.

But Streisand's *Way We Were* recital is known for a marketing snafu, as it was released at exactly the same time as the official soundtrack recording of the *Way We Were* movie. Now, this soundtrack really looked like a soundtrack, adorned by a shot of Streisand and Robert Redford walking along the southern California beach as they do onscreen. The studio album, on the other hand, struck an odd note, as it bore a photograph of Streisand wreathed in black and looking like an Iranian kindergarten teacher.

Both discs were Columbia releases, but Ray Stark, as the film's producer, resented losing sales of "his" recording to confused buyers. He had to organize a legal sortie to get Columbia to retitle Streisand's studio recital. And Columbia surrendered.

Yes. But Columbia then simply removed the words *The Way We Were* from the recital's cover, replacing them with a sticker reading, "including the hit singles THE WAY WE WERE and ALL IN LOVE IS FAIR." Yet the album *didn't* include the "Way We Were" single, Streisand's first 45 to reach Billboard's top-seller slot. And that single has never been transcribed to either LP or CD. The standard Streisand studio cut (as opposed to the movie version) of the song is the one that is always used, here and on compilations, and though both it and the single used the same orchestra track, the vocal on the single is just different enough to impress Streisand fans as being preferable. You can tell them apart on the line "Smiles we gave to one another" in the second A. On the single, Streisand goes up and then up again on the word "another"; in the standard version, she goes up and then down.*

The next recital to appear was *ButterFly* (1974), a victim of Streisand's inexplicable professional partnership with Jon Peters, credited as the album's

---

* On CD, the album is now called *Barbra Streisand—The Way We Were*. The disc itself reads "Featuring the hit single [sic] The Way We Were and All In Love Is Fair," though these two titles came out on two different 45s—and, again, that "hit single" of "The Way We Were" is not the one on the album.

producer. Perhaps this alone put *ButterFly* into disrepute, as the producing of records is a specialized art, a vocation demanding experience, technical expertise, and a dense knowledge of the pop-music field, none of which Peters could claim.

So critics and some of the public saw *ButterFly** as appointment catastrophe: you had to hear it because you knew it couldn't be good. Yet the first cut, "Love In the Afternoon," is beguiling, with "He showed me" repeated intensely three times, cutting through the sultry-ballad feeling with the typical Streisand naturalism, her way of individualizing the song's abstract pop flavor. It's Streisand as she has always been, Jon Peters or no Jon Peters. Whatever his effect on the physical act of recording, he could not influence the way Streisand relates to a song.

But he could program numbers better left alone. The second cut, Bob Marley's "Guava Jelly," is vulgar, not at all the Streisand we know, and the following "Grandma's Hands" finds Streisand trying out the gospel "shouting" style** that so entranced George Gershwin when, during the composition of *Porgy and Bess*, he visited black churches to experience authentic African American vocalism. Bill Withers, who wrote and introduced "Grandma's Hands," delivered it very evenly, to electric guitar and drums, but Streisand makes it fierce and nuanced—telling the story, as she loves to do, and letting her shouting rise to perhaps the highest notes she ever sang in chest, on G and A, as a Caribbean band pulsates behind her.

From Marley and Withers we move to the Carpenters' hit "I Won't Last a Day Without You," and we realize that *ButterFly* is featuring covers of songs associated with specific singers. The menu is extremely eclectic—the Carpenters, no less!—and of course Streisand generally sang covers in her early years in that she didn't "create" (as the French term the premiere rendering of a pop tune) "Stouthearted Men" or "Second Hand Rose."

ButterFly, however, is a veritable covers showcase. Streisand's "Jubilation," a Paul Anka specialty, is rather like Anka's, with its piano solo and backup choir. But Streisand's "Since I Don't Have You," a hit in the 1950s for the Skyliners quintet, veers far from the original, which was presented in the

---

* The upper-case *F* denotes a combination of "Butter" and "Fly": the album's cover art, of a fly visiting a stick of butter. Right. And Superman won't wear the suit or be seen in the air. Streisand is to blame for all this as well, however, for filling the LP jacket with thirty-six photos (cut back for the CD) of the sessions featuring Streisand and Peters snuggling, though we occasionally see Streisand discussing musical matters with conductor Tom Scott. These virtual honeymoon shots disguised backstage squabbles—the constant re-staffing of creatives, replacement of songs and arrangements, problems with the sound. *ButterFly*'s studio chaos makes it unique in Streisand's output.

** This antique term was the direct forerunner of "soul," describing a vocal delivery, unique to each singer, inflecting the vocal line with high-lying phrases.

shuffling beat of the dance called the Stroll and emphasized the lead sing-er's stylized falsetto laments, so much a part of fifties group pop. Streisand reinvents the music, making it sweetly sad and then (at the release) explo-sive, in another of her miniature dramas.

Yet some of these songs can't be so easily transformed—David Bowie's "Life On Mars," for example, free-flowing dada banged out in a hectoring manner. Streisand's version, the seventh track, is not too dissimilar, even given that Bowie uses the gulpy hiccups of rock vocalism and Streisand doesn't, and that she sees it as another of her gradual-build-in-intensity dramas with an agonized climax, and he lays it out more evenly. Still, Bowie seemed to regard her cover as an incursion. "Sorry, Barb," he said, very publicly, "but it was atrocious."[54]

More to the point, the album fails to hold together as a unit. It isn't just eclectic: it's an accidental panorama, a garage sale of pop, and it may never live down that "Produced by Jon Peters" line.

The next recital, *Lazy Afternoon* (1975), dispensed entirely with *ButterFly*'s wish to turn Streisand into a gizmo of hip—Bob Marley, no less!—and we note with relief that it opens on Streisand's surest ground, a Broadway clas-sic. It's the album's title cut, from *The Golden Apple* (1954), a modern retell-ing of Homer. "Lazy Afternoon" is Helen's seduction of Paris, tempting and fanciful, with superb lyrics (by John Latouche) and a bosomy, long-lined melody. Unlike most of the cuts in *ButterFly*, this one boasts a masterly scoring, so that a line about hearing "the grass as it grows" arrives as the orchestra seems to shimmer in the air at the very wonder of the green world, so still yet so alive, just like this music, Broadway music. It's a mar-velous rendering, and all of *ButterFly* is forgotten.

In fact, with this album we encounter an innovative format we can call New Barbra, creating a matrix for many of her successive recitals. From now on, more often than not, Streisand's best releases will include:

(1) A taste or two of the Bergmans' insipid bittersweet, set by various compos-ers, here Dave Grusin, for "A Child Is Born."

(2) Numbers drawn from classic pop, such as, here, Stevie Wonder's "You and I," which Streisand presents as something like a hymn tune, slow and steady. Soft at first and strong later, she finally pushes into fortissimo at the top of her range, only to die out in a sudden piano of voice and orchestra alike.

(3) New numbers written especially for Streisand, such as, here, Rupert Holmes' "My Father's Songs."

(4) A chance novelty, here a disco piece, "Shake Me, Wake Me."

(5) One or two show tunes. Besides "Lazy Afternoon," Streisand takes up Ralph Rainger and Howard Dietz's "Moanin' Low," a torch number from *The Little Show*

(1929). This was an intimate revue, the adjective denoting "adult" subject matter. That meant, in this case, an abused woman and her lover (Libby Holman and Clifton Webb, both in light blackface), who, after her vocal, went into a dance that culminated in his strangling her. Whether or not Streisand knew of this dire history, she truly sings this number *back*, to charts that suggest a combination of roughhouse forties swing band and the smooth Frank Sinatra-Nelson Riddle string sound of the 1950s. This is one of the best cuts in all of Streisand's Second Period, a real barn burner.

(6) Though there isn't one on *Lazy Afternoon*, the Duet With a Star soon becomes one of Streisand's favorite genres.

Something else defines New Barbra: a unique orchestral sound unifying certain albums. Here it is the work of the just-mentioned Rupert Holmes, who found an identifying style to reach across the silence separating the selections. Holmes and Streisand established a fine rapport that lasted till, right after *Lazy Afternoon*, Holmes was commissioned to write songs for *A Star Is Born*, in preparation at the time. Holmes quickly left the project out of distaste for Jon Peters' shock-and-awe approach to producing.

Before further pursuing the New Barbra format, Streisand tried out her most unexpected release, **Classical Barbra** (1976), venturing into the world of the "art song," from Debussy and Fauré to Schumann and even that most rarified of *Lied* composers, Hugo Wolf. Streisand's approach (with both piano and orchestral accompaniments) is scrupulous in all matters, yet the disc is a resounding failure, because crossover can work only in one direction, from classical to pop, not the other way around.

That is: a classical singer who has an ear for the vernacular music of her people can adjust from the high style to the low. Our old friend Eileen Farrell is a perfect example, superb in Wagner and Puccini but also in Harold Arlen. However, pop singers cannot move into classical territory, because there is a *physical* bar. To sing pop, one simply opens up and lets the notes out. Classical singing, however, is *produced*, which is why all classical singers must study voice before they can perform. Then, too, while they observe pitch and note values very strictly, they can effect subtle variations in the "feeling" of a phrase, coloring the sound, accenting it, all the while working with more sheer body of tone than pop singers can command.

Streisand is thus out of her depth. She is respectful but stiff, and her thin tone sounds like crooning. More: it has no give, no lyricism. This is an album of homework. To compare Streisand's "Beau Soir" (the Debussy chanson on the disc) with those of classical singers reveals how undernourished her version is. And note that she sings "Beau Soir" in C Major (the key that baritones favor in this title) rather than the E Major that sopranos use. It robs the music of its delicacy and sparkle; it comes off as turgid and dull. One might say that *Classical Barbra* was probably something Streisand had to attempt, given her explorer's mentality. Still, she had neither the training nor the background to fulfill the experiment.

Streisand then resettled in her natural habitat, with three successive issues of the New Barbra format, in **Streisand Superman** (1977),* **Songbird** (1978), and **Wet** (1979). The last named gathered up songs relating to water, so the show tune is "Come Rain Or Come Shine," the novelty is the old Bobby Darin hit "Splish Splash," and the duet (with Donna Summer) is "No More Tears (Enough Is Enough)," a disco piece long enough to be called a sequence rather than a song. Unlike many later Streisand duets, wherein the voices originate separately and are then blended, creating music with an air of fake news about it, "No More Tears" was recorded by both singers in the same studio at the same time. Ironically, disco is so processed a form that it wouldn't have mattered if the two had ever even heard of each other, much less actually met. A huge hit, "No More Tears" features the pair holding out their notes over the pounding rhythm, a useful way to excite the fans.

But then there are fan favorites on all three of these discs—*Superman*'s "My Heart Belongs To Me," for example, or "New York State Of Mind," covering Billy Joel's paean to, after all, Streisand's hometown. *Songbird* is especially notable for its Bergmans cut (to Neil Diamond's music), "You Don't Bring Me Flowers," because an impromptu remix of Diamond's own track and Streisand's version, played on the air, excited such interest that Columbia had the two singers get together for a single of the tune, another of those Streisand Duets and one of her biggest hits ever. It also provisioned a Famous Streisand Moment when she and Diamond suddenly appeared on opposite sides of the stage of the 1980 Grammys, without a warning announcement, to sing the number while slowly approaching each other, Streisand at length to caress his cheek. If not great art, it was certainly great show business.

Now comes another departure, as Streisand sought further rejuvenation with an arranger who, like Peter Matz and Rupert Holmes, would help her tape a recital with its own *tinta* (an Italian term describing a "coloring," a

---

* Fun (at any rate Odd) Fact: Streisand *Superman*'s cover art offered, against a solid blue background, the diva in her outfit from the "building a house" sequence in *A Star Is Born* (released the previous year): a sleeveless white T bearing the red and orange Superman logo, with matching knee-length socks.

unique sound style). The original plan had been to invent yet a Newer Barbra by partnering her with the Bee Gees, the Australian Gibb brothers Barry, Robin, and Maurice, who had written and performed the soundtrack accompaniment to the iconically youthful John Travolta dance film *Saturday Night Fever* (1977). As it happened, the Bee Gees' management demanded a prohibitive amount of money, so Streisand negotiated, in her characteristic high-middle Show Business Blunt, with "How much for just one of them?"

Barry was the one, and not just as an arranger but a writer, creating or co-creating (mostly with Robin Gibb or Albhy Galuten) all the numbers. Gibb's use of the Bee Gees sound—a kind of rhythmic wind blowing into floating clouds of pink puff—made this release the very opposite of Streisand's First Period discs, with their long-established show tunes in the old show-tune style.

Entitled **Guilty** (1980), the recital reaffirmed Streisand as the singer of the age in, commercially speaking, her most successful recording. Interestingly, it is the one that most emphasizes the singer over the actress. There really is nothing to "act" in Gibb's songs: they're about mood, not story, in idylls about love, more love, most love. There are no supermarkets in old Peking here, no secondhand Roses. "We are devotion" is a line in the first cut, the title one, but every song in *Guilty* is We are devotion.

This suggests monotony. However, the elusive nature of the music lends a certain variety, especially when Gibb uses the modal harmonic structure of rock rather than the more traditional tonic-dominant relationships of the Songbook. Thus, the first track, "Guilty" itself, a Streisand-Gibb duet with a backup chorus in gently rocking ballad form, never really establishes a home key. It would appear to be in C Major and E Minor at the same time, giving the music an airy suspense that the pedestrian lyrics lack. If Gibb's harmony were a whodunit, we would never find out who did it.

Streisand sings solos as well, and some of Gibb's compositions do use traditional Western harmony. The third cut, "Run Wild," is in a clear-cut e minor, which then moves into E Major at the title words, as if in the last A of Cole Porter's "I Love Paris." Porter often recorded himself in demos of a new score to teach the performers their numbers, and Gibb made comparable recordings of the *Guilty* songs for Streisand in the breathy, semi-androgynous style he and his brothers made famous, along with a ton of reverb. This led to an industry joke that *Guilty* was a Bee Gees release with Barbra Streisand.

It isn't. The *music* is in the Bee Gees manner, but Streisand's vocals have direction and clarity—not Bee Gees qualities—and she knows how to make a phrase tell, as when, in the fifth track, "The Love Inside," at the line "And we were cruising for the ride," she hits a B over an A Major chord (thus creating a somewhat unusual A⁹) that centers the piece. The Bee Gees don't accent pitches that way; their homogenized sound treats all phrases equally. Streisand gives the melody a stronger profile, so that a recital that might have been merely catchy and pleasing becomes something more. *Guilty* is not one of her more distinguished albums, but one can see why it is her bestselling one.

The next recital, *Emotion* (1984), is a step backward, lacking *Guilty*'s overriding vision, though almost all its numbers were written for Streisand, in the *Guilty* manner. Nor is *Emotion* one of Streisand's classic releases, though it did go platinum (that is, selling at least a million copies). But, in any case, Streisand then had another change of habit in mind, which brings us to

THE THIRD PERIOD

The Broadway Album (1985) returned Streisand to her initiating repertory, with contributions from Rodgers and Hammerstein, Kern, Gershwin, Frank Loesser, Leonard Bernstein, and especially Stephen Sondheim. In fact, another of those undoubtedly apocryphal Streisand Stories involves her supposed phone chat with someone (possibly a Columbia staffer, or orchestrator Jeremy Lubbock, or even her boy friend of the time, Richard Baskin, who was working on the new album with her):

STREISAND: I want to include that Sondheim number about…It's like (singing) "Nothing's gonna harm you…"
OTHER PERSON: "Not While I'm Around."
STREISAND: Not while *you're* around? What are you, the music police? Listen, if I want to sing Sondheim, I'm going to—
OTHER PERSON: No, Barbra. The title of the song is "Not While I'm Around."

(Pause.)

STREISAND: Oh.

False as the tale may be—and there are plenty of false Streisand tales—Streisand chose to launch *The Broadway Album*'s program with a number about confrontations with frustrators (presumably Columbia suits), and we hear them (in spoken "voiceover" simulations by David Geffen and actors Ken Sylk and Alec Baldwin) scorning the very idea of this return to the Songbook. "Sweetheart, it's just not commercial," one says, and "We've got to appeal to the kids."

The number Streisand is singing during this is Sondheim's "Putting It Together," and the author was happy to reimpose the number's view of the artist's vulnerability in a business atmosphere by writing new lyrics to fit Streisand personally. One of the frustrators even touches on the singer's wary PR policy by asking if she'll finally give the press interviews. ("Maybe one," she concedes.)

This "Putting It Together" is an authentic cri du coeur from Broadway—and note Randy Waldman's dashing flibberty-gibbet synthesizer figurations, in hommage to the "New York scurry-up" accompaniment that Sondheim conceived for an older number, "Another Hundred People." The irony in all this lies in how obdurate the frustrators are even as Streisand is giving us the album they want to discourage her from making. We do note one sympathetic voice, though he is immediately countered:

SPEAKER 1: But she's an Original.
SPEAKER 2: *Was.*

The Broadway Album's second track, "If I Loved You," is the calm after the storm. But now we worry that Streisand's Second Period, spent among the fleshpots of pop, has led her into inflecting theatre music with decorations that don't belong to Broadway, as with a kind of rock appoggiatura on "loved you" in the second A and a bluesy howl of a higher-than-written note on the last word of "never to *know*." The following three tracks, all by Sondheim (or by him with Bernstein), attest to Streisand's bond with Sondheim for the dramatic opportunities he provides. This supports the first principle of Streisand's vocal art: tell a story. One of the trio, "Being Alive," is classic Streisand in her trademark emotional structure of a subtle start ceding to a penetrating rhythmic pulse and on to a smashing climax with a long-held final note.

Track six offers a *King and I* medley, as "I Have Dreamed" and "We Kiss In a Shadow" vie with each other in interspersed bits.* (A Sondheim medley in track nine does the same thing, in a challenge match between "Pretty Women" and "The Ladies Who Lunch," so mismatched in tone that they might be opposites.) Interestingly, when the *King and I* group reaches "Something Wonderful," the band cues it in with the strange "Eastern" chords Rodgers wrote for the number—a pet peeve of Hugh Martin, who had composed chords very much like them ten years earlier for "Ev'ry Time" in *Best Foot Forward* (1941), a show that Rodgers co-produced

---

* As we know, Streisand recorded "My Lord and Master," from the same show, on *People*. With the two present cuts, she completes taping Tuptim's entire vocal part in *The King and I*—an odd achievement, as Streisand would be miscast as the simple slave girl, who in any case sings (in the show's original keys) soprano.

(unbilled) and knew very well. In Martin's eyes, Rodgers had hijacked the music as being vaguely Asian in character, though Martin composed it for the lament of a young girl in northeastern Pennsylvania on a prom weekend. That Streisand's arrangers, Paul Jabara and Bob Esty, troubled to retain Rodgers' introductory chords, so much a part of the *King and I* sound, reminds us that well-informed arrangers were a feature of Streisand's studio work from the very start.

By track seven, "Adelaide's Lament," Streisand is well into her Broadway ID, giving us what could be a cut from the cast recording of a *Guys and Dolls* revival, from the opening sneeze (Adelaide has a cold) to the Noo Yawk accent and spoken ad libs—and Adelaide is a role that, had Streisand never gone Hollywood, she could easily have played on stage. At Adelaide's imagining of yet another aborted elopement with her boy friend, she speaks of the train ride to Niagara Falls, in a "mood sublime." The original stage (and film) Adelaide, Vivian Blaine, slows up to dilate upon the word *mood*. But Streisand forges on at that point, playing Adelaide's exasperation by giving *mood* an unwritten too-high note that fairly screams in pain. In all, *The Broadway Album* is a definitive Third Period release, telling us that Streisand's Second Period pop persona—her *Stoney End*ness—influenced but did not wholly change her style.

The next three studio recitals adhere to Streisand's established formats. *Till I Loved You* (1988) is New Barbra but rather over-burdened with ballads, *Back To Broadway* (1993) continues to revive the Songbook, and *Higher Ground* (1997), also New Barbra, adds in the increasingly essential Streisand Duet, here with Céline Dion.

Back To Broadway is the most ambitious of the trio, if only because the material itself demands narrative focus. The program is replete with summoning names—Gershwin, Loesser, Bernstein, Streisand's new fave Sondheim, and Lloyd Webber. Streisand does more inflecting this time around, except on the two numbers from *Sunset Boulevard*, which she sings almost entirely in the "purer" Broadway style, as if auditioning for the film version. A Streisand Norma Desmond in the Lloyd Webber incarnation, coming around the time of *The Prince Of Tides* and *The Mirror Has Two Faces*, would have found Streisand at the same age as Gloria Swanson was when she created the character. And Swanson, though a superb soprano, could not have grounded the songs in the belt range Lloyd Webber demands. Indeed, Streisand's "As If We Never Said Goodbye" is quite thrilling, returning us yet again to Jule Styne's hearing, in a Streisand interpretation, the unfolding of a three-act play, here made of intimate confiding of her anxiety at being back on a soundstage, then of eagerness to reclaim her movie career, and at last of sovereign grandeur, from mere actress to Queen Of the Paramount Lot. As Streisand sings, we realize how much we have needed her in musicals, but at least while *Back To Broadway* is on, Dolly's back where she belongs.

On the other hand, one of the duet spots—another Lloyd Webber, "The Music Of the Night" with the original Phantom of the Opera, Michael Crawford—finds Streisand inflecting while Crawford sings the music straight. This approach rather stuffs the ear with dueling musics—his following the written notes against her pop figurations. This approach dramatizes for us a problem in today's music theatre, for many in the field (especially those under a certain age) disdain the sing-as-written ethic as square, corny. They want the music sung as pop music is sung—freely, in a limited imitation of rhythm-and-blues vocalism. However, this emphasizes the singer's ID over that of the character: it isn't correct for the theatre. We note this effect in Streisand's more recent performances of the *Funny Girl* songs, as she no longer delivers them the way she did in the stage show or the film. Now they bear a touch of pop in the vocal line.

Meanwhile, Streisand had produced a four-disc box set comprising as many unusual or even previously unheard items as vintage Streisand cuts, **Just For the Record** (1991), so while we aren't dealing with compilations in this survey, we have to except this one. Her first recording is here—not from her early Columbia days, but set down in 1955 on a private disc in a studio-for-hire when she was thirteen. It's a Songbook selection, as we might have expected, Harry Warren and Mack Gordon's "You'll Never Know," from the Alice Faye–John Payne movie *Hello, Frisco, Hello* (1943). There are as well eight tracks from the unissued Bon Soir live album, one of them "Value," from *Another Evening With Harry Stoones*, in effect Streisand's first own personal show tune. Her famous medley duets with Judy Garland on the latter's television show are here, with a bit of dialogue from *espontanea* Ethel Merman, who surged out of the audience to join them in song. (The intrepid may find the actual singing of this trio of extraordinary Songbook adepts online. Merman all but buries them.)

Among the curiosities on *Just For the Record* is "You Wanna Bet," originally the B side of a single promoting the show *Sweet Charity*, still in rehearsal at the time of release. After Streisand recorded it, "You Wanna Bet" got new lyrics and turned into *Sweet Charity*'s title song, so this track is a double rarity. Streisand's high-flying reading of the number has the *zing!* the song seldom gets on stage (from the leading man, almost always an actor rather than a singer).

Further, *Just For the Record*'s booklet is quite elaborate, filled with not only photographs but Streisand's own musings on all the tracks. Her first

Columbia releases—under her control, remember—offered very little liner information. But by the Third Period she had changed her mind and was giving the listener track-by-track creatives' credits and little blips on how she related to each number. *Just For the Record* is the epitome of box sets, almost an autobiography in music.

We sometimes speak of a good "date movie," and **A Love Like Ours** (1999) is a good date CD. Streisand's first recital after her marriage to James Brolin, it might have suffered from the mawkish cooing of *Till I Loved You*— and we note the booklet's many photographs of the Brolins, mainly strolling along the lush California sunset beach but also dancing at their wedding (and there's one of Streisand alone, in her bridal gown). Still, while Streisand let Jon Peters cakewalk all about the recording studio when *ButterFly* was taped, Brolin is content to marry his love and not produce her, and this album is a success.

In modified New Barbra mode, without a novelty or a classic pop tune, *A Love Like Ours* ranges from the Gershwins and *Funny Girl* to a Legrand–Bergman number written when the *Hello, Dolly!* film came out and a song so new that (as Streisand says in her liner notes) she didn't get the lyrics till her wedding day, when she premiered it. Of course, all the songs treat the thrill of new love and, even, the regret that it didn't come sooner—the Gershwin number, from *Pardon My English* (1933), wonders why destiny kept Boy and Girl apart for so long. "Me at the Prado," she muses, "you in Colorado," and by then Streisand has opened the number up, decorating the vocal line and jumping the key a step higher for the last A. As so often, she joins a sophisticated cabaret style (in the first chorus) to a more beseeching dramatic style in the reprise after an orchestral interlude (here given almost pictorial lyricism by Tommy Morgan's harmonica).

Everything about this lovely CD seems to celebrate the Brolins' nuptials. Even the Bergmans' lyrics to "The Island" usher in an enticing tropical visit, with an insistent drum beat, Kenny G.'s honeymooning tenor sax, and the band sounding like the paddling of a secret pleasure canoe. Note how the music fades out on an unresolved "suspense" chord.

As I've said, Christmas albums are common. But Streisand made a second one, **Christmas Memories** (2001). Unlike the no-carol-left-behind attitude one might expect, however, this songfest's plan is to avoid traditional Yuletide tunes. Instead, Streisand offers a very vaguely holiday-themed recital in New Barbra mode (though without the duet track), with, of all things, a Sondheim in the Broadway slot and, for the novelty, a kind of remake of Sarah Vaughan's "Snowbound." No, not a cover—Streisand's track uses the original Don Costa orchestrations, and while Streisand doesn't imitate Vaughan's sporty slithering up and down in her vast vocal range, Streisand does allude to the way Vaughan slides into her near-bass *chalumeau* register for "So deep is my love" with her own underwater dive. And note that critic Gary Giddins speaks of Vaughan's "fearless caprice," which really describes Streisand's singing (in general, if not here) as well.

Actually, Streisand has her elementary moments in this release. The Sondheim "I Remember," from his television musical, *Evening Primrose*, is one of his few genuinely innocent numbers, and Barbara Mandrell's old hit "It Must Have Been the Mistletoe" is the simplest of compositions, running a very basic melodic cell over and over through the A sections and lifting only in the release.

Is this Christmas or is it merely pop music in December? Target stores offered the CD with a second disc containing just "God Bless America," which is neither Christmas nor pop music (in any real sense). After the seldom-heard verse, Streisand sings it in black soul style, which was becoming an on-and-off feature of her Third Period.

There is but one overtly religious track, in Franz Schubert's setting of the Ave Maria (to match Gounod's, on the earlier album), which gets something of a pile-on of fervor with a heavenly choir and two Streisands (through overdubbing) singing harmony. We get as well the pietistic "One God," the "Feelings" of the Christian community. Written by Ervin Drake and Jimmy Shirl (co-authors, with two other miscreants, of the equally five-and-dime-holy "I Believe"), "One God" attempts to objectify the spiritual, making show biz out of something that should be personal and private. Streisand's reading is sincere, but the song itself really is near to blasphemy. Mind the Light, Friend.

The Movie Album (2003) obviously complemented the two Broadway "returns," though there seems to have been a wish to capture the overkill sound of the old Hollywood musicals in some of the arrangements. The second track, "Moon River," is prim, featuring the guitar, but the third track, "I'm In the Mood For Love," brings out tuttis from some seventy-five instruments. Note an extremely unusual change of key in the second (rather than the last) A, when Streisand goes *down* a step rather than up.

Somehow or other, she found a way to bring Sondheim into the program, using the lyrics he wrote for the love theme from *Reds*, known as "Goodbye For Now." This somewhat shy melody, so lightly scored, is hard to present; it's one of the very few genuinely delicate numbers Streisand has tackled. She's more at home in the following track, "You're Gonna Hear From Me." A determined march through the fields of cliché by André and

Dory Previn, it was used in *Inside Daisy Clover* in a movie-within-the-movie as Natalie Wood's debut short, risible and cheap and completely out of sync with the outer film's setting. Wood, dubbed, gave it as a typical sixties heroine anthem, but Streisand cleverly makes it more of a ballad. It's still a piece of nothing, but, as with "Summer Me, Winter Me" on the *Way We Were* recital, Streisand brings it off by concentrating on the musical values.

Thus far, Streisand's recitals have all tended to observe a particular format; these are more than a chance agglomeration of songs. Some adhere to the model of *The Second Barbra Streisand Album*. Some observe the guidelines of New Barbra. Some order their content by theme—the French and classical discs, the two Christmas collections. *Stoney End* was Streisand meets Pop. *Guilty* was Streisand meets Barry Gibb.

The three recitals that succeeded *The Movie Album* similarly followed precedents. **Guilty Pleasures** (2005) was a second collaboration with Gibb. **Love Is the Answer** (2009) was sheer New Barbra with an extra allotment of show tunes and, for the novelty, a Jacques Brel (sung partly in French), albeit one of his ballads rather than his more characteristic turbulent narratives. And **What Matters Most** (2011) was a descendant of *The Broadway Album* in its all-Bergmans program, its numbers all drawn from one source.

Guilty Pleasures is the least imposing of the trio by far, because while the Bee Gees style worked well for *Guilty*, Gibb (writing now with his sons instead of his brothers) gives us nothing but fresh leftovers, new yet strangely stale. In *The Importance Of Being Barbra*, Tom Santopietro memorably called *Guilty Pleasures* "a marketing concept in search of an album."

Put on **Release Me** (2012) at the third cut, Ann Ronell's old standard "Willow Weep For Me," and you time-travel back to the Streisand of her first decade, the 1960s. She sounds young and devoid of experience, seasoning, seniority—everything but her native genius in delving deeply into the soul of a song. On the word *stream*, you hear an indescribable lift that is uniquely hers, and at "Listen to my plea" an extra something on the *plea* somehow bonds with the entry of the piano and flute to put us inside the number with her as no other singer can.

How did this happen in 2012? It's Streisand as she once was: because the track was taped in 1967 for *Simply Streisand*, which we covered some twenty pages ago. And note Ray Ellis' scoring, featuring, as the older albums did in general, the *concertante* charts that characterized Streisand's first LPs. From the lower strings at "Willow"'s opening to the pungent harp glissando at the end, you hear air around all the orchestra's sections, an antique sensation in our modern age of overmixed sonics.

Release Me is a collection of rescues, some old and some more recent (and one from the year before), of tracks left off recitals they had been planned for. It's an extremely eclectic gathering, bonded most apparently by the inclusion of the engineers' warning statements just before the tape rolls. "Take eight," one announces as the disc begins, though—as an amused Streisand points out—she hasn't sung yet. The album's cover art gives us only the diva's eyes in a frame of black, alluring and provocative, The Lady From Whoknowswhere. Yet here in the studio Streisand is very down to earth. Take eight when there hasn't really been a take so far? "You have a cockeyed system, I'll tell you that," she says.[55] A bit more tech stuff, then silence, then the music slides its way in, giving us a heady taste of the backstage of music-making.

Something else holds the disc together, though, even with such distinct selections as a country number (Larry Gatlin's "Try To Win a Friend"); Randy Newman's solo piano accompanying Streisand in his "I Think It's Going To Rain Today"; and a 1947-musical-fantasies-for-$200-Alex medley of "How Are Things In Glocca Morra" and "The Heather On the Hill." None of these relates in any way to the others. Yet there is the wonderful resuscitation of Streisand before her absorption of rock and pop styles led her to inflect everything she sings, even the Songbook.

Ah, but in *Release Me*'s final track, "Home," from the all-black show *The Wiz*, you hear a different Streisand. Instead of the *concertante* scoring, she works with a jazz trio inserted into a very large orchestra, and, as "Home" is intensely pop rather than Broadway in conception, she sings the piece in rhythm-and-blues style. In all, *Release Me* is a remarkable album, at once unified and scattered, and in part so nostalgic it startles the ear with its historical review of Streisand's growth as an artist.

Streisand's fascination with the duet as a format of its own takes over her most recent CDs, **Partners** (2014) and **Encore** (2016). Oddly, Streisand's notion of a duet is really that of a trio—her voice, her partner's voice, and the trendy technology that allows the (in effect) effigy of the Other Singer's Vocal to be imported remotely. Thus, Streisand can lay down a track that will then be boosted by a second voice from somewhere else—from a studio on the other side of the country; from an iPhone; from the beyond. Streisand can thus duet with Elvis, and does so. It's not unlike singing "April In Paris" with Napoléon: is it real or is it Memorex?

Perhaps because both were live in the studio, *Partners*' first track, "It Had To Be You," wherein Streisand swings with Michael Bublé against a forties big-band arrangement, is the best of this lot. It boasts the zesty interplay of two pros having fun with an ancient tune that still has juice in it.

We even get the seldom heard verse, after which the two singers take turns on the lines. Then she leads and he echoes, till they unite on the last A. Wilding a bit in the second chorus—he breaks the fourth wall by calling her by name—they top off the cut with aplomb. And note a smashing upward piano glissando on "Nobody else gave me a thrill."

Partners' other tracks vary in effectiveness. In "Come Rain Or Come Shine," John Mayer sings in rhythm-and-blues style; Streisand doesn't. So it's an odd match. "New York State Of Mind," with its author, Billy Joel, sounds very processed and, worse, gets apocalyptic. This isn't "I Happen To Like New York," the Cole Porter number that became for a bit the anthem of the city's survival after the Islamic terror attacks in 2001. Joel's song, from 1976, is instead a lazy eulogy of Manhattan culture, the musical equivalent of spending Sunday morning in pajamas doing a lot of nothing.

Later, "The Way We Were," with Lionel Richie, also gets too strong, as if the album wants to chase perfect storms instead of charming us with its ballads the way a raconteur spins a yarn. So the following "I Still Can See Your Face," with Andrea Bocelli, mostly on a smaller scale, comes as a relief. It's a strange duet, because Bocelli's operatic tenor keeps pulling focus: he sounds great but, especially given the rock-beat arrangement, he is wrong for the venue.

And how we can no longer avoid noticing that Streisand's instrument is truly in decline, starved of tone at the high end and thick and rough in the middle voice? On "Somewhere," partner Josh Groban sounds so youthful that, by comparison, the devolution of Streisand's vocal presence is almost stunning. One first became aware of it in *What Matters Most*, the Bergmans disc of three years earlier; was this the reason for *Release Me*, with its concentration on the younger Streisand?

It's not fatigue: it's age. A flute or violin will play indefinitely, but the voice physically gives out over time. Maybe Streisand likes duets because they allow her to share the spotlight cosmetically, using her partner as an *aide-chanter*, so to speak. On *Encore*, she does sing four numbers sola (in bonus tracks on a special edition made available only at Target stores), and she also brought in a new diversion, spoken lines before most of the numbers, to give each one a theatrical context, a practice introduced on a few Decca show albums in the 1940s and Columbia's *Finian's Rainbow*.

Oddly, Streisand's voice is as lugubrious in the dialogue as in the singing, and she is not as dramatically engaged as we would expect. On the first *Encore* track, *A Chorus Line*'s "At the Ballet," the music doesn't kick in till 1:10, which gives Streisand, as tart-tongued Sheila, enough time to establish her persona. We even hear a line about it. Yet Sheila, ordinarily so striking that in the theatre she's the first character we pick out as an individual, is almost a nonentity here.

We have another problem: her duet partners are by a generation (or more) her juniors. There are only two ages in American show biz: one, young; and two, invisible. And while Streisand is still too big to vanish, her singing pales next to, for example, Patrick Wilson's in the second track, "Loving You." And, as before, Streisand arranges for separate tapings; on the third track, she is paired with Anthony Newley, who died long before. This sort of thing only underlines the "canned music" music feeling of these long-distance "partnerships."

Encore's four solos come off better than the duos, as with "I Didn't Know What Time It Was," Rodgers and Hart in an after-hours jazz club feeling, with an entrancing trumpet interlude by Chris Botti and a playfully clipped pronunciation of "Warm like the month of May it was," as Streisand once again leaves her mark on a phrase both musically and emotionally. "Losing My Mind," the classic torcher from *Follies*, is here as well, in a scoring that echoes Jonathan Tunick's Broadway original even unto the rising celesta line (starting at "I dim the lights") in the last A of the first chorus. The song, ideal for Streisand's familiar three-act-play approach, gives her one of her best cuts in her own real-life three-act play.

Nevertheless, it is *Encore*'s final track that makes the disc climactic in Streisand's recording career. It's "Climb Every Mountain," with Jamie Foxx, and the number epitomizes Streisand's journey from the Songbook to pop. Because while *she* sings the Rodgers and Hammerstein anthem more or less in Broadway style, *he* gives his line the rhythm and blues treatment: the two main strains of American popular music joined together and at length sounding—in a coda unique to this CD—like a Hollywood apotheosis. Streisand and Foxx "commit" to the music as none has committed before, while the huge orchestra crashes into glory and the words THE END flash before our eyes.

STREISAND'S CAREER:
A PICTURE ESSAY

A Life in Art

This moment from *Funny Lady* encapsulates Streisand As Performer. Omar Sharif, playing Nicky Arnstein, may be Fanny Brice's great love (returning from *Funny Girl*), but note that Streisand is surrounded by the accoutrements of not romance but her profession: good-luck telegrams and flowers; jars of make-up; a shot of her onstage (just left of center above Sharif, the tiny figure on the cigarette holder); a Victrola; a wig for a comic skit. *Funny Lady* is a backstager, and so is Streisand's life, because we know her only through her achievements in music and movie-making. Streisand is not a Warholian figure, famous for her fame rather than her work. On the contrary, Streisand *is* her work.

Now for a chronological tour through her career...

Funny Girl

The real funny girl, Fanny Brice, adorns song sheets from revues produced by Florenz Ziegfeld, including Brice's theme song, "My Man," which *Funny Girl*'s producer, Ray Stark, wanted to interpolate into the stage show. *Funny Girl*'s composer, Jule Styne, supposedly bought Stark off by reminding him that he could always add it to the film version, because no true son of Broadway cares "what's in a movie anyhow."

Yet Streisand's performance of the number, so defiantly loving, gives the film an extraordinary sense of fulfillment that the stage show lacked. On Broadway, Streisand and Fanny left us with a bit of show-biz hotcha. In Hollywood, Streisand turned "My Man" into the establishing number of a movie star: exactly what Streisand had been planning to be all along.

Above, "Cornet Man" on Broadway, as Streisand leads the ensemble in the Chicken Scramble. Carol Haney choreographed it as Act One's first production number, and Styne and lyricist Bob Merrill wrote it as semi-pastiche, to recall old-time show business without copying it. The number was a knockout—that was the problem. When Jerome Robbins joined the production in tryout, he thought "Cornet Man" threw *Funny Girl* off balance, with too much brilliant dancing for its own sake. Robbins was turning *Funny Girl* into a Big Lady Show for Streisand, so he thinned "Cornet Man" down to an exhibition vocal for the star and a bit of movement with the dancers, as we see here. *Funny Girl* on stage and film is the key Streisand event, so let's spend extra time with it.

We're now in Hollywood; Walter Pidgeon's Ziegfeld is irritated with Streisand's Brice because she refuses to sing "His Love Makes Me Beautiful." She's skittish about appearing as a showgirl, only confident as the clown: a *funny* girl. In a way, this is Streisand's career in synecdoche, though in different terms: she wants to act in movies as a glamour star, not sing in them as a talent star. But Hollywood says, "Shoot Streisand singing six numbers and we'll make sixty million." Note Anne Francis (*far left*), fourth billed yet almost entirely edited out of the release print, supposedly at Streisand's instigation, though Francis eventually exculpated her. Anyway, Streisand didn't have that kind of power. Yet.

Ziegfeld forces Brice to sing the "Beautiful" number, absurdly overproduced in the movie (*above*). His shows were eye-filling, but not gargantuan. *Below*, gambler Omar Sharif plays penny poker with the neighborhood ladies after Brice's Ziegfeld opening, then romances her, for even a funny girl must love, if unhappily.

Still, all the best parts in the film find Streisand goofing around (as she destroys the skating number that replaced "Cornet Man"), while the "love" sequences in the second half tend to drag. *Funny Girl* was exactly what Streisand needed to jump-start her movie career, but it's faithful to the stage show, and the stage show is flawed. Still, Streisand observes the first rule in The Prima Donna's Handbook: Your last act is your best. And the aforementioned "My Man" leaves us with that wonderfully startling conclusion—one woman, one song, The End.

Hello, Dolly!

This movie has everything: not only a First Couple (Streisand and Walter Matthau) but second and third couples (*above*, Danny Lockin, E. J. Peaker, Marianne McAndrew, Michael Crawford). Also (*below*) a parade...

...a Waiters' Galop (*above*), and a finale (*below*) in a church by the sea...

...and somehow they even found room for Streisand (*above*, in the title number). *Hello, Dolly!* is a much-criticized but very enjoyable film, featuring a sunnier Streisand than we usually get and in her funniest script by far. Many are those who disdain the movie because Streisand is too young for the role, but whom would you have wanted instead? Betty Hutton? Really? You really would?

The Glamour Diva

Streisand's third film, *On a Clear Day You Can See Forever*, turned her inside out as a Total Movie Star in fabulous fashions; she never looked quite so *designed* again. *Above left*, the egg helmet she wears at the banquet where she sings "Love With All the Trimmings" while staring at John Richardson (*above*, in another scene) in the hairdo that devoured Brighton.

The Way We Were

Love both happy (*above*, with Robert Redford) and disrupted (*below*), as politics intrudes on the personal.

Later Streisand

Concertizing in *A Star Is Born*, Streisand reminds us that her music is what draws us ever back again, because there are many fine actresses but no one else sings like Streisand. Yet she *must* act, and even direct. Now she has that power: she came, she saw, she conquered. So we see her in charge of *Yentl* (*opposite bottom*) in street clothes with Mandy Patinkin and ebullient Amy Irving. Mandy loves Amy and Amy loves Mandy, but both love also Streisand (who they think is a boy), which makes *Yentl* a very modern piece. It is as well suffused with period atmosphere, as (*opposite top*) Patinkin and Streisand (in men's garb as the religious scholar Anshel) ride through their own particular Anatevka—in real life, the famous Charles Bridge in Prague.

Family becomes increasingly important in later Streisand films. Earlier, there is the occasional mother (in *Funny Girl* and *Up the Sandbox*), but from *Yentl* on we get a great deal of parents, siblings, and in-laws. In *Nuts* the parents are villains—in fact, our *Nuts* still (*above*) shows the story's only decent characters: Streisand's defense attorney (Richard Dreyfuss) and the unbiased judge (James Whitmore) at her insanity hearing, and of course Streisand, whose mother and stepfather want to put her away to hide his sexual predations. An uncomfortable offering when new, *Nuts* now screens as au courant in our growing awareness of this once hidden problem. The sight of the bathroom door's knob turning while an adolescent Streisand trembles in the tub plays as if a moment in Hitchcock.

The Prince Of Tides overflows with family (*above*), for good or (mostly) ill, as mother Kate Nelligan protects but also terrorizes her offspring. Is it coincidence that Streisand's last films—even the execrable *Fockers* pair—place her as daughter, mother, mother-in-law? Or is it a case of Younger artists seek liberty and Older artists seek stability? Streisand's own role in *The Prince Of Tides* is that of a psychiatrist—a healer of souls wounded by bad parenting, which makes it less coincidence and more a consequence of Streisand's expanding humanist perspective.

A Fond Farewell

Streisand's is a talent in which many arts are combined, not just as singer and actress but as personality as well. She is the madcap but also the political activist, or let us say Dolly and Yentl at once. As Walt Whitman said of himself, the Great American Originals "contain multitudes." Our Mona Lisa photo, taken during the filming of *The Prince Of Tides*, emphasizes the humorous Streisand, a surprising player who, showing up for a sex dinner with Nick Arnstein in *Funny Girl*, whips out her fan before we're ready for it and ruthlessly flashes it open as much to startle as to delight. As Martha Raye put it in *Hold On To Your Hats*, a long-forgotten musical of 1940, she came, she saw, she can-canned.

Streisand's Cinema

*F**unny Girl** (1968), a roadshow release, with reserved seats, an intermission, and a souvenir book, followed the show's narrative structure while dropping eight of the numbers, including the best title, "The Music That Makes Me Dance." However, three songs associated with Fanny Brice were added, most notably her "autobiography" piece, "My Man." Further, Styne and Merrill wrote a new title tune, a lament for the clown who "may be all wrong for the guy" but "good for a laugh"—which does at least essentialize the story's conflict between Fanny the comic and Fanny the lover.

Isobel Lennart—still the scriptwriter, as on Broadway—added to this meme with a bit when Fanny wants to accompany Nick to a high-stakes poker game on which their shared future depends. But Nick fears Fanny will go crazy with suspense:

NICK: Can you watch with no expression at all—whatever happens?
FANNY (faking blasé confidence): Can I watch with no expression?

So of course we immediately see her agonizing at the game, biting her glove in frustration and trying to signal Nick. He shoots her a severe look and she instantly freezes.

Odd as this sounds, *Funny Girl*'s second half mirrors that of *Show Boat*, as a gambler husband suffers a bad turn of fortune, wrecks his marriage, and, after a separation, shows up near the story's end. Of course, events in the heavily plotted *Show Boat* tumble over themselves, while *Funny Girl*, all but starved for narrative, concentrates on Fanny's character, especially the way she takes success in her work for granted but never quite believes in her success in love. On stage, *Funny Girl* ended with a reprise of the feverish

"Don't Rain On My Parade": Fanny the conqueror. But the film ends, star-tlingly, with Fanny singing "My Man": Fanny the unhappy lover, and so in the moment that Streisand insisted on filming the first chorus viva voce, using the pre-recorded track only for the second.

Though Ray Stark would occasionally fight with Streisand over which of them "owned" the very idea of *Funny Girl*, and though she must have known that Columbia Pictures wanted Shirley MacLaine's Fanny for the movie, it couldn't have been made without Streisand. Not only was she the spit and image of Fanny Brice: Streisand was by then one of the biggest stars in show biz.

Nick, however, was easy to cast, and most of the usual suspects in the line of romantic leads were considered. One innovative choice was David Janssen, known for the television series *The Fugitive*, but the studio finally went with Omar Sharif, prominent in a series of "big" pictures that culmi-nated in *Dr. Zhivago*. Playing most of his scenes with a contentless smile, Sharif gets interesting only here and there, as in the toxic look he shoots at Streisand during that high-rollers poker game.

Still, he and Streisand manage a valid chemistry, another of the film's bonding elements. In fact, Fanny's self-deprecating passion for Nick Arnstein so drives the story that in the sequel, *Funny Lady*, James Caan's Billy Rose can very persuasively excuse his cheating on Fanny with another woman by saying, "To her, I'm Nick."

Meanwhile, there was quite an uproar in the Arab world from the day Sharif's casting was announced. A shot of an onscreen Streisand–Sharif kiss on the cover of an Egyptian magazine was indeed the shot heard around the world, though a few writers noted that Sharif, born in Egypt but of Lebanese Catholic family, had exiled himself to Europe to protest laws that hampered his ability to film with Western studios. CAIRO ENRAGED was the headline of the day, but Streisand, taking a rare chance to comment to reporters, replied with *"Cairo* is enraged? You should see the letter I got from my aunt Rose!"[56]

The third-billed Kay Medford as Fanny's mother, held over from Broadway (and the London run as well), does some expert underplaying. But the fourth-billed Anne Francis' bad experience on the shoot took a toll on Streisand's public persona. Coming off the not terribly successful televi-sion series *Honey West* (as a private detective, an arresting innovation for the day), Francis played Fanny's fellow Ziegfeld girl and confidante, in the perilous "subplot" slot that the stage *Funny Girl* suffered from. When the show ran long, the confidante, played by Allyn Ann McLerie, was written out; now the movie ran long, and Francis' screen time was edited down to almost to an "under five" (that is, one notch above an extra, with less than a handful of spoken lines). Francis did end up with one cute bit, after Fanny has infuriated Ziegfeld by spoofing herself in what is supposed to be a romantic number—again, she's only sure of herself when she's the funny girl. In her dressing room, Ziegfeld (the fifth-billed Walter Pidgeon) is in the middle of ripping her apart when Francis opens the door a crack and, unseeing, asks, "Did he fire you?" Pidgeon growls, "Not yet," and Francis gets the heck out of there.

Unfortunately, an article in *The Hollywood Reporter* quoted Francis blaming Streisand for Francis' demotion. "Every day Barbra would see the rushes" was the most killing line, "and the next day my part would be cut."[57]

Did Streisand really have that much power? On her first movie? Over a generation later, Francis told James Spada that *The Hollywood Reporter*'s wording came from not Francis but her PR representative, "an old dear friend" whom Francis was reluctant to correct publicly. It was the movie's director, William Wyler, who limited Francis' screen time.[58]

On the other hand, being New In Town didn't inhibit Streisand's controlling instinct, and she relentlessly backseat drove Wyler, despite his distinguished Old Hollywood résumé. I don't relate to the line that way. Something's wrong with the set. Do they have to stand so close to me? Streisand's "Everybody else is wrong" worldview did not respect Hollywood's chain of command, in which the director is the sole authority on the set. When Anne Francis was (falsely) quoted as saying, "Barbra ran the whole show,"[59] gossip from those working on the production seemed to support that. Here's Randall Riese on the matter: "If Barbra's credo was perfectionism, [the company's] was professionalism, and the two were not always compatible."[60]

Between the stage and screen versions, we've spent a lot of time on *Funny Girl*, so let's move on to **Hello, Dolly!** (1969), which Streisand shot even before anyone knew how moviegoers would respond to the new star in *Funny Girl*. The familiar *Hello, Dolly!* "thing" that precedes all discussion is Streisand's youth. She turned twenty-six barely one week after the start of principal photography in a role specifically written for a widow who has been knocking around on her own for quite some time, living on odd-job scraps. Still, does age matter as much as talent? No one else in show business would have been as good as Streisand, as while Dolly didn't give her *Funny Girl*'s occasionally dense "acting" moments (as in the rendering of "My Man"), Dolly remains one of Streisand's best portrayals, because the playfully manipulative fictions with which she bosses everyone around precisely match Streisand's sense of humor.

There's another question (for some) about Streisand's Dolly, on the notion that Carol Channing, who created the role on stage, was unfairly passed over. But there was no rule that movie adaptations must honor Broadway casting. For every Robert Preston preserving his *Music Man* role, there was a Mary Martin losing *The Sound Of Music*'s Maria to Julie Andrews—or, for that matter, Andrews losing Eliza Doolittle to Audrey Hepburn and Guenevere to Vanessa Redgrave.

Besides, Channing's Dolly was a theatrical concoction, brilliant in its way but too steely and gestural for the screen. Nor could Channing (or anyone) have rivaled Streisand's singing, in a score amplified with extra numbers for the star by the show's songwriter, Jerry Herman (including a ballad cut during *Mame*'s Philadelphia tryout, "Love Is Only Love").

Streisand looks terrific in Harry Stradling's photography, merry and smiling more than in any other of her films. *Dolly!* was her chance to expand her ID from the bedeviled Fanny Brice to the all-conquering Dolly, endlessly resourceful from first coffee to evening prayers.

Streisand even changed her plastique for the role. She moves in a way we haven't seen before, as in the title song, where it seems her hips are on springs. Some have complained about the many different voices she affects, including Mae West's. But these are like the various business cards ("Mrs. Dolly Levi/Painters Taught How To Dance") she hands out. A jack of all trades, she's a living version of the traditional sex worker's question, "Who do you want me to be?"

Dolly! itself is prized above all for its sequence in the Harmonia Gardens restaurant, centering on the title song (enriched here by Louis Armstrong's star cameo). However, Streisand's key sequence comes earlier, starting in the millinery shop, where we see her taking charge of her own future while initiating the birth of romance in the film's young people. Critic Erick Neher has noted how Ernest Lehman's screenplay tidies up a sloppy coincidence in *Dolly!*'s stage script: how do Cornelius (Michael Crawford in the film) and Barnaby (Danny Lockin) happen to be in the millinery shop of Irene (Marianne McAndrew) and Minnie (E. J. Peaker) just when Vandergelder arrives? They just do; and that's show biz.

But Lehman's rewriting has Dolly specifically sending Cornelius and Barnaby to be where she needs them—in the hat shop when Vandergelder troops in. There are even new lyrics to that point in "Put On Your Sunday Clothes."

And once these principals are in place amid the chapeaux and closets, Streisand seizes the film, all sweeping arm gestures and confidential smiles. In a cross-hatched mauve dress with matching feathered picture hat, she's a play-within-a-play, improvising script and ever moving all her supporting players to that essential musical-comedy thing, a happy ending to a wonderful day. *Funny Girl* didn't have one, but *Funny Girl* is serious while *Dolly!* is zany. So it makes perfect sense for Michael Crawford to hide in a closet, for an outraged Vandergelder (Walter Matthau) to menace him, and for Streisand to tickle Crawford with a feather. And of course:

CRAWFORD: (sneezes)
STREISAND (in a comically flat tone): There's nobody in there.
CRAWFORD: (sneezes again)
STREISAND (in exactly the same tone): God bless you.

Nothing like this could have occurred in *Funny Girl*, because that film is the story of Streisand not getting what she wants. *Dolly!*, so traditional that it runs the same plotline as *A Trip To Chinatown*, a once famous musical of the 1890s, is about Streisand getting what she wants (a rich husband) while giving everybody else what he or she wants as well. Nor could *Funny Girl* have hosted the number that takes us from the millinery out into the world of young people having fun, "Dancing." Here choreographer Michael Kidd presents a park full of densely layered groups of dancers in competition as they at times literally tumble over one another.

This can only lead to a suddenly intimate moment, as Streisand starts "Before the Parade Passes By"—but *this* explodes into the spectacular yet boring parade finale (of Act One, in the roadshow prints), which utilizes a studio-built panorama of old Fourteenth Street and enough extras to populate a good-sized town. The parade itself goes on endlessly, yet the professional and recreational gatherings (grumpy women teetotalers, circus clowns, meat-packers, and so on) are of absolutely no pictorial interest. It's nothing but big.

The story goes that the film's director, Gene Kelly, had no sympathy for the material and had taken the job on the theory that *Dolly!* might be the next *Sound Of Music*, the most *seen* movie musical in history. But at least Kelly—or Kidd—smartly gave the last bit of the parade's colossal boringness to Streisand, who tops off the melody at its coda ("When the whistles blow...") while marching with a red-coated wind band. On the last line, she resorts to one of her patented long-drawn-out notes on "pa-*rade*" and interpolates a lower mordent on "passes *by*" as the camera pulls back to give us a thrilling view of the whole dopey shebang. At the last moment, Streisand celebrates with a twirl just before the visual goes black for the intermission.

Though the film ended in the red because of all the unnecessary spectacle, for many spectators Streisand scored a personal success. True, Dolly was another talent-star role, like Fanny, not a movie-star role, which you deserve not because of what you can do but because of who you are. Nevertheless, Streisand was building her reputation on what the public expected of her. The personality and acting roles could come along in due course.

It would be irresponsible to fail to point out that, eight years after the filming, Danny Lockin, then aged thirty-four, took the wrong man home from a bar and was tortured to death by the use of a knife and publicly unnamed "instruments." The murderer was sentenced to a mere four years in prison (for "voluntary manslaughter"), and everyone in this country should know about this.

Streisand's third movie was a third adaptation from Broadway, *On a Clear Day You Can See Forever* (1970), with a score by Burton Lane and Alan Jay Lerner and the latter revising his stage script. It's one of Streisand's unsatisfying films, but its premise is arresting: a medical man in the psychiatry phylum falls in love with a patient before she was reincarnated. That's right: he becomes besotted with who she was back in Regency England. She's what used to be called an "oddball": she can make flowers grow fast, hear an incoming phone call before the ring, and even read your mind. That's all so much ESP, which, for some reason, Lerner associated with reincarnation, though the two have nothing in common.

That was Lerner's second mistake; his first was in failing to come up with a valid story with which to develop the premise. Perhaps he thought the many flashback scenes—the best thing about the original stage show, riots of color and droll extravagance—would fill out the evening, but in the end *On a Clear Day* was a classic case of a musical without a second act. Lerner tried a revision for the show's national tour and then rewrote once more for Paramount's filming.

It still didn't work, and Streisand is not consistently successful playing period English (at that with a grandly British cast all around her) in the flashback scenes. Her predecessor in the role on Broadway, Barbara Harris, was very persuasive as her former self, because Harris always seemed a bit Martian; that otherworldly air was her passport into the past. Instead, Streisand reminds one of John Malkovich in *Les Liaisons Dangereuses*, a bit hard to believe in the long-ago clothes and rococo attitudes.

True, *Funny Girl* and *Hello, Dolly!* were set in the past, but an American past, a relatively recent one at that. The *Funny Girl* narrative ends about forty years before its first audiences were taking it in, so it was hardly the archeological dig that *On a Clear Day*'s flashback sequences were.

Besides, if Streisand is too modern for Melinda Tentrees, the other half of *On a Clear Day*'s modern-day heroine, Daisy Gamble, she's still more interesting than the rest of the movie's players, who range from wasted to wrong. Larry Blyden is the main one wasted, in another of his countless who-cares-about-him? roles as Streisand's fiancé, but then he always was a sort of unlikeable Tony Randall. Jack Nicholson is the wrong one. Absurdly young and trim as Streisand's stepbrother (a part new to the story for the film), Nicholson is completely without purpose in the action and seems to know it, which may be why his screen time (and even a song, "Who Is There Among Us Who Knows?") was cut to almost nothing in editing.

And then there's Streisand's vis-à-vis, Yves "The Walking Dead" Montand, as the doctor. To say Montand has no chemistry with Streisand is like saying Julie Andrews has no chemistry with King Farouk; more precisely, Montand has no chemistry. Further, his vocal style, French *fantaisiste* cabaret, is too *intime* to balance with Streisand, who sings almost all the songs in any case.

Unfortunately, Lerner decided to cut the stage score back almost entirely to the present-day pieces, leaving the flashbacks without the musical definition of their stage numbers: "Ring Out the Bells"; the patter song "Don't Tamper With My Sister"; and the harpsichord-accompanied, "Greensleeves"-like "Tosy and Cosh"; not to mention a marriage-contract number ("The father of the bride shall free and willingly provide..."), a vivacious ensemble cut in tryouts but restored for the tour.

These numbers lent the show color and flair, while all Lane and Lerner gave to these scenes was "She Wasn't You" (revised as "He Isn't You") and the new "Love With All the Trimmings," which has virtually no sense of period. Still, the tune does bring us to an understanding of how the film, poor as it was, worked well for Streisand's wish to establish herself as a movie—not a talent—star, even as her next five features were all non-musicals, anyway.

Of course, a song spot calls for talent. But "Love With All the Trimmings" is more than a song. It is first heard at a banquet where Streisand, holding a wine glass, is staring relentlessly at a blond hunk (John Richardson). Okay, that much is plot and music. What really matters here is what Streisand is wearing, perhaps the most flamboyant outfit ever designed (in this case by Cecil Beaton) to declare an actress a top Hollywood beauty. It's all white with silver trim, surmounted by bosomy décolleté and a mob cap in the form of a vast egg—the kind of thing planned to entice the public into staring at the star just as Streisand is staring at Richardson: with enchantment. At one point, to warn her quarry that her intentions are strictly dishonorable, Streisand runs her wineglass down her cleavage with maximum prejudice—and we realize that we are witnessing a career transition. Fanny was awkward in love and Dolly a cut-up rather than a romantic figure. But Melinda is a femme fatale, decked out and ravishing.

Clearly, director Vincente Minnelli sees Streisand as a glamour star, especially in Cecil Beaton's Regency costumes and not least a red number with a long silken back panelling falling from her top hat (which, by the way, she wears to court when on trial for her life). *On a Clear Day* thus marks Streisand's emergence as a movie star in the purest sense, because the film is terrible but when she is onscreen it works—entirely because of *who she is*. Meager fare that *On a Clear Day* is after the hyper-active *Funny Girl* and *Dolly!*, this third Streisand film nonetheless counts as a major event in her career because of how she was presented to the public.

Bill Manhoff's 1964 Broadway hit, *The Owl and the Pussycat*, was a two-character comedy about a prostitute who rooms with a nerdy would-be writer as the two bicker and eventually come to an understanding. It was unremarkable, save that black Diana Sands (whom we recall from *Another Evening With Harry Stoones*) played opposite white Alan Alda, though her role was not written for a black actress.

In other words, this was pure color-blind casting, highly unusual in 1964. Interestingly, while the national tour reaffirmed the cross-racial presentation with Eartha Kitt and Russell Nype, the Broadway production's two standbys were both white, Rose Gregorio and Robert Moore (later a major director). Again, there was no "race" in the action. Doris and Felix make an odd couple entirely because they are temperamentally antagonistic—even if the original owl and pussycat, in Edward Lear's Victorian children's poem, are of different species and get along quite well.

The play is a trifle with a soupçon of emotional content near the end, but Streisand wanted something different—not just a non-musical role but an offbeat one. A test. Ray Stark, who still had her under contract, gave her this 1970 release, with George Segal as her Felix under Herbert Ross' direction. Buck Henry (very trendy after writing *The Graduate*) opened up Manhoff's stage script, transferring the setting from Los Angeles to New York to take in the cultural advantages and executing a cameo in an on-location shoot at the (now defunct) Fifty-Third Street Doubleday's. All of this worked well enough, though the movie, too, is a trifle, famous above all for Streisand's see-through mesh outfit, each breast embossed with an open palm and a little valentine at her privacy.

In truth, Doris (especially as Streisand plays her) is an acerbic and raucous character with the usual soft center to be revealed in the final reel. However, Streisand did try out a topless scene—again, very rare for the day and deleted from the release print—and highlighted an encounter with a car full of irritating hoods with the line "I would appreciate it very much, if you don't mind, if you'd just *fuck off!*" Here was another defiance of the cautions of the era; some prints scrubbed the line, and the bowdlerization was carried over for the DVD.*

---

* At this writing, the uncensored version can be seen on YouTube.

Next, Streisand tried screwball farce in **What's Up, Doc?** (1972), playing op-posite Ryan O'Neal and directed by Peter Bogdanovich. The plan was to pay hommage to the format of Howard Hawks' *Bringing Up Baby* (1938), in which Cary Grant was an academic square (his field is bones; O'Neal's would be rocks), too repressed to enjoy life, and Katharine Hepburn was his dash-ing love-nemesis who teaches him to embrace not only life but anarchy. Add to this two leopards, one tame and one dangerous that gets mistaken for the tame one, changed in *What's Up, Doc?* to four plaid suitcases with contents of dire importance that keep getting mistaken for one another. In both pic-tures, the fun is amplified by offbeat characters sowing merry confusion.

Remember screwball farces? Bogdanovich didn't, because their essential quality was wit. Many of Hollywood's screenwriters in the 1930s made political statements in all sorts of ways, and one of these was the use of playful brilliance to delight and hearten the intelligent and confuse the overlords of DC. For any time the authorities realize they aren't getting a joke, they know that somewhere, somehow, someone is making fun of them. Indeed, while *Bringing Up Baby* is a classic today, it failed on its original release. Maybe it was too smart even for the intelligent.

What's Up, Doc? wasn't. A huge commercial success, it doesn't hold up well. The writing itself is the central problem. Bogdanovich gets a credit, along with Buck Henry again and the team of David Newman and Robert Benton, and while they give their characters the rhythm and accents of wit, the verbiage itself is doltish. A sample, as Streisand continues to call O'Neal by some name of her own concoction and disparages his fiancée (Madeline Kahn):

> STREISAND: You have got to stop repeating yourself.
> O'NEAL: I am not repeating myself; I am not repeating myself; Oh,
>   God, I'm repeating myself.
> STREISAND: Steve, you don't want to marry Eunice.
> O'NEAL: I'm not Steve, I'm Howard.
> STREISAND: Neither of you wants to marry Eunice.

Well, at least the writers observed proper subject-verb agreement on the last line. Bogdanovich has to establish Streisand as a devil-may-care icono-clast, but he does this by, for instance, having her cross busy San Francisco streets without looking out for traffic. She even causes a motorcyclist to wipe out while trying to avoid her. Bogdanovich is mistaking a lack of common sense for joie de vivre and recklessness for nonconformism.

No. Hector Berlioz is nonconformism. Eleanor Roosevelt is noncon-formism. Walking into moving traffic is stupidity.

The handling of Ryan O'Neal is worse. Streisand, as a comic, is a self-starter. O'Neal, at least in this stage of his career, is not a comic, and Bogdanovich had to guide him through his paces using a counting system. We see this notably in a farcical set piece in which O'Neal's hotel room is more or less destroyed, involving a room-service waiter, Streisand hanging on a ledge outside, a villain with a golf bag balancing perilously on the same ledge, Madeline Kahn hectoring O'Neal, and so on. O'Neal has to try to turn off the television but he will be defeated, and Bogdanovich apparently directed O'Neal to work according to a number count learned by rote, as the TV control knob comes off. O'Neal then:

(1-2) stares rigidly at the knob in his hand, then
(3-4) stares intently up in the air at nothing, then
(5-6) stares pointedly at the TV screen.

O'Neal "let Peter place him, his body and his voice," Buck Henry told James Spada. "Ryan was playing Peter." It's an approach common in the directing of "activity" show biz, such as comedies and musicals. One thinks of Jerry Mitchell, a Broadway dancer turned director-choreographer, who, when staging a show, frequently acts out what he wants to see by telling a performer, "Let me be you" and demonstrating what he needs. Bogdanovich mistakenly tried this on Streisand as well. She shot him one of her looks and said, "Are *you* . . . giving *me* . . . line readings?"[61]

If O'Neal was out of place in all this, the supporting players lack the picturesque quirkiness of Hollywood's screwball stock company in the 1930s. Austin Pendleton, as a philanthropist whom O'Neal seeks to impress, does display an amusing "love at first sight" appreciation of O'Neal and Streisand (who is masquerading as O'Neal's consort) that energizes his scenes, and Kahn was a captivating sprite with great comic resources, even when playing, as here, a dowdy nag who is supposed to exasperate us. On the contrary, the picture would have been a lot poorer without her. At the first-day table read, the entire cast was grinning simply at the way she pronounced O'Neal's character's name—a "Howard" filled with bustling suspicion. Somehow, Kahn managed to pack all of "Are you up to something I don't approve of?" into just those two syllables.

What's Up, Doc? cost about $4 million and grossed more than $65 million in the United States alone, and we won't argue with success. Still, from Streisand's standpoint, the picture expanded her persona only in linking her romantically with the first of her more or less all-American hunks in a file that would grow to take in David Selby, Robert Redford, Michael Sarrazin, James Caan, Kris Kristofferson, Nick Nolte, and Jeff Bridges. In terms of comic delivery,

Streisand was funnier in both *Funny Girl* and *Hello, Dolly!* (admitting that they offered her sharper lines). Further, while pursuing a non-musical series of films, Streisand nevertheless included a taste of the Songbook here, singing Cole Porter's "You're the Top" (in duet with O'Neal) in the front and back credits and reviving at least part of *Casablanca's* "As Time Goes By" (which is actually a show tune, from *Everybody's Welcome* [1931]), sung atop a grand piano as O'Neal fingers the keys. ("G minor seventh," she helpfully prompts.) It's one of the few times in the film that the two stars seem genuinely to relate to each other, though they were supposedly romantically involved offscreen.

Up the Sandbox (1972) was Streisand's initial release for First Artists, and as the outfit existed to give its founders unimpeded self-expression as auteur-performers, she bears praise and blame alike for this film, poorly received by many critics and a commercial flop as well.

Streisand clearly wanted something with bite: a feminist commentary on contemporary society in the plainest naturalism. The heroine is a housewife with two kids and a loving but busy husband. Nothing stimulates the heroine, so she slips into a fantasy life—as a terrorist operative, or on a wild goose chase in Africa. Yet dreams evaporate. She imagines getting a *Time* cover, as "dust mop of the year" and "expert on Tinker Toys."

"I thought love was enough!" she wails—no, complains. Better: rages, and this is one of Streisand's best acting performances, albeit in a setting so mundane it gave Streisand's randy-pandy show-biz appeal no playing room. This is Streisand the acting star, but it isn't regarded as a collectible performance because the boredom of the heroine's life seeps into and thus creates the boredom of the movie.

And there is a vexing narrative problem in those fantasies, as director Irvin Kershner gives us no way to separate them from the film's day-to-day plotline—no shift in lighting, dialogue pacing, or anything else. On the contrary, the fantasies were integrated into the real-life narrative, a suicidal violation of storytelling protocol.

As it happens, this is true as well of the movie's source, Anne Richardson Roiphe's bestselling 1970 novel *Up the Sandbox!* (yes, with the exclamation point that Streisand's version retired): Roiphe doesn't highlight the fantasies. She wants the reader to figure out for him- or herself that half her tale is imaginary. However, a literary conceit doesn't necessarily play well when the lit has been animated. Paul Zindel, who adapted Roiphe's novel, shows admirable respect for Roiphe's sophistication, but it so to say blundered the movie, and neither Kershner nor Streisand appears to have intervened. It may be that both were too beguiled by Roiphe's technique to realize how ambiguously it would work on film.

For example, early on we find Streisand in the hall outside the office of her husband (David Selby), an academic. His attractive young teaching assistant comes out and Streisand startles us with:

STREISAND: Are you having an affair with my husband?

But the assistant isn't startled. Handsome man, pretty me. It makes sense, really. She looks Streisand right in the eye and replies:

ASSISTANT: Well, as a matter of fact, I am.

And while we're absorbing this, Kershner runs the assistant's entrance again *exactly as before*—but this time Streisand doesn't say anything. So the first go-through must have been a daydream. Or was the second time the dream?

Thus, Kershner has established that his heroine has fantasies—but he doesn't make it clear where they begin and end. A later dream gives us Streisand's interfering mother (Jane Hoffman) cutting the front-door chain link with gigantic bolt cutters to force her way in. Is that actually happening? At least a big set-piece fantasy, in which Streisand takes part in a black-power assault on the Statue of Liberty, is too outlandish to be anything but imaginary—though, to repeat, it is not *presented* outlandishly. Later, when Streisand physically attacks her mother at a family party, it's so believable that, again, we're confused. Does she *really*?

In fact, the party sequence is wonderfully persuasive, giving us all the corny reality of a parents' anniversary celebration, with the ceremonial bestowal of a trip to Italy (STREISAND'S FATHER: I wanted to go to Miami) and the little niece running around snapping candids of everyone (STREISAND: You're going to look really funny with an Instamatic up your ass). To ensure audience approval of Streisand's going after her mother, who wants her to leave Manhattan for the suburbs, Paul Zindel's script gives the mother derogations of New York's "Spanish-speaking" and "colored" people. So even those of us who don't already hate mothers can thrill to the moment when Streisand pushes Hoffman's face into the anniversary cake. Yet even when the two end up rolling around on the floor, this fantasy might well actually be happening. It's a bit rowdy for the occasion, true, but it's physically possible if culturally unlikely—and certainly less extreme than the assault on the Statue Of Liberty.

Up the Sandbox was Streisand's most "personal" film to this point, the first one she planned for herself (and one that she does not regret making, despite its failure). So let us spend some time with it, starting with a blueprint of the fantasies in the order in which they appear, to see if we can discern a pattern—some theme that draws them together and turns a key into the thinking of Streisand's character, Margaret Reynolds.

(1) First, *the brief confrontation with the teaching assistant*, who ends in telling Margaret, "He loves you very much," followed by a sororal embrace.

(2) *Margaret attends a speech by Fidel Castro*, who, in a private tête-à-tête, reveals that he is a woman.

(3) *Margaret's mother breaks into the apartment*, so she can inspect the refrigerator. "Where's your soup stock?" she cries. "Where's your fresh vegetables?"

(4) *The Statue of Liberty caper*. Margaret takes avid part in it, lighting the bomb fuses—but she complicates the program to rescue someone up above inside the statue. Nevertheless, the very symbol of American freedom topples before our eyes.

(5) *The family party*, with Margaret in a tartan skirt and sweater, as chic as she'll look in the entire movie. As if warning us that she's going to cake her mother, nagging as always, Margaret cries, "Don't you ever shut up? I don't come around here and tell you how to live!"

(6) At another party, *Margaret becomes "pregnant,"* forces the bulge down, and instead develops a notable rack. She sails over to her husband, chatting avidly with a perky blonde, but he scarcely notices Margaret, and her new breasts deflate.

(7) With a trench coat over her party gown, *Margaret is now on a mission in Africa* (filmed on location) with an idiotic academic (Paul Benedict, a longtime specialist in amusing eccentrics). They are taken prisoner by a tribe ruled by women and are about to be executed when the fantasy ends.

(8) *Margaret's husband turns on her*, enraged at the prospect of a genuine pregnancy and tossing the pages of Margaret's novel out the window.

(9) *The finale*: but is this in fact a dream? We find the Reynoldses in Central Park, hard by the carousel. Margaret drives off in a car, leaving her family behind. *Or will she?*

One theme runs through it all: women cannot be empowered in society as it is currently constituted. Even Margaret's marriage—the one thing a housewife ought to be able to count on—is a sham, for between real life and the fantasies, Mr. Reynolds presents an unstable entity. David Selby is at once smart and attractive but elusive and unavailable; we never get to understand him. Margaret's mother is actually more vivid, though she gets relatively little screen time, and note that, alone among Streisand's co-stars then, Selby was little known next to Sharif, Matthau, Montand, Segal, and O'Neal. The idea, apparently, was to keep Margaret's mate accessible yet insubstantial: intimately remote. And if a housewife isn't at one with her husband, she has nothing.

In one of her rare sensitive moments, Margaret's mother warns her daughter that "Marriage is a 75–25 proposition. The woman gives 75." Even then, the man gets to do what he wants while Margaret gets to do nothing. Then why is it so exhausting? "I don't have time enough to be an interesting woman," she explains, because there's always another chore keeping her from . . . what? Where is she driving off to at the picture's end?

Perhaps this was the wrong project for Streisand's ID as it was in the early 1970s, too radical for a performer just coming out of musicals and comedies. The serious *Yentl*, *Nuts*, and *The Prince Of Tides* hold worthy places in Streisand's catalogue of films, but they arrived later, after she had enlarged her persona. And, in some ways, her very next film was crucial in that transition.

"Why don't you have a Nazi prom?" Streisand snarls at golden-boy Robert Redford over the luncheonette counter at which she labors as he orders a meal for himself and his dressy, moneyed friends. It's college, it's *The Way We Were* (1973), and it's the extended flashback sequence that tells us who Katie Morosky (Streisand) and Hubbell Gardiner (Redford) are and how, in some indescribable manner, they develop an interest in each other.

Well, she finds him beautiful and he finds her bemusing, puzzling, an intellectual challenge. He isn't used to challenges; the beautiful seldom experience them because, as a line in Arthur Laurents' screenplay tells us, "Everything came easily to him."

Nothing comes to her; everything is a fight. "The Kremlin is worried about the Civil War in Spain!" she tells her fellow students at an outdoor speech rally. "Are you?" Actually, the Kremlin was planning to turn Spain into a Stalinist jail-country like Russia, only Katie is the "useful idiot" (in Lenin's terminology) who doesn't appear to know that. And she is beginning to win her fellow students over, till a prank—signs behind her spelling out "ANY PEACE BUT KATIE'S PIECE"—provokes her to slap the mic with her hat.

Her crusades are not just political but personal, because after she and Redford become a couple she urges him to stay with fiction and not tread the easy path of Hollywood screenwriting. "I'll keep on making [waves] until you're every wonderful thing you should be and will be!"

She's scolding him, badgering him. The movie really could have been called *The Way She Nagged*—yet this is Streisand's first major picture as a glamour star who doesn't have to sing to collect a public, needn't dress in *On a Clear Day*'s east-of-the-sun-and-west-of-the-moon couture. This movie is a charisma gig, centered on two fascinating personalities. There is no spectacle, no supporting player baiting an Oscar nomination, no visual magic from a High Maestro director: just the two stars at their most compelling. And we should note that although Redford had already burst into the top echelon of the Hollywood *nomyenklatura*, it was Streisand who got top billing. This is her *Casablanca*.

And in fact Redford foresaw that *The Way We Were* was bound to end up as Katie's story, not his and not even theirs, for all the shots of the two of them rapt on the sun-kissed Angeleno sands. True, Laurents wrote his character sympathetically while disapproving of him. Hubbell may be a hack writer, but he's eloquent when out and about. "You don't speak," he tells Katie. "You lecture." And, because he's not only a natural-born grandee but an athlete (and we see him in competition on the field): "You still think a Varsity letter stands for 'moron.'" And (even if he does give this one a humorous spin) "Are you really so sure of everything you're so sure of?" And, climactically, though the film is but half over, "I don't think we're going to make it."

They don't, as we all know, for this is a tale of hostile worldviews in conflict. Redford resisted playing Hubbell because he saw the guy as "spineless" and a "pin-up." These are the words of the movie's director, Sydney Pollack, a close friend of Redford's but all the same smart enough to know that no one else in Hollywood had the looks control for the part.

Yes, Hubbell is a pin-up; Redford was a pin-up, whether he liked it or not. In the movie's wartime sequence, he's in the navy almost certainly because the uniforms flatter Redford's fair coloring. In the DVD's documentary feature, Laurents recalls the case of a little boy sent from classroom to classroom in his school bearing a note that he hadn't read. It asked each teacher, "Did you ever see such a smile?"

Redford had to do it, because the theme of the movie was conflicting absolutes: the physical versus the moral. And Redford was wrong in seeing Hubbell as spineless. On the contrary, he is a deep well of powerful opinions. But he underplays his way through life while Katie bangs out her observations like Rachmaninof at the keyboard. So we always know her—from the portrait of Lenin on the wall of her room (later, in a different place, it's Roosevelt and Stalin), from her membership in the college Young Communist League (and, we later learn, in the Party, though this comes up only in a scene that was cut).

But we don't know Hubbell/Redford, because that's how Redford wants it. Had *The Way We Were* been made in the Studio Age, say with Bette Davis and Errol Flynn, we would know their characters through the personas they had established in earlier films.* Actors of that era most often played

---

* There actually was a movie vaguely anticipating *The Way We Were*, *Ann Vickers* (1933), based on Sinclair Lewis' novel and starring Irene Dunne and Walter Huston. The heroine's crusade was prison reform rather than leftist politics, and there was a happy ending, but both actors played somewhat against their type, Dunne flouting middle-class cautions in quite serious ways (including having an abortion) and Huston lighter in tone than usual.

who they (supposedly) were, occasionally innovating, as when outlaw Jimmy Cagney goes song-and-dance man in *Footlight Parade* (1933).

Redford, however, had been forging his career outsmarting the paradigm. From whimsical gay to predatory creep to frontier fighter, in *Inside Daisy Clover* (1965), *Little Fauss and Big Halsy* (1970), and *Jeremiah Johnson* (1972), respectively, he evaded detection: he could be anybody, and that was his power. It's bizarre to think that producer Ray Stark, impatient with Redford's reluctance, threatened to cast Ryan O'Neal, who was much too lightweight to counter Streisand in so intense a narrative. An old-fashioned movie-star movie like this one reveals the radiance of It and how It dwarfs the rest of us. It's not only larger than life: it's larger than fantasy.

And isn't that what Streisand had wanted right from the start—to be the ultimate movie star like Redford, more enchanting than the movies themselves? Thus, the romance of these two avatars transcends *The Way We Were*'s many faults, especially its clichés and bathos. Look, for example, at how obvious even the names are: Katie Morosky. Hubbell Gardiner. Hubbell's college friends J.J. (Bradford Dillman, a forty-three-year-old undergraduate, which is superannuated even by Hollywood standards) and Carol Ann (Lois Chiles). One half expects Katie's political friend at college to be Ivan Samovar. Actually, he's Frankie McVeigh (a very young James Woods).

Frankie McVeigh. *Remember that name!* Though Woods appears only in the college flashback scenes, he figures importantly later on—in fact, in the film's most chilling line. More on this presently.

Meanwhile, why did Redford see Hubbell as spineless if he really isn't? Perhaps because Laurents' screenplay failed to justify the character till it was amended by ghost writers. On the DVD, Pollack mentions David Rayfiel and Alvin Sargent, and there apparently were others. But *someone* gave Redford, near the end, a crucial speech in which we learn that he believes political activism is a foolish vanity that may destroy lives but never effect a change in society.

"*What* Bill of Rights?" he cries. "We don't have any free speech in this country and we never will have!"

He's angry—not at the System, but at Katie, who ran off to DC to support the Hollywood Ten, getting her picture in the papers and compromising his professional stability in a business that Hates People Who Get Involved In Controversy.

Meeting her train as the Ten's allies arrive in a bunch, Redford socks a heckler and ends up alone with Streisand in the station commissary, where, finally, the movie gives Hubbell a chance to make his policies clear. And he is anything but weak: his argument that nothing whatsoever will dislodge the ruling class—or, as we now call it, the swamp and its operatives in the Deep State—is powerfully articulated in, unquestionably, Redford's best scene.

What have the Hollywood Ten accomplished, after all? They'll go to jail and become unemployable and then, a bit later, some "fascist" producer, says Hubbell, will have a problem with a movie and he'll hire the "Communist" writer to solve it. Oh, yes: "They'll make movies. They'll have dinner, they'll play tennis, they'll make passes at each other's wives."

So nothing changes, because it's never about principles. It's about people. And Katie replies, "People are their principles."

Which is either so maddeningly clueless or so persuasively correct that Hubbell smashes everything off a nearby tabletop. *Impasse!*

Is this a political film or a romance? Is it Redford's acting style—so interior, the face a curtain drawn over the soul? Or is it Streisand's—so transparent, abundant, revelatory? Seldom if ever before have two actors been so fascinatingly incongruent in the way they behave. Yes, incongruent *characters* are elemental in the movies, as with the classic pair, Rhett Butler and Scarlett O'Hara. The actors, however, usually observe a certain stylistic agreement on the rules of engagement.

Streisand and Redford do not. You see it at its most effective during the college sequence, when they encounter each other alone, she so plainly hungry for his affection yet terrified of showing it and he so locked up that he's apparently vacant till he suddenly confides in her: he sold a story. He is now a *writer*, and we sense that this is something he won't share with his J.J.s and Carol Anns. They're good for other things—but Katie, only Katie, will understand the exquisite ego-gratification of getting published.

The golden Hubbell has everything, we thought. Yet now he reveals that he needs a certain kind of respect. Not for his looks or athletic prowess but for his talent (even though we never learn whether he is truly gifted or simply capable). And note that he needs that respect from Katie, who has nothing. She's resentful and unpopular, but she has the intellect and sensitivity to be able to share his victory. It's a terrific part to play, and one could say that *The Way We Were* changed the course of Streisand's career. This extraordinary bonding of two superbly unalike sensibilities lifts the experiment out of the recesses of genre and tells us why it was such a huge success and continues to be so despite a chorus of scorn from cinéastes.

This film is a mystery, too, ever drawing us back to try to collect its observations. A great love fails, and Arthur Laurents thinks it's Hubbell's fault and Sydney Pollack thinks it's Katie's. Again, we have incongruent collaborators. The audience is unclear as well, because some call it a nostalgia picture though it tells us that nostalgia is a lie, as when Katie looks back on her and Hubbell's youth, when life was "uncomplicated":

HUBBELL: Katie, it was never uncomplicated.

Unfortunately, *The Way We Were* is also incoherent, made so by a huge cut near the end, just when the romance and the politics come together. Legend tells us that a preview audience got restive during the political scenes and Pollack, grabbing his editor, Margaret Booth, ran up to the projection aerie and cut the entire business out with a razor blade. Some eleven minutes supposedly disappeared, though on the DVD's documentary the director says it was half that: and we get to see the cut footage in this bonus feature.

What a mistake it was to delete those scenes! "The climax is missing," says Arthur Laurents, and the result leaves us to infer that Streisand and Redford parted because he had a fling with Carol Ann, sheer soap opera. But people aren't their adulteries. People are their principles, remember? And one of the omitted scenes gives us the picture's central event:

HUBBELL: Who is Frank McVeigh?

Streisand is taken aback—that name, from all those years ago? Good old Frankie McVeigh, my only friend in college. You cut in on him to dance with me at the Senior Prom. And Frankie just stood there while we moved to-gether, confused and distracted because he knew that beautiful men like you get everything they want, and he wasn't willing to just . . . but why bring him up after all this time?:

HUBBELL: He informed on you.

Well, as they say in the Marine Corps, *there it is*. Most immediately, for plot purposes, this tells us that Katie has been Named, and no studio will employ a writer whose wife thus compromises his loyalty. More generally, the moment recaptures the age* of Naming: of those who actively sought to bring a Stalinist tyranny to this country; of those who joined the Party but then turned away; of those who attended just a few meetings and only out of curiosity; of apolitical guys who went to meet chicks; even of those who had nothing to do with Communism at any time but were on someone's hate list. I saw Goody Proctor with the devil.

---

   * We refer to this time, vaguely, as the McCarthy Era, though the Hollywood Ten's hearing occurred in 1947, before Senator McCarthy hijacked the anti-Communist movement, giving it a mark of Cain from which it has never recovered. Note, by the way, an odd little link with the real-life Streisand, in the aforementioned announcer on the Hungry i bootleg mentioned in the chapter on Streisand's Recordings: Alvah Bessie, one of the Ten.

"He informed on you" is *The Way We Were*'s most crucial line, and we should note that Streisand doesn't rage at McVeigh's treachery. She laughs. "The little rat," she calls him. Because it's so... absurd. So abstract. This name from the deep past now able, just by referring to her in a public hearing, to terminate Streisand's happiness forever. And there's another great line in this scene, when Streisand first tells Redford who this Frank McVeigh is:

> STREISAND (with a rueful smile): We went to college with him. At least I did.

That is: even though you had some interaction with him, he was invisible to you. But somehow I wasn't. You liked me. You confided in me, to whatever extent a self-protected and mostly unavailable being like you can confide. "At least I did" reminds us that Hubbell and Katie aren't simply different personalities: they come from different planets. He didn't go to college with the Frank McVeighs. He went to college with the Bradford Dillmans.

Hubbell doesn't remember Frankie McVeigh because the Hubbells of this world pass through your life without knowing you exist. The Katies, on the other hand, want the world open to all—that's why she says, "At least I did." *She* went to college with everyone who was there, while Hubbell scarcely went to college at all. He went to Hubbell. His life is himself just as Katie's life is everyone's, and that's why their romance must end.

It isn't really about politics, this story. It's about how accessible or how inaccessible people can be, which is why *The Way We Were* is one of the most searchingly well cast movies of its time, and why Sydney Pollack fought so hard to get Redford to play Hubbell: because Pollack knew how *privately* Redford performs—as if even the movie's audience didn't deserve to get close to his character.

Streisand is just the opposite, which is why she plays well with other very open actors, such as Walter Matthau (even though they hated each other), James Caan, and Richard Dreyfuss. But again, it's the gulf between Streisand and Redford that makes their teaming so provocative. "At least I did," she says: because I was part of something. I knew what Franklin Roosevelt meant as a maker of history; you thought he was just another president.

In short, Katie has always been alone, and never more than now. McVeigh has opened the lions' cage, and now Hubbell—the only one she understands and who understands her, so close and closer still—is telling her he will not protect her.

As Laurents says, this is the climax of the tale, and it's missing from the release print. No wonder many see the work as an ignoble tragedy, based around figures of little moment.

Still, this was the first interesting film to fulfill Streisand's need to carry a role on personal magnetism, the first title with "Mirror, mirror, on the wall" impact. Who's the fairest one of all?: the romantic lead opposite Robert Redford. It's that simple, because in cutting the stuffing out of the film, Sydney Pollack left us with little more than a pugnacious social critic, her dream lover, and a beguiling title tune, by Marvin Hamlisch and the Bergmans.

Nonetheless, Streisand got what she needed, as a movie star in its purest sense, the Garbo and Monroe sense—whereby everyone knows who you are—and she achieved it by playing, very often, mysteries: the working woman in *Dolly!* with a multitude of contrasting business cards but no clear business; the *What's Up, Doc?* polymath who acts like an idiot; the *Up the Sandbox* housewife with secret fantasies; *Yentl's* boy of ulterior gender. She has to say, "Hubbell, it's Katie" to Redford when they're in bed because otherwise how will he know who she is?

True, he's asleep. And in fact he knows who she is all the way along: that's why he chose her when he needed to share the news about his writing success. It's not Redford who needs reminding but Streisand's audience, because she's confusing. In *The Way We Were*, she's a fanatic social agitator with hurt feelings. In real life, she's a unique singer who nonetheless wants to be another of the countless dramatic actresses.

To repeat, she is not a Warholian figure bearing the household ID of a household name, known to all. She's elusive, a coat of many colors, but she doesn't necessarily seem so because she behaves as if she weren't. And, in this particular movie, it's more complicated yet because Redford is even more elusive than she is. Fanatics are not aware of anyone else; that's part of the fun. So "Hubbell, it's Katie" is a very telling moment in this popular yet critically underrated (and also flawed) work, the moment when the mystery guest signs in on the chalkboard and, for a few seconds, no one has to guess who she is.

We'll mention **For Pete's Sake** (1974) only to keep this chapter on Streisand's movies complete, because this is a meretricious and even stupid film that could have been made with anyone in Streisand's role. And that is hardly true of any of her previous seven films.

A comedy without a single laugh, *For Pete's Sake* finds Streisand trying to raise money to support her husband (Michael Sarrazin) through various schemes from prostitution to cattle wrangling in the streets of New York. There are some unusual touches, such as the casting of Molly Picon, a doyenne of the Yiddish-language stage, as a procuress named Mrs. Cherry. Overall, however, the picture is mirthless trash. It was a hit even so, if only because it followed *The Way We Were*.

"Over my dead body," says Streisand when Ray Stark (to whom she is con-tracted for a last film) suggests a sequel to *Funny Girl*, to be called **Funny Lady** (1975). And many are those who denounce what was obviously con-ceived as a commercial rather than artistic project.

But hold. It's always gratifying to see Streisand in a musical (especially after her string of talkies), and if she can make *For Pete's Sake*, she can make anything. Besides, there were the legalities to consider: *Funny Lady*'s co-writer Jay Presson Allen told Judith Crist at one of Crist's talkback retro-spectives that Streisand was "figuratively speaking...escorted to the set every day by a team of lawyers."[62]

Of course, *we* see it as a musical—Streisand sees it as another "door-mat" role, as a woman who lives for the attention of a man rather than for her own achievements. And, indeed, the Fanny Brice of *Funny Lady* was, arguably, the last doormat role Streisand would play (with the possible ex-ception of Cheryl in *All Night Long*), and we should note that Brice was a great show-biz achiever and a complete Original in her own right. Interestingly, *Funny Lady* marked a rare time when Streisand wasn't all that eager to meddle in the making of a film. For one thing, she was impa-tient to get it over with; for another, she was distracted by her new liaison, with Jon Peters.

Actually, *Funny Lady*'s Brice is less of a doormat than *Funny Girl*'s, though she starts the film still mesmerized by Nick Arnstein. We even hear the "falling minor third" Arnstein Leitmotiv from *Funny Girl* on the *Funny Lady* soundtrack. And when Streisand and, returning from the earlier film, Omar Sharif kiss, the underscoring plays a bit of "People."

At least that scene finally cures Brice of her Nick infatuation, though by that point the story is all but over. Anyway, if she was still involved with the dream of Arnstein, why did she marry Billy Rose, her vis-à-vis in this go-around? Rose had qualities, but they were almost all bad ones. He was a Gregg shorthand champion, a sometime "lyricist" thought to have attached his name to songs written by others by agenting the publishing deal, an imitator of Florenz Ziegfeld who thus produced revues and spectacles (and even bought the Ziegfeld Theatre); but who was above all a cheap chiseler who became a multimillionaire but would steal your cigarette lighter.

Rose's biographer, Earl Conrad, suggests that Rose married the very social Brice for the cultural advantages: he wanted to go places and Brice *was* places. Rose moved into Brice's apartment, "where," says Conrad, "she entertained the celebrities that Billy so seriously wished to cultivate." So now he had what he needed, but what was in it for Brice? Because (though the movie doesn't let us know this) he was not considered a good fellow. As the famous New York joke ran:

Q: Who has the biggest prick on Broadway?
A: Fanny Brice.

"I fell in like with him" is *Funny Lady*'s analysis of the affair: they married for companionship. And, indeed, James Caan's Billy plays well with Streisand's Fanny. Both are natural-born kidders, and somehow her direct line delivery fits nicely with his mannerisms—the lopsided grin, the odd silent hesitation when you feel he should say something, the gestures to nowhere. It emphasizes that she knows everything and he's a clutzy outsider. Yet he spars with her like a know-it-all; their styles meet at the shouting level.

True, Caan was too tall to resemble the tiny Rose in any way, but then *Funny Lady* is not a studied retelling of Brice's later life. Perhaps its main purpose, from Streisand's point of view, lay in reifying her revisionist notion of who gets to be a movie star and who doesn't. Everyone told her she was wrong for the job, but she seized the position, and on traditional terms, making a parade out of playing romances with Hollywood's Lochinvars. Thus, while the short and feisty Robert Blake was seriously considered to play Billy Rose, ultimately Ray Stark had to go with Caan because Blake wasn't cute or famous enough to play opposite Streisand.*

With Caan as Rose and Herbert Ross to direct and choreograph, Streisand had, in effect, "her" team in place—as if, even given the importance of *Funny Lady*'s male lead and a pride of production numbers for Ross to execute, everyone in Streisand's orbit was the help.

But what about the music? As this was a period piece, it was decided to combine old numbers (mostly) associated with Billy Rose with a new set of six songs by John Kander and Fred Ebb, specifically to promote character and situation. To give but one example, a rehearsal of Harold Arlen and E. Y. Harburg's "It's Only a Paper Moon" (and, yes, Rose shares byline credit, but no one believes he did any of the writing) runs that melody concurrently with new Kander and Ebb "asides" for the two stars, "I Like Him" and "I Like Her."

Further, Herbert Ross broke the rule that Hollywood's Broadway sagas present theatre numbers on outsized sound stages, giving us effects beyond the theatre's logistical possibilities. In *Funny Lady*, all the stage numbers were shot on a theatre stage, lending the movie unusual thespian atmosphere.

There are a few authentic small touches as well—the original color three-sheet poster of Rose's circus musical, *Jumbo*, on the wall of his office, for instance. Still, too much of the action lives in Neverland, as when chorus

---

* Ironically, just before *Funny Lady* was released, Blake's television series *Baretta* appeared on ABC, and with his catchphrases (e.g., "That's the name of that tune!") and pet cockatoo, Fred, Blake became one of the best-known people in the country—arguably more so than Caan.

girls in "If You Want the Rainbow (You Must Have the Rain)" dance in pastel tutus with matching umbrellas under thick see-through plastic shortcoats, a ravingly anachronistic concept for the period.

Funny Lady doesn't even know which period it's in. Various dialogue clues early on tell us it's 1929, just after the Wall Street crash. "See you on the bread-line," Streisand tells a fellow performer, as it's closing night of the *Follies*, established with a view of the New Amsterdam Theatre marquee heralding the show's eleventh month. However, no *Follies* ran anywhere near that long. Ziegfeld opened his annual in very late spring as the last big event of the the-atre season, did more or less sell-out business for four or five months, then sent it out on tour. And Streisand's Fanny shouldn't be in a 1929 *Follies* in the first place, because there was no *Follies* that year, and in any case her last appearance in a Ziegfeld-produced *Follies* was in 1923. (She appeared in two posthumous editions mounted by the Shuberts, in 1934 and 1936.)

No doubt Hollywood's rationalization for the inaccuracies in these musical biographies—and *Funny Lady* is far from the most unreliable of the lot—is that the form offers not facts but entertainment loosely drawn from the facts. But what's the excuse for the script, which veers from smart and funny to vapid and clumsy, as in Fanny's first reunion with Nick:

FANNY: I just want to climb into your back pocket and stay there all the time.

That certainly doesn't sound like Jay Presson Allen, who wrote the very pointed screenplays to *The Prime Of Miss Jean Brodie* and *Cabaret* (and she was called in to help regulate the disorderly scripts of Streisand's *A Star Is Born* remake). Presumably the line is the work of *Funny Lady*'s other writer, Arnold Schulman, who capped a spectacularly undistinguished career in his screenplay to *A Chorus Line*, which reduced a Broadway classic to a Bark Box.

Then, too, *Funny Lady* suffers from the same second-act trouble that bedev-iled *Funny Girl*: after a highly theatrical first half filled with backstage *geschrei*, the second half devolves into a dreary love story. It's all the worse when, after James Caan regales us with his finagling rascal of a Billy, we have to sit through that cameo of Omar Sharif's Nick so Streisand can finally realize that he isn't marvelous after all. Lady, it took you two whole movies to figure that out? And then Caan reappears, his mustache neatly aged by Hollywood's never-fail Acme Powder Company, and now even Caan is boring. The movie leaves us with Brice cut off from her staff of life, performing: Funny Retiree.

One very odd thing is the lack of star treatment in the way Streisand is made up and costumed. The archival hairdos don't flatter her, especially after *Funny Lady* starts with clips from *Funny Girl*, all of Streisand in her most attractive moments, such as her entrance for her first date with Nick, when she produces a fan out of nowhere and instantly snaps it open. It's a cute parody of glamour-star filmmaking, though it in fact originated in the stage *Funny Girl* and was simply carried over for the film.

Funny Lady is starved for such moments, whether as parody or seriously meant. Its salient glamour spot arrives in one of the onstage numbers, "Great Day," wherein Streisand appears in full diva kit of gold-and-silver-spangled dress slit up to the waist, matching cap, and bodice pushing up her splendid bosom. Herbert Ross stages the number with black dancers (the music, by Vincent Youmans, suggests a gospel rave-up, especially in Peter Matz's arrangement for the film), while Streisand performs independently, upstage and cut off from the dancing. The whole thing is out of sync with the era and drags the movie down in any case. It's one of the reasons the film got a lot of bad notices. Pauline Kael, once a Streisand supporter, was scathing on *Funny Lady*, calling Streisand's performance akin to "a female impersonator's imitation of Barbra Streisand."[63]

Still, the movie did good business. Even Kael enjoyed the "wittily staged" "I Found a Million Dollar Baby In a Five and Ten Cent Store," another onstage number, in which a miniature Streisand in white tails dances on a very long cigarette and holder held by a gigantic redheaded woman painted on the scenery. In fact, the music—along with some of the early Streisand-Caan bickering—is the only reason to see *Funny Lady*. So it's all the more curious that the soundtrack album doesn't offer exactly what is heard in the release print—and there are further differences between the original LP and the later CD.

Although all of Streisand's recitals were made by Columbia, her *Funny Girl* show album and a few soundtracks came out on other labels, *Funny Lady* on Arista. One can see why the disc uses a non-movie taping of "Million Dollar Baby," because, in the film, something goes wrong with the scenery and Fanny lets out a few sarcastic ad libs and doesn't sing every note. The orchestral track doesn't vary, but, obviously, Streisand recorded a "clean" reading for the album.

The album differs also in the track for "Blind Date." *Funny Lady* was to have started with a flashback frame, as an older Fanny contemplated seeing her beloved but so vexing Nick again, and Kander and Ebb wrote an arresting little soliloquy for her. This then cued in the earlier Fanny, onstage in the *Follies*, singing Kander and Ebb's loving recreation of a Fanny Brice number, a comic version of the serious soliloquy in that neither Fanny knew what sort of man was going to walk through the door.

The movie dropped the flashback and the little soliloquy, running "Blind Date" during the opening credits, but Arista retained the intro along with a longer version of "Blind Date" itself, with a nimble scoring trick right after the line "Shirley ain't sittin' on no shelf": plucked strings on three crisp beats. On the disc, Streisand's ad lib comments are not what we hear in the film, and her spoken dialogue with the audience (because she hid from the date, thinking he would be a dud, and now has to learn that he was a "Rudolph Valentino, from the movies") becomes, on the disc, a conversation with just one voice, that of a man who sounds exactly like George Segal, from *The Owl and the Pussycat*.

Now, just to make things difficult for us, the *Funny Lady* CD, while getting the cuts into story order (as they were not on the LP), substituted a less interesting "Great Day" for the one heard on the LP. That track adhered to what was used in the film, with a vocal that begins as a voiceover during a transitional dialogue scene as Billy's revue, having finished its Atlantic City tryout, heads for Broadway. As Streisand reaches the refrain's second A, on "Angels in the sky," her voice leaps up to a big high note while the movie gives us a view of Times Square fading into Streisand onstage in mid-number. It's one of the few really exciting moments in the film because of what Streisand does on the word "sky." Yet the CD uses a different take, without that wonderful effect. Who on earth makes these bizarre decisions?

Streisand didn't like doing sequels or remakes, but her next title, *A Star Is Born* (1976), was the fourth filming of the story. Hollywood writer Adela Rogers St. Johns started it off with the idea for *What Price Hollywood* (1932), the tale of a waitress (Constance Bennett) who charms a director (Lowell Sherman) who's hitting the skids on alcohol and general Weltschmerz. Fearful of dragging her down, he sets her up with a handsome playboy (Neil Hamilton) and shoots himself.

The plan was to give the public a taste of the show behind the show—the waitress begging to trade tables with a co-worker specifically to get Discovered by Sherman; the fans rioting at the sight of the new young star, even at her wedding, where they tear away at her bridal outfit till she is forced to seek sanctuary back in the church.

Only RKO would have been willing to produce such an unhappy look at Hollywood, a company town that disliked criticism by its own kind. But RKO was the nonconformist studio, the one where the early and very affected Katharine Hepburn was a Queen of the Lot and where Fred Astaire and Ginger Rogers redefined dance as a medium of dressy democracy. There was always a feeling of the East Coast and even New York itself in the RKOs, and if you were having trouble landing a script on a touchy subject, RKO was your safety.

This will come up again when we get to the Streisand *Star Is Born*. Meanwhile, the second version (1937)—the first of three so-entitled *Star Is Borns*—gave no credit to Johns and the seven writers who worked on *What*

Price Hollywood's shooting script, which is truly shocking. Less surprising was the new film's blatant celebration of the movie colony, as this was a release by David O. Selznick's indie studio, and Selznick loved the place. There's a feeling in *What Price Hollywood* that sorrow is implicit in the way the movie industry operates, whereas in 1937 Fredric March's suicide derives from his own troubled soul. We sense that as well in James Mason's portrayal of the same character in the 1954 *Star Is Born*, now a Warner Bros. musical for Judy Garland. Thus, in the first three films, the heroine was played by, first, a glamour star, then a personality star, then a talent star.

In Streisand's very own *Star Is Born*, she is a talent and acting star, as is her sweetheart, Kris Kristofferson (though he was allegedly too stoned to do much acting and his singing lacks spark). This fourth version was conceived—impulsively, off the top of his head—by John Gregory Dunne, and he and his wife, Joan Didion, wrote it for Carly Simon and James Taylor, obviously changing the background from movies to the music world.

But were the (then married) Taylors ready for dramatic roles? Even today, some forty years later, theirs are not careers rich in acting gigs. The project started hopping around in the Hollywood manner, and at one point it appeared that Cher—also a talent and acting star—was going to do it. Then Streisand became interested. Warner Bros. would have to yield ownership of the property to First Artists, retaining only distribution rights, but the studio couldn't resist getting in on the "Streisand singing six numbers and we'll make sixty million" rule.

Unfortunately, by this time in her career, Streisand had become a compulsive ditherer on all projects of which she was in charge, endlessly changing her mind about everything, demanding another script revision, a different location shot, a correction in the lighting of her right cheek. ("I can feel the heat is different! A bulb must have burned out!") Some people nag their partners; Streisand was nagging an industry. Something like a dozen different scripts were prepared, by which time nobody knew what the movie was anymore. In the end, the third and last of the Dunne-Didion scripts was the one that was shot, apparently with contributions from Jay Presson Allen, as I've said, and the usual Streisand amendments.

Worse than all this was Jon Peters' intrusion into every aspect of the film. A STAR IS SHORN was one headline from the incredulous Hollywood press, seeing Streisand's talent clipped by "a hairdresser" (though, as we know, Peters was the proprietor of hair salons, not an employee). As if protectively taking on the coloration of her sidekick, Streisand became raucously contrarian on this film as she had not been before and would not be after, even seconding Peters on his characteristically impetuous suggestions. "Full of mad schemes"[64] is how *A Star Is Born*'s director, Frank Pierson, described Peters, who at one point wanted to play Kristofferson's role despite having no singing ability and at another wanted to direct.

So we find Streisand (who took three credits on the film, for her acting, as "executive producer," and for "musical concepts") hectoring Pierson on almost every shot and regarding herself as a co-director. Watching all this with caustic detachment, Kristofferson accused Pierson of giving in to the diva and making "a Barbra Streisand lollipop extravaganza,"[65] but in fact Pierson was the one actually in charge. Streisand would become enraged at his habit of letting her tell him how a scene should be shot, nodding in response, then going off and doing it his way.

It would seem that Streisand had a vision of How Music Treats Our Anguish, whereas Pierson was just directing a movie, urging along the story and filling out the characters. And yet, to an extent, Streisand's idea for the retelling does come through, with a feminist slant, as we see two artists meet in their music even as hers carries her upward and his cannot help him.

Was it because her songs (that is, those specifically written for her in this film) were *hers*, on her personal topics, while his were anyone's? Yet his theme tune, "Watch Closely Now," is supposedly about himself. "Are you watching me now?" he sings—but it doesn't mean anything, even to him. He can't even remember the lyrics.

Streisand thought the songs' content was so important that she was constantly giving notes to the film's prime lyricist, Paul Williams (working with composer Kenny Ascher), making it all but impossible for him to finish anything. "There was *so* much input," he later explained. It was like "having a picnic at the end of an airport runway."[66]

A smash success though a critical catastrophe, *A Star Is Born* suffered a unique setback when the premiere was shadowed by Pierson's dryly scathing article, published in both *New West* and *New York* magazines, "My Battles With Barbra and Jon." It seemed almost to hope the picture failed.

In the event, half the film is a lot of fun and half of it is stupid. The fun lies in the many views of the backstage of the pop-music industry, where life is just as mean and driven as it was in *What Price Hollywood*. We see the harried road manager (Gary Busey) trying to get a professional attitude out of Kristofferson, who just doesn't care anymore. We see the entourage of people who serve no particular function (except the groupies), the opportunists frantically pitching ideas to Streisand as she comes offstage after her first big performance. We see Streisand's personal bête noire, the greedy paparazzi. ("Don't you ever have enough?" she cries, when they close in on another of the self-inflicted disasters of her lover's career.)

We see as well that wonderful show-biz phoniness, when a crass disc jockey with whom Kristofferson has been feuding (he actually hurls a case of Jack Daniel's through the glass wall of the guy's cubicle) joins the national mourning party after Kristofferson's fatal car crash, saying, "He was like a brother to me." In a very striking scene, we get the obnoxious fan who treats his idol as if they were intimates, his worship a mask hiding a seething hostility. ("Lots of crazy strangers" is how Kristofferson's rock star defines this sector of the public.)

We get the "everybody's on the make" view of the wannabees hanging on at the fringes, when Kristofferson finds a young woman swimming in his pool. A "journalist" (meaning she carries around a tape machine), she wants an interview with a star, and Streisand arrives to find the two of them in bed. Hurt to the point of being stunned, Streisand brings the whole movie to a halt, but the girl is all set for business: snapping on her recorder, she extends her mic toward Streisand and simply says, "Go."

More: the concert scenes have atmosphere, especially one with a crowd bigger than a DeMillian exodus, in a somewhat grainy look, as if Pierson wanted the effect of real-life stock footage. One has to imagine the director mustering his forces despite crushing technical difficulties, while Peters kibitzes with unhelpful suggestions and Streisand continues to berate Pierson for defying her.

As it is, it's difficult to judge Pierson's work, as First Artists owned the negative and, as soon as Pierson signed off on his edit, Streisand reportedly commandeered the footage to create her own *A Star Is Born* to favor her shots and cutting back on Kristofferson's. Apparently, she eventually restored much if not all of the original Pierson edit, though we still see some strangely static scenes between the two leads in which the camera placement is simply wrong, even amateurish.

In fact, it's the film's romantic half that seems terrible, with dead (and sometimes ludicrous) writing and hackneyed situations. Worse, it's one of Streisand's least impressive acting performances, while Kristofferson cuts an impressive figure as the self-destructive John Norman Howard, the first rock star in history with three first names. As I've said, Kristofferson felt so alienated from the proceedings that, supposedly, he seldom hit his marks sober. Still, he has a natural sense of humor combined with a resigned sadness that brings the character to life.

Then, too, a scene in which Kristofferson joins Streisand at the mic in the recording studio as she tapes "Evergreen" has a certain love-match validity. For once, the two seem really attuned to each other. Streisand picked out the melody in her head and Paul Williams laid words atop it, achieving a sentimental piece on the pedestrian side yet somehow beguiling enough to catch the national ear. It won Streisand and Williams an Oscar, Grammy, and Golden Globe.

Perhaps that moment stands out precisely because otherwise the romance appears to have been patched together out of scrips and scraps of the too-many-cooks library of screenplays that were collected during the development stage. This is not even to bring in how the unbalanced love plot clearly wants to favor Streisand. We don't even see Kristofferson's climactic car crash, as the sequence fades on a view of Kristofferson speeding off to a distant nowhere. Just as Sydney Pollack kept having to raise Robert Redford's profile in the *Way We Were* narrative, Frank Pierson tried to give Kristofferson's participation in *A Star Is* Born more presence. Perhaps one could say that, just this one time, Streisand's "Everybody else is wrong" credo failed her, because she ended in fashioning a love story with only one person in it.

As to the film's score, "Evergreen" is actually one of the less interesting numbers. Unlike Streisand's earlier musicals, this one doesn't feature character pieces like "People" or "Just Leave Everything To Me"; the principals open themselves up to us in their performing spots. Thus, Streisand's "Queen Bee" (by Rupert Holmes) and "Woman In the Moon" (by Ascher and Williams) touch on the assertive new version of the story's heroine. The latter song is so slight in content as to be almost meaningless. However, Holmes' patter number, marked "Slow and funky," rattles off a load of amusing images in sixteenth notes, some of them on the whimsical side, as in "Little Nefertiti used to consummate a treaty in the bed as much as on the throne."

This is Streisand's first number in the continuity, when she's yet to be discovered, still just the lead singer of the Oreos (with two black women partners), working small clubs, and we notice that, as Streisand's career blossoms, she sings only simple songs with little verbal content. In fact, "Queen Bee" is the movie's only truly arresting number, suggesting that, to Streisand, stardom means dropping one's quirks and intensities, those markers of the unique performer. Is this because originality is a bar to the accumulation of a huge public or because it's too protean to sustain over decades at the top? Does the Original inevitably become part of the Establishment?

Upon the movie's release, the New York *Village Voice*'s A BORE IS STARRED was only one of the ridiculing headlines. Scorning the show as a vanity production, the critics were savage, but the movie was a whopping hit, proving that adage about "Streisand singing six numbers" was absolutely right. She wanted to act, not sing, but the public seemed to insist that she was less an actress who sings than a singer who acts. And there's a rude story that goes with that, though like them all it may be apocryphal.

The first *King Kong* remake was in production at the same time as *A Star Is Born* (both films came out in 1976), and Jon Peters was in some Hollywood lair when he spotted *Kong*'s producer, Dino De Laurentiis, and went over to his table to say, "I'm Jon Peters. I'm producing *A Star Is Born*. I'll bet a million dollars my movie makes more money than yours."

De Laurentiis looks up at Peters with an unreadable expression. Then he answers, "It should make more money. Your monkey sings."[67]

But here, now, is a valid idea for two glamour stars in a popcorn movie, something light and insignificant that can work only if the stars enjoy good chemistry. For color, let's go with a boxing theme, and for plot the two leads will meet cute and take instant dislike to each other because their respective backgrounds and styles are so antagonistic. Yet for business reasons they have to keep company even so, snarking all the while. It's love at first hate, of course, because of Hollywood's Second Rule for movie stars: Opposites Attract.* As the film approaches the happy ending, it terminates a climactic boxing match when someone "throws in the towel" (which by boxing rules is an automatic surrender), even though our fighter star was winning. That's all right, though, because he'd rather be in love, after all.

And that's Streisand's eleventh feature, coming right after *A Star Is Born*: *Cain and Mabel* (1936), starring Clark Gable and Marion Davies.

All right, no: the actual Streisand release was **The Main Event** (1979). It gave no source credit to *Cain and Mabel*, but the Streisand film is in effect a remake, if only in the most strategic particulars. This includes the throwing of the towel, though in *Cain and Mabel* a trainer does it and in *The Main Event* the honor goes to Streisand, protecting her boxer love from harm.

The Main Event is a comedy, so the action begins with a premise so unbelievable it's part of the fun: Streisand's financial man has absconded with everything she owns. Till this point Streisand was a perfume tycoon, but now:

> STREISAND (to her accountant): Do you mean I have to be careful at
> Saks or I can't afford toothpaste?

She can't afford toothpaste, because there's nothing left except an objet trouvé—a contract with a boxer, which prompts Streisand to make a living by becoming his manager. He's Ryan O'Neal, as one Kid Natural—so natural that in fact he hates boxing. He prefers to give driving lessons, albeit officed in headquarters shaped like a gigantic boxing glove.

Anyway, now we have our two opposites, separated by not only stylistics but her need to make him fight and his reluctance to. We have as well that

---

* The First Rule is: Be Accused Of Murder But Innocent. Streisand was to get to that one, too, as we'll soon see.

color of the boxing setting, which in *Cain and Mabel* was show biz by other means—the marquees! the lights! the merriment! *The Main Event* gives us a more honest view of the fight community: multiracial and starved for cash. Its backstage is sweat and poverty, quite devoid of light and merriment. Still, this is a comedy, so the overall view is only gently gritty.

Directed by Howard Zieff, *The Main Event* gave Streisand a role she relished: all about her looks, her energy, her comic delivery, her Streisand-ness—not a glamour role, but a personality part that puts nothing between the actress and the public. She found plenty of chances to shoot scenes in shorts, to emphasize her figure and even (in a playful, "everyone's in on the joke" way) her bottom. In fact, there is very little in the film besides the two stars hacking around with each other, unless it be Patti d'Arbanville's comically tough-edged girl friend of O'Neal, with a smoker's cough dense enough to slice; everyone who talks about the movie mentions it.

Back in the days of *Cain and Mabel*, Hollywood knew exactly how this sort of movie should go, with flavorsome supporting people and the usual stacking of writers to add wit to the official screenplay. When somebody wants to scorn Marion Davies' latest Broadway show, it's "The ushers are quitting because they're afraid to be alone in the dark." *The Main Event*, written by Gail Parent and Andrew Smith (with the usual Streisand editing pep sessions) is thin in wit. The jokes are obvious rather than twisty, as here during during a comic car chase:

> O'NEAL: Well, I've got two words for you and they're not "Happy birthday!"
> STREISAND: Well, I've got the same two words for you!
> O'NEAL: Watch your mouth!

At least the two stars work a pleasant chemistry together, and O'Neal is a much more agile comedian than in *What's Up, Doc?*. Having trained as a boxer in youth, he knows his way around the ring, but it appears that his work on the Depression piece *Paper Moon* (1973)—with the same director, Peter Bogdanovich, as on *What's Up, Doc?*—broadened his grasp of character. Oddly, in *Paper Moon* O'Neal is playing what he played in the earlier film, the male exasperated by the female. But it ran flat in *What's Up, Doc?* while it informs *Paper Moon* with a loving sorrow. Perhaps this was because he was working opposite not an adult but a little girl (who was of course his own daughter, Tatum O'Neal). However it developed, the Ryan O'Neal of *The Main Event* meets Streisand on an equal footing as a comedian, and whether one likes or disdains the movie, the pair's interaction substantiates the narrative far more delightfully than what we get from Gable and Davies in *Cain and Mabel*.

Rotten Tomatoes treated *The Main Event* to a mere 38 percent rating, but it was a hit in 1979, perhaps because of its then trendy inquiry into gender roles. The poster art showed both stars facing off with the gloves on, their legs braced to land a knockout blow, and at one point O'Neal complains to Streisand, "What do you think I am, a piece of meat?" Actually, this wasn't all that new. In *Cain and Mabel*, Gable says, "To tell the truth, I'm scared to death every time I crawl between the ropes."

All the same, Streisand was never a trend opportunist, looking for Zeitgeist-ready properties. Like Stephen Sondheim, an artist with whom she has much in common, Streisand gets involved with projects she finds irresistible through some personal sympathy, not because they are bound to succeed. Thus, as we've seen, she was hostile to *Funny Lady* from start to finish, making it under legal duress even though it had fierce commercial validity.

And now she was deeply committed to making *Yentl*, a tricky prospect because of its cross-dressing heroine (some thirty years before cross-dressing, too, became trendy) and meticulously articulated Old World Jewish folkways. It wasn't even a musical then—and, after all, Streisand had just made *Funny Lady* and *A Star Is Born*. Even *The Main Event* closed with a lengthy Streisand disco vocal.

So Streisand was obsessively dedicated to producing and starring in *Yentl*—and directing it as well, in her first time in that role. But then something else happened.

Streisand was not even cast in her next film—not at first. This was to be a little European-style piece in which character and atmosphere mattered more than plot. The French do this very well; it was the sort of thing you'd take in in an "art house" in the coastal cities in the 1950s and 1960s—a curiosity, really, because you and your party would come out of the cinema unsure of what you had seen and not even clear on whether you liked it or not. Something by Alain Resnais, for example, with just enough Gallic charm and observation to earn money but not respect. A failure d'estime, we might say.

Of course, the art houses were gone by this time, the early 1980s, and the "art" audience was no longer extensive enough to play to exclusively. The *New York Times*' influential movie critic Bosley Crowther, who championed small European films he thought worthy, had destroyed his credibility crusading against *Bonnie and Clyde* for its use of glamour stars to subvert traditional morality, and Crowther's passing was, in effect, the passing of the little art film. The cinemas wanted *Bonnie and Clyde*, not Alain Resnais.

Now, it happens that the Hollywood agent Sue Mengers was married to the Francophone Belgian movie director Jean-Claude Tramont, who was directing one of those "little" films, ***All Night Long*** (1981), about adulteries among the southern California middle class. Gene Hackman was the protagonist, the executive of a drugstore company suddenly demoted to night manager of one of the firm's outlets. Hackman gets involved with a vapid but attractive young woman named Cheryl, played by Lisa Eichhorn. And Eichhorn has a firefighter husband (Kevin Dobson) and Hackman has a coarse and dopey son (Dennis Quaid, two years after *Breaking Away* and still quite young), both of whom are also involved with Cheryl. Dobson's even married to her. And then Hackman's wife finds out about Cheryl and sues for divorce while carrying on with her divorce lawyer.

There's almost as much love intrigue as in one of Handel's *opere serie* for London, but even as the principals trade and share partners, much of the action occurs in Hackman's drugstore, where everything leans toward dumb physical farce involving incompetent employees and criminals seeking a payday.

So already there are two very different kinds of film going off at once— one based on character interaction and one based on low-comic stunts. Further, W. D. Richter's screenplay is so dim that not a single line strikes a light, and Hackman, the star who's supposed to hold everything together, is simply retailing his patented half-smiles and sly grins. Sue Mengers could see that her husband's movie was not going to succeed.

Hmmm, but what if? Mengers' favorite client and, she thought, best friend was Barbra Streisand, just then busy getting *Yentl* ready for principal photography and thus, as the old thespian phrase has it, "at liberty." What if Streisand replaced Lisa Eichhorn, thereby promoting a "little" film into a Streisand blockbuster?

It would still be little in its narrative scope, though, wouldn't it? A Streisand blockbuster was lavish *Funny Girl*, or cast-of-thousands *A Star Is Born*, or even *The Main Event*, full of personality. *All Night Long* was . . . quiet. Worse, Streisand's role was quiet, too, with none of the sarcasm that was an essential part of her ID, at least to that point in her career.

Yes, yes, yes, because what if Universal promised Streisand four million dollars, the highest salary ever offered till then? Streisand might find the precedent itself alluring out of sheer prestige: she would be the Constance Bennett of the 1980s.* More important, Streisand's *Yentl* contract held her

---

* In 1931, Bennett's agent negotiated the biggest deal in Hollywood's early history: two films with Warner Bros. for $300,000—and, rumor had it, the studio had to pay Bennett's agent's commission and her IRS assessment on top. It was the most anyone had ever been paid, and we note an interesting parallel with Streisand in that Bennett was regarded by the Hollywood community as demanding and uncompromising. Too, like Streisand, Constance Bennett had no filter when speaking her mind. The major *Photoplay* journalist Ruth Biery called Bennett "honest to the point of being

financially responsible for any overtime in the shooting schedule, and Streisand the perfectionist knew there would be no way to bring to term a complex piece like *Yentl* without incurring overtime charges. Thus, *All Night Long*'s $4 million was an inducement, and Streisand said yes. She even accepted second billing, after Hackman.

The movie had already started shooting, so Lisa Eichhorn was fired, with the cover excuse that she had been miscast. Still, changing the leading woman did not solve the problem of the terrible script, especially in the loony drugstore "comedy" sequences. These not only sabotage the film's overall tone, as I've said, but also defy realism. A shoplifter, threatened by the security guard's gun, makes funny faces instead of . . . oh, I don't know, surrendering or running away? A vast Amazon of a woman also tries to rob the store, but her defeat is played as slapstick.

Lamest of all is the use of a toy helicopter worked by remote control, which Hackman uses to taunt his corporate nemeses. This scene starts cutely enough, with Wagner's "Ride of the Valkyries" on the soundtrack, referencing a comparable moment in *Apocalypse Now*. But then Tramont fails to connect Hackman's use of the flying toy with his anger at the men who humiliated him. He's surely supposed to be bombarding them, but the machine just flies around aimlessly while Hackman does his grin and the two executives make unhappiness noises. No wonder Sue Mengers felt her husband's movie needed an emergency infusion of some kind.

Rather, it needed a new script and director. To repeat, none of the characters ever says anything interesting, and Cheryl manages to be nonconformist and ordinary at the same time. This just isn't a Streisand role—not after the one-of-a-kind strivers like Fanny and Katie. Even in the frivolous *Main Event*, Streisand was as much a fighter as Ryan O'Neal was.

It is hard to imagine Streisand's agreeing to play Cheryl if she hadn't needed that cash-flow boost to enable *Yentl*'s going into overtime. Cheryl believes that sex settles everything, because it tells you whom you're compatible with. Well, that's sensible, but so what? Fanny learns that sex agitates everything, and Katie sees politics as defining compatibility. They give us something to think about.

Cheryl doesn't, which makes the part—despite Streisand's consistently well-observed portrayal—absurdly inert for a star turn. "You think I'm stupid, don't you?" she asks Gene Hackman. "Well, I'm not. I just do stupid things." Her idea of dinner (and we actually see this come to pass) is

---

rude" and quoted a typical Bennettism in explaining why she abandoned stage acting: "I couldn't bear the people looking at me. That's why I prefer pictures." Coincidentally, it was Bennett who played the "Streisand role" in *What Price Hollywood*, the aforementioned source of the *Star Is Born* films.

condensed mushroom soup mixed with tuna and served on bread. She even flourishes a chef's master stroke: you use the soup fresh from the can, without adding liquid. Dennis Quaid quite gobbles it down.

In short, *All Night Long* is a complete waste of Streisand while, paradoxically, being one of her best performances. It's the unidentified flying object among her movie roles, with line readings, look (in a curly blond wig), and plastique utterly unlike her other characters. And not once does she break training to signal us that it's really our Barbra underneath the assumption. Even a bit of singing is executed in Cheryl's lackluster vocal style.

Streisand was so sure she had reinvented herself that, according to a tale that ran through the Beverly Hills gossip circuits, she dressed herself in Cheryl garb, topped it with Cheryl's wig, and dropped in on a country-music bar in the Valley, to get a feeling for the kind of people Cheryl would have come from. It's like something in the theatre, in *Die Fledermaus* or Puccini's *La Rondine*: the sophisticate passes as an alternate being, and no one suspects a thing.

So Streisand enters the bar and someone immediately calls out, "Hey, look, everybody, it's Barbra!"

All Night Long did poorly on release, and Streisand was especially unhappy with the advertising poster, which featured a very lifelike drawing of her sliding down a firehouse pole (though in the actual footage it's seen only in long shot, and is over in two seconds) while, below her, the likenesses of Hackman, Dobson, and Quaid smirk as they reach up to nab her. It suggested a sexy comedy rather than, again, a little character piece. Worse, Streisand was shown with her dress flying up, in the cheap va va voom manner.

She felt betrayed, and not only by the poster art; it so hurt her relationship with Sue Mengers that they split up both socially and professionally. Possibly there was more to it than just how dismally the film played—it opened well but the box office fell quickly and most critics thought it a far miss. More pertinent, however, there are times when those we love initiate projects of intense personal import; to withhold support feels to them like treachery. Mengers had got Streisand involved in *All Night Long* yet Mengers didn't get *Yentl*. Right. And which would better define Streisand, some floopadoop about shallow Californians having cheat sex or the desperate tale of a woman subverting authoritarian rule to express her independence?

If you knew Streisand, then you understood why she had to make the desperate tale. And if you didn't understand, it was because you weren't listening to Streisand when she explained why *Yentl* matters. You were listening to yourself.

Or, worse, you think any business-as-usual movie with nothing on its mind is preferable to something experimental and needful and driven because the actress who sings has found a subject worth banking every-thing on, something that's *hers. All Night Long* wasn't anybody's, which is another way of saying it didn't need to be made, while many of the films we most admire so needed to be made that the artists who needed to make them were willing to give up a piece of themselves.

There's a tale about this. In the early 1940s, director William A. Wellman pitched his adaptation of the anti-lynching novel *The Ox-Bow Incident* to every studio in Hollywood, and no one would touch it. That picture would-n't make a cent, they said, and it was topically dangerous to boot. At length there was only one studio left, Darryl Zanuck's 20th Century Fox—and Zanuck and Wellman hated each other. A man as proud as Wellman would-n't have asked Zanuck for a match, let alone a business deal. But this movie wasn't business to Wellman: it was why he was alive, to make a formidable attack on hotheads quick to tie a noose around your neck and hang you till you pop.

Yes, this picture wouldn't make a cent, and Wellman loathed the notion of having to face Zanuck as a suppliant. Still, Wellman needed this film as he needed to breathe. His wife and kids knew that about him. People who like you know what you're made of, and people who don't know—because, again, they aren't listening to anything you say—are not your friends in any real sense.

Sue Mengers was not listening. If she had been, she would have noticed how *Yentl* had driven a wedge between Streisand and Jon Peters, another one who deprecated the project because it wasn't...what? It wasn't Hollywood. It wasn't glitz. It wasn't money. A number of factors were sepa-rating Streisand and Peters, not least his violent temper. But *Yentl* was how Streisand saw the world, and if Mengers can't see it, too, and wish her well of it, then what role does Mengers play as her agent? Streisand already had glitz and money. Mengers was deaf to anything she heard that she couldn't use, and when she lured Streisand into the feckless *All Night Long* while still ragging on *Yentl*, it really was time for the two to part company.

Incidentally, Zanuck said yes.

Yentl (1983), the tale of a young Jewish woman in the old country who cross-dresses in order to study rather than keep house, is actually about all of us. Everyone wants to live as a free being, to defy the tyrannical rule of fathers, with their folkways and pieties—all fronts for fascist control, whether the fascists are religious fundamentalists or political overlords. Even their minions on the lowest level seek to oppress anyone who breaks out of lockstep.

We see this in Yentl's first scene, in which she is nauseated by the smell of the fish she has to bring home from the market (not to mention the chattering of the professional housewives) but is eager to purchase something from the traveling bookseller. He wants her to stick to picture books—empty and pretty, perfect for a young girl, no?—but she wants a *book* book. He virtually refuses to sell her one till she says it's for her father.

As we'll see, the entire film revolves around the theme of book learning versus tradition: around the intellectual life as opposed to tribal practices. It's the Word on one hand and Life on the other, and note that, as hard as Yentl will push to dwell within the intelligence of the Word, Life will keep happening to her.

We can see why Streisand became so ferociously bonded with this story, why she *had* to make this movie to her personal specifications, which meant not only playing Yentl herself but producing the film, writing the film (with others), directing the film, editing the film. It is all but unbelievable that they—there's always a they—let her get away with it. Of course, that happened, it seems, only because she agreed at some point to let *Yentl* be a musical.

The screenplay, credited to Jack Rosenthal and Streisand, is so rich in the telling lines that develop the theme of this battle between the Word and Life that the movie becomes something of a thriller: will Yentl—or Anshel, as she becomes—actually succeed in her quest, despite getting hijacked by a marriage to another woman, Hadas (Amy Irving)? And Hadas is in love with Avigdor (Mandy Patinkin). And, lo, Yentl is in love with Avigdor herself. Again, Life will intrude upon the Word, yet the Word somehow never gets to intrude upon Life.

Ironically, Yentl's own father (Nehemiah Persoff), a learned man, encourages her wish to study. He is not one of the controllers. But he knows that graduating a woman from picture books to a genuine education will antagonize archons of the culture they dwell within. Here's one of those telling lines, when father and daughter settle in for some study and discussion and he closes the shutters on the windows:

YENTL: If we don't have to hide my studying from God, then why from the neighbors?

PAPA: Why? Because I trust God will understand. I'm not so sure about the neighbors.

Here's another—and note how closely it is linked to Robert Redford's big speech in *The Way We Were* about the uselessness of social agitation, about having any politics at all:

PAPA: Go on, turn the world upside down and inside out, you won't have a moment's peace.

Yentl's source is a thirty-page story by Isaac Bashevis Singer, "Yentl the Yeshiva Boy," and if we turn to it to isolate the origins of this very pointed dialogue, we are disappointed. Singer apparently doesn't have any politics, either: he isn't dealing with The Issues. Instead, he is simply observing how a culture operates, in a picturesque tale filled with fizzy details. For instance, there's the little pack of perquisites expected of a wedding (as translated by Marion Magid and Elizabeth Pollet): "the banquet for the poor, the canopy [over the bridal couple] before the synagogue, the musicians, the wedding jester, the Virtue Dancer."

It's quite colorful and surely authentic, as Singer uses literature as cultural anthropology. However, Singer's Yentl herself is not at all the driving force that Streisand made of her, as a real-life Original seeking communion with a fictional Original. To put it another way, Singer's Yentl is not a Streisand. Rather, she is bored with a woman's lot in a very narrow society, and thus undertakes her disguise more out of playful mischief than revolutionary idealism.

Indeed, Singer is not interested in the creation of a unique and noble character, as if in a *Bildungsnovelle* by Goethe or Thomas Mann. Again, Singer's scope is bounded by customs and attitudes defining a way of life, one that survives because it is a fascism without a dictator: the people themselves are the autocrats, so they believe themselves free.

Of course, they aren't, for in their society all behavior not sacred to tradition is forbidden, even a woman who wants to read a book. And Singer, unlike Streisand, accepts this without criticism. He simply finds an amusing story in the eternal triangle, because in his twist on the theme, one of the three is both male and female. And this inspires in him a lovely little piece of folk wisdom: "The harder you look for [truth]," he explains, "the harder it is to find."

So Streisand's *Yentl* is almost a new work using Singer's story and characters. Look how differently they end: in Singer, Avigdor and Hadas name their firstborn, a boy, Anshel, while Anshel "himself"—Yentl, of course—vanishes from the continuity. But wasn't it *her* story, not theirs? In the movie, all the *other* characters are removed from the action, as we see Yentl on a steamer crossing the ocean to the New World, where the Word and Life, she believes, collaborate in harmony. She has disposed of Anshel, though we notice that she is dressed between the genders, so to say, in a plain, dark, long coat, a heavy muffler, and a woolen cap.

Is this because of the cold weather out on deck, or because she has been too deeply affected by her religious studies to slip back into the woman's "role" (whatever that is now for such an independent character), even woman's dress? If this were a stage musical, everyone would be singing "Oklahoma," but, earning her sixty million, Streisand sings "A Piece Of

Sky," because that's another term for liberty. The sky is a future of limitless possibilities: in America, where the culture *admires* the Original. Just ask Barbra Streisand.

Still, we should keep in mind that, even while shifting the contours of Singer's character interaction, Streisand respects his atmosphere so powerfully that this could be the most faith-centered movie ever made. Even *Fiddler On the Roof* is not so insistently limited, with its Christian neighbors, its tsarist Chief of Police, its Jewish rebels who flout the rules. *Yentl's* society, so absolutely Jewish and conventional, hasn't a single stranger in its midst; even on the steamship at the end, Streisand's deck promenade is surrounded by men in the traditional black religious dress.

For relief, some moviegoers might long for a few Methodists in the dramatis personae, or at least someone named Marjorie. Really, *Yentl's* only stranger in its hidebound social construct is Yentl herself, challenging the prevailing mores with her eternal "Where is it written?" and getting into a disguise so utterly revolutionary—so unthinkable—that they probably never thought to devise a punishment for it.

And the rebellion never stops: after Hadas' parents terminate her engagement to Avigdor (because his brother was a suicide, a source of disgrace) and are now styling Anshel as the substitute bridegroom, Anshel protests the edict. True, he gives in. Still, after the wedding, Anshel starts to school Hadas in the art of being a free soul, too.

Where Streisand breaks away from Singer most intently is in her central theme of The Word versus Life. "Where is it written?" she keeps asking, whenever someone tells her that what she wants to do is never done. Seeking a way forward, Yentl dismisses community practices and fastens on community law. If it's written down in some legal code, it has authority; everything else is gossip.

Ironically, what Yentl wants is transparency even as she goes about in her Anshel masquerade. And she really does fool everyone: when Hadas' father rejects Avigdor as a son-in-law, he says he prefers "someone with no secrets to hide," and he means Streisand, the town fraud (did they but know). And she clings to her obsession about The Word even as she begins to see that Life is more powerful, even more useful. We can't control The Word, as it was set down many years before us: but we do create our lives. As Avigdor tries to get Anshel to marry Hadas (thus to keep all three of them close), he urges her on with "It's fate, it's meant to be!" Whereupon Anshel replies with the credo of the Original:

STREISAND (who could be talking about herself, more than about Yentl): Nothing's meant to be—we *make* what's meant to be!

Another aspect of the movie's revision of the Singer text lies in the relationship between these Old World bros Anshel and Avigdor. Singer does tell us how intensely they bond, but the movie translates this into visuals in very nearly worrisome terms. Avigdor is so physical with his pal—horsing around, grabbing him, wrestling with him, trying to get him to skinny-dip with the gang—that we wonder if Avigdor has figured it out without figuring it out. Is it possible that he has sensed that Anshel is a woman yet cannot process it intellectually because it so antagonizes the conservative in him?

Because that would explain his ferocity when the action finally reaches The Scene, the moment when Yentl tells—shows—him who Anshel really is, and he reacts with the demented self-righteousness of which Mandy, of all actors, is the uncontested master. "You're a devil!" he shouts. "You spit on the Torah!" He is all but hands-on violent, and, like so many others, he accuses the truthteller of having been dishonest when he himself couldn't have dealt with honesty in the first place—like the homophobic parents who get mad that gay sons and daughters put off coming out to them. Why didn't Yentl tell him before this?:

YENTL: [Because] I was afraid of this! Of exactly this!

He subsides, and they end embracing on the floor. Still, we're left with the belief that he was enraged because he had been in love with her all along, *even when she "was" a man*. What are we to call this? Straight panic?

More: it is highly questionable in sexual terms that Avigdor wanted Anshel to bed Avigdor's sweetheart, Hadas. What do psychiatrists say about a man who would share his woman with his buddy?

After so much Sturm und Drang, calling *Yentl* "a Streisand musical" trivializes it. And while it does have a full set of songs (by Michel Legrand and the Bergmans), no one but Streisand sings, making this a musical in a strictly limited way. As for the music itself, this is the least distinguished group of songs of all Streisand's films, and all of the numbers are interior monologues. There is no "Queen Bee," no "Blind Date." Again, this is a score made of nothing but Heroine's Wanting Songs; for comparison, imagine *My Fair Lady* giving numbers only to Eliza Doolittle, all of them "Wouldn't It Be Loverly?" or replicas of it. *Yentl* even removes itself a bit from the way songs inhabit musicals in that Streisand performs only part of the score by lip synching: the rest of it is heard in voiceover.

But then, Yentl is "a character with a secret," in Marilyn Bergman's explanation, quoted in James Spada's Streisand biography: "There is nobody else she can talk to, to whom she can reveal her essential self." Thus, her songs can't work the way songs normally do in movie musicals. If Yentl were in psychotherapy, these songs would constitute her sessions.

Legrand's soundtrack score (that is, the music we hear as accompaniment to the action generally) is not Jewish in flavor except for a riff here
and there. At that, nor are the songs themselves ethnically purposed, in the
Fiddler On the Roof manner. They do help propel Yentl on her quest, which
is at once a universal one and a personal one, a Streisand one. "Papa, can
you hear me?" she cries, as if disclosing the source of but also the drain on
her strength. We keep being told that the *Yentl* project was so very dear to
Streisand because she lost her father in her infancy—and he, like Yentl's
father, was apparently a man of learning. Nevertheless, we don't really
know how his death influenced her art. But we do know that the Original is
bound by destiny of character to execute and then acculturate the unthinkable—as did Dante, Beethoven, Wagner, Picasso.

Have we gotten too grand? Let's slip back into a bit of housekeeping: one
of Yentl's songs, "No Wonder [he loves her]," actually functions as a plot
number, during a dinner at Hadas' parents' house, when Yentl gets her first
view of Avigdor and Hadas together. The action is so inveigling that we
wish Streisand's voiceover would cut out so we can hear the dialogue, even
as director Streisand's many eliciting camera shots pick up how much *there*
there is in the scene.

This brings us to *Yentl*'s direction, which is, I have to say, shockingly
good. This being Streisand's very first time directing, one would have expected a partly qualified result, with something of the learner's permit
about it. Surely a beginner—who may have plenty of imagination but no
practical experience—will stumble here and there. But Streisand doesn't,
neither in her coaching the players in the intricacies of gender interaction
nor in framing the shots. Clearly, she had been absorbing tradecraft while
she was still simply an actor on the set in her previous twelve pictures—
learning, for instance, how to let the story "tell itself" rather than exagger-
ate it with unrealistic emphases.

Thus, when Anshel and Avigdor arrive in town and make it into the
ghetto just before it is locked up for the night, Streisand does not try to
make a point about the sequestration of the Jewish population after dark,
because to these two characters there is no point to make. This is what happens in their part of the world. Nor does either of the pair make a remark
about their close call: they are speaking to each other, not explaining the
historical background to the audience.

And yet. There is a slight hint in the way they carry themselves that they
have absorbed this humiliation as a people, not as individuals. They can't do
anything about it, but they resent it. It's just a nuance, easy to miss, and
Streisand must have known that a goodly portion of the spectators would have
no idea what was happening under the surface visual of Anshel and Avigdor
returning home. Indeed, few of them would have understood how perilous

Jewish life could be in the movie's setting—"Eastern Europe," as a screen print-over tells us early on, "1904." The words themselves, so apparently neutral, are a warning. But Streisand doesn't belabor the point. She narrates from within the reality of her characters' lives, not externally, to comment on them.

Or take the movie's opening shots. Traditionally, these are establishing moments, what we might term "specific in a general sense." One thinks of the early Hollywood talkie set in New York, with its cityscapes (especially of Times Square, with "bustle" music or a quotation of Tin Pan Alley's latest Manhattan anthem) or prairie vistas. A moving train. Morning on the farm. Look: chickens.

This is primitive material, obviously. Directors today move hastily into the storyline, and so does Streisand, because she's heading right for Yentl's first "Where is it written?," her characteristic challenge to the rule of fathers, to the ordering of things that keeps the individual in lockdown.

So *Yentl's* first shot isn't a long view of a little town. Instead, we see books. They lie on the cart of the aforementioned bookseller, traveling from place to place. He brings learning, but—as Streisand presently shows us—only to those in the club: men.

Or consider the death of Yentl's father, a genuine loss to the movie, as he alone among the elders encourages her need to live intellectually. As he prays to God for his daughter's happiness, the camera picks up a nearby tree, big and green, flourishing: as if to say that Yentl will flourish, too. Then, without losing the shot, the camera reconsiders the tree with withered leaves—and, instantly, we understand that Yentl's father has died.

Naturally, this is business casual for today's directors. But, again, Streisand hadn't been a director before this. And she does know how to tell a story, speeding along to the funeral: who will deliver the traditional prayer for the dead? Yentl immediately says she will, to general consternation, because of course a woman can't. But she's already doing it, and no one dares stop her at such a reverent moment.

Thus, very early in the continuity, all the themes have been placed—the question of gender fairness, The Word versus Life, the rebellion of the Original. "Papa, can you hear me?" she sings, because he was the only one who understood her. Even Avigdor and Hadas, though loving her, did not get her in even the remotest way. This is a story about isolation, and, much later, as Yentl's voyage nears its completion, we suddenly realize that "Papa, can you hear me?" was the script's key line, a mission statement that finally reaches fulfillment when she cries,

"*Papa, I can hear you!*" as she launches one last Heroine's Wanting Song on the ship taking her to America, the aforementioned "A Piece Of Sky." Many feel that this finale doesn't match the rest of the movie, but isn't that the point? The village and its rules are gone; Yentl is on the way to the start of her life. The ship is neutral territory, far from Eastern Europe and 1904, because in protean America everything constantly changes, whereas in Yentl's abandoned homeland nothing has changed for a thousand years.

Now bonding with her father as never before with that "I can hear you!," Yentl has taken over in their relationship. She, now, is the one who leads. "There *better* be thirty cents in it," she told Mike Wallace back on *PM East*. Mere bravado. But here, some twenty-two years later, Yentl/Barbra has the mastery of her medium, as versed in Life as in The Word.

With a domestic gross of $40 million on a negative cost of $12 million, Yentl was a hit.* The reviews were very rangy, though, from raves to a few pans with phrasing chosen to ridicule. Streisand believes the attacks on a woman director are gender-based (even when they come from women), though I say again that Streisand's tour de force in directing Yentl lies not in a woman's meeting the challenge but in a newcomer's doing so. Directing—while simultaneously producing, co-writing, and starring in—a production is not an appropriate task for on-the-job training.

Thus, to have navigated such intricate character psychology while keeping the socio-religious background in focus in her very first shoot as CEO on a movie set made Streisand look "too" brilliant to some eyes, following the ancient show-biz adage of They love to build you up and they love to tear you down. At a certain point, even those who once adopted you as a pet talent can become infuriated when you reach a height of power that makes them feel insignificant.

Well, they are insignificant: or they wouldn't feel personally diminished by someone else's success. More pertinent, they would be making movies instead of simply watching them. One writer spoke of Streisand's "pillbox-contoured designer yarmulke,"[68] though, as Streisand herself pointed out, she had researched Yentl for some ten years with her usual obsession over details, and therefore was sure to get the skullcap right.

Most rejecting of all was Isaac Bashevis Singer, who (correctly) pointed out that this wasn't his Yentl anymore: it was Streisand's. As I've said, Singer's Yentl is motivated less by an adventurous self-belief than by a mild distaste for housework, and, unlike Streisand's heroine, who closes her film with her anthem on her victory ship, bound for glory, Singer's title character

---

* The worldwide gross has not been made public except in part—Australia here and Sweden there—even as some biographies compute it at $100 million. One wonders how appealing so ethnic a story would prove in foreign climes, but then *Fiddler On the Roof* traveled profitably, too. The Japanese impresario of the first Tokyo staging told Hal Prince, the show's original producer, that it was astonishing that *Fiddler* played well in America: "It's so Japanese!"

is scarcely even a genuine protagonist (in the ancient Greek sense of the one character in a dramatic work whose ego needs drive the story).

But Pauline Kael, who had vacillated from loving Streisand to denouncing her, praised *Yentl*, with an odd encomium: "It's a movie full of likable people."

That cannot be said of Streisand's next film, **Nuts** (1987). Indeed, it's a movie filled with villains. This is the one in which Streisand is accused of murder, as a classy, high-priced prostitute who has been reduced through incarceration pending trial into a belligerent ragamuffin in hospital gown and robe. *Nuts* shows us a hearing to determine if she is sane enough to stand trial, and almost everyone is out to put her away forever:

> The first judge (Dakin Matthews) she encounters, who is interested in not justice but keeping cases moving swiftly along, no matter whose rights are nullified.
>
> Her parents (Karl Malden, Maureen Stapleton), who pretend to want what's best for her even as Malden, enabled by a pathetic rather than vicious Stapleton, seeks to see Streisand buried alive in an asylum.
>
> The attorney (William Prince) the parents have hired, a hypocritical, condescending foodledoo.
>
> The psychiatrist (Eli Wallach) assigned to the case, a loathsome quack toadying to the parents.
>
> The prosecutor (Robert Webber), also in league with the parents, it seems.

Is anyone on Streisand's side? Richard Dreyfuss plays the lawyer who takes on her case, and the new judge (James Whitmore) is at least neutral, as befits his office. True, as the nature of those ranged against Streisand becomes apparent—not only worrisome but outraging—we wish Whitmore would express less neutrality and more advocacy. But Dreyfuss, at any rate, is Streisand's fiery partisan.

Oddly, considering the dire circumstances, Streisand and Dreyfuss meet cute. In fact, he is forced into the role of her defender against his will after Streisand decks the foodledoo right in the courtroom:

> STREISAND (to Dreyfuss): Are you any good?
> DREYFUSS: You had good. Now you've got me.

That sounds like a screwball comedy, but *Nuts* is as dark as can be and its heroine is far from the Streisand we dote on. There is no singing, no self-deprecating New York humor, and she scarcely ever gets out of her hospital attire. At one point, we see her apartment: sophisticated and uptempo, with volumes of Lawrence Durrell here and a Raggedy Ann doll there along with high-tech lifestyle gadgets and the inevitable food-delivery menus. The film's opening sequence tips us off to her physical appeal: women prisoners, on their way to court, pass by jailed men who call out crudely at them—but then the scene changes to an upscale bar as a line of dressy bons vivants gaze appreciatively at a passing female.

We later learn that this is Streisand on her way to a professional meet, but we note how director Martin Ritt has analogized louts in prison cells with gentlemen in their suits. Both groups are openly appetitive around women, as if to say that all males are dangerously alike. *Nuts* isn't going to be about class or sex. It's going to be about gender.

Ritt and Streisand battled endlessly during the shoot, which may explain why a film made almost entirely on a single set—the courtroom—took four months to photograph. *Nuts* ended up with a negative cost of $25 million, more than twice the cost of *Yentl*, a much more complex project and one that was meticulously lit (by David Watkins) to suggest at times a near-fantasy in an exotic storybookland. *Nuts*, with its everyday costuming, much smaller cast, and industry-standard lighting, should have been less expensive, not more.

But while lighting is one of the most time-consuming (and therefore expensive) elements in filmmaking, so is the wrangling between director and star, with controversies over every scene, every line. Ritt told the *Dallas Morning News* that each day, everyone came on set anticipating "a huge fight between Barbra and myself. They were never disappointed."[69]

Ritt wasn't the first director attached to the film, in the modern post-studio-era manner in which a project will be pulled this way by the first director, that way by his or her successor, and so on. Writers, too, came and went by the drove, as Streisand was *Nuts*' executive producer and Streisand, we know, never met a script she felt was ready for shooting.

Based on a play by Tom Topor, *Nuts* was originally to have been adapted by Topor himself, with Debra Winger as the heroine. But Topor was put through draft after draft, and, finally, feeling that those in charge of the movie were tearing his story apart, he withdrew, leaving then-director Mark Rydell to bring in writer after writer.

Universal, the contracted studio, saw *Nuts* becoming a runaway production with a crowd of scripts. Doesn't it seem that some directors deliberately commission extra screenplays because in fact they don't know what they want and are searching for someone to show them? "I have a version of *Nuts*," a Universal bigwig told Topor, "with more [writers'] names on it than the New York telephone book."[70]

Then Rydell, Universal, and Debra Winger were out of the picture and Warner Bros. was running the project with Streisand and Ritt. But using whose script? Going by remarks the participants have made at various times, it would appear that Streisand sat down with scenarists Alvin Sargent and Darryl Ponicsan to amend one of Topor's scripts. ("The structure is mine," Topor says.)[71] Ultimately, though, *Nuts* was written to Streisand's specifications, as she was the executive producer. It seems odd, after *Yentl*, for Streisand to step back from directing as well—which probably accounts for the antagonism with Ritt: in effect, he had appropriated "her" authority.

Like *Yentl*, this movie has one of those Scenes, and like *Yentl*'s, the one in *Nuts* gives us Streisand trying to tame a wild man. In *Nuts*, it's Leslie Nielsen, as a john who demands more than Streisand is willing to give. He has already had his money's worth, but now he needs control. A man who has to pay for it is giving up control—giving up, really, the egotism of his masculinity. Taking more from his date, whether he cajoles her into it or forces it upon her through violence, reasserts his sense of self.

With the pleasantry of the seasoned pro, Streisand tries to ease him down, but he becomes aggressive, then enraged, then berserk, and he tries to murder her as they struggle on the floor. Finding a shard of glass from a mirror, shattered in the fight, she plunges it into him. So, as I've said earlier, she ends up accused of murder but innocent, on grounds of self-defense.

Note that *Nuts* uses Nielsen, heretofore a palsy-walsy romantic lead and then, starting with *Airplane!* (1980), a goofy comic. It's an arresting piece of casting, for if nice-guy Nielsen can turn vicious when his will is thwarted, then the subtext is that no man can be trusted.

Not even your stepfather, Karl Malden, because it turned out that the battle with Nielsen wasn't The Scene. Later, during the hearing, Malden is on the witness stand and Dreyfuss, examining him, seems to hear something in his testimony, something alarming. A *tell*. Slowly he turns. How old was Streisand when Malden stopped "bathing" her? Yes, daddy bathes his little girl. But she wasn't so little, was she? And Ritt then shows Streisand in the tub, terrified and quite well along in years. We see the knob on the bathroom door turning against the lock. *How old, Malden?*

With the courtroom in an uproar, everything suddenly stops short as Dreyfuss at last puts it together—and *now* we get The Scene, with more flashback bits to guide us:

DREYFUSS (to Malden): Didn't you make your stepdaughter your lover?

and:

STREISAND (sobbing on her knees, restrained by a police offi-
cer): Don't let him hurt me!

Note how different this father is from the one in *Yentl*.* That parent not only
indulges his daughter in needs the surrounding community frowns on but
also understands that she is an Original and thus must be encouraged because Originality enriches the culture whether the culture knows it or not.

Meanwhile, Dreyfuss becomes the surrogate father as Streisand's pro-
tector; in a less realistic delineation of the story they would end up in each
other's arms. And Dreyfuss is no fool in sizing up the role Eli Wallach's
doctor plays, either, revealing him as not just a mealy-mouthed incompetent but actively destructive under the front of professional grandiosity.
When Dreyfuss realizes that Wallach has zonked Streisand with debilitat-
ing drugs just before her all-important testimony—of course in order to
destroy her case—he confronts Wallach in the courthouse cafeteria, calling
him out for the evil freak that he is:

WALLACH: Don't threaten me, you lawyer son of a bitch!

Whereupon, with a slice of his hand, Dreyfuss launches Wallach's tray of
food into kingdom come, a terrific moment:

DREYFUSS (leaving): Bon appetit!

Wallach gives a fine performance in an ugly part, yet he himself felt that the
doctor was doing only what he thought best for the patient. This is an outra-
geously idiotic statement given what we see, but who knows what Wallach's
role was like in the edit that Martin Ritt signed off on? Because, after that,
Streisand recut the film herself, as always when she was the boss. In Hollywood,
there's the studio cut, the director's cut, and sometimes the unreleased longer
cut. But there's also the Streisand cut, executed on her own elaborate editing
console at her Malibu property that may have cost as much as $500,000.

Streisand, we know, has been accused of vanity cutting, robbing her
fellow actors of their best shots and filling the screen with more and more
Barbra. But there is no way to document this when we don't know what the
director's cut looked like in the first place. "Don't Believe What You Read,"

---

* Note as well that *Nuts* directly succeeded *Yentl* in Streisand's movie output, albeit
by four years. She has said that commingled duties in micromanaging *Yentl* so drained
her that she couldn't even think about moviemaking for a long time thereafter. Still, we
can't miss observing that the calendar of Streisand's movie fathers went from wonderful dad to monster dad without a break.

a number on the *Streisand Superman* album, warns us of what celebrities have been telling us for decades: somebody out there is making everything up.

In any case, Wallach's attempt to sabotage Streisand's testimony fails, and the judge frees her, though of course she will have to stand trial for murder. Nevertheless, she has a strong case given the circumstances, and she knows it. Still in her hospital gown and robe, she heads for the courtroom door as a mystified Dreyfuss asks where she's going:

STREISAND: Out!

And then we see her, resplendent in the sunlight of the New York streets, grabbing a red scarf from a passing garment-center clothing trolley for a dash of color on her institution-blah outfit. We note a crazy man in the crowd, singing gibberish, and the movie seems to say to us, *That's* nuts.

So the story is over. But a printover tells us that Streisand's character—whose name, by the way, is Claudia Draper—was acquitted of murder, fulfilling that first rule of Hollywood stardom.

Pat Conroy's bestselling novel *The Prince Of Tides* runs to almost Dickensian length and is in love with language. Here's the narrator, Tom Wingo, a southerner with a powerful family problem, on his mother:

> She could smile one moment and make me think of the shy commerce of angels;
> the next moment the same smile could suggest a hermitage for morays or an
> asylum for terrorists.[72]

Tom leaves the riverruns and island hideouts of rural South Carolina for New York, where he is to assist in the recovery of his sister, a would-be suicide. Her psychiatrist needs his input on their life-destroying family, and, as the novel unfolds, Conroy moves back and forth between where he comes from and where he's headed, between what occurred before and what is occurring now. "You dwell too much on the past!" his terrible, interesting, not entirely unhelpful mother cries—but then, the entire narrative dwells on the past, and of course psychotherapy (which is what Tom undergoes while he tries to unravel his sister's sorrows) runs on autobiography: the past created you, so tell the doctor what happened.

In this, her fifteenth feature (1991), Streisand plays the doctor and Nick Nolte the hero, so the movie version will have its romance—adulterously, as both leads are already married. The many flashbacks will give us a chance to figure out what went wrong for the Wingos as if in a mystery, and we will note that, as we meet Tom's family—his rough, angry father; that formidable mother; Tom's brother, Luke; and the sister, Savannah—we encounter the doctor's family as well.

The doctor's husband is a world-class violinist and their only child a sullen jerk who finds a friend (and enabler of positive character transformation) in Tom. Directing and co-producing again, Streisand had cast the role of the son when Pat Conroy (who was writing the screenplay with Becky Johnston) thought her choice wasn't suitable. Riffling through the résumé shots of the also-rans, Conroy found someone who looked perfect: Jason Gould, Streisand's son. He does a very nice job.

Still, his is not an admirable character. He's a spoiled rich kid, totally unlike the three Wingo children, who are forever trying to turn their tightly budgeted life into a fabulous dream of a place. Again, *The Prince Of Tides* is a long novel, and much of it obviously would be lost in adaptation; the "secret" life of the Wingo kids is largely missing from the film.

Streisand emphasizes instead her love affair with Nolte, though she does get in a great deal of the contrasts between South Carolina (in other words, Tom's past) and Manhattan (his transitional space, where he learns how to come to terms with the past, thus to return, appreciatively, to his homeland). This is a movie made of geography, because Streisand's Manhattan doesn't have any: it's all steel and fashion with a touch of Central Park. The south that she shows us, on the other hand, is water and sky, a holiday-postcard look, for all its terrors.

Further, this south is populated by folk of small dimension—villagers tending to village matters (along with three escaped convicts). On the other hand, Manhattan teems with grandees and their professions. In South Carolina, Tom's mother is a homemaker, no more. But Streisand is not only a doctor but the independent sort, working under her own surname, Lowenstein, in place of her husband's.

Throughout the film, we are constantly jarred by the contrasts between these two "settings"—but one element binds them: the two fathers in the story. Both are monsters, highly different in personal style. Mr. Wingo (Brad Sullivan) abuses everyone, even vulnerable little kids. One of those people of very narrow tastes who likes a few things and hates everything else with a passion, he throws a tantrum at something interesting for dinner. Who cares what it is? It's slop!

So Mrs. Wingo and the kids dash into the kitchen to rustle up a new dinner for him, a blue plate special of dog food right out of the can. Now, that's what he calls dinner! And we note a sly comic touch when the family dog, thinking there must be a mistake somewhere because that's his order, tries to scarf it up and gets swatted away.

Doctor Lowenstein's husband, Mr. Woodruff (Jeroen Krabbé), is much smoother in manner, plying a hostile smile and a dainty flip of a European accent. A tyrant, he insists that his son master the violin whether he wants to or not and deeply resents the bond that has sprung up between the boy and Tom through their football practice sessions. Again, Tom's athletic coaching is improving the boy's attitude, but all the father can see is an uncultured oaf interfering in family matters. When the Woodruffs host a fancy Manhattan dinner party, Mr. Woodruff pulls out his fiddle and hurls a savagely brilliant rendition of "Dixie" right in Tom's face, complete with power smile and glaring eyes.

Note that the Woodruff father is very good-looking and moves with the stalking tread of a man who has had his way all his life. By contrast, Tom's father is brutish and sour—so, really, the two settings differ once again. Interestingly, director Streisand utterly reveals Mr. Wingo but keeps Woodruff as a surprise, showing him to us very briefly early on but not letting him speak till ninety-five minutes into the continuity.

Most inaccessible yet is the title character: Luke, Tom's older brother. We never even see him grown up, though Conroy uses the older Luke—whose murder sets Tom's sister over the edge of despair—throughout the novel. The Prince of Tides is the ruler of the natural world, its lover and spouse as a deeply committed environmentalist, and the heart of the story is missing from the movie because Luke is.

This puts great pressure on Nick Nolte, because he must therefore carry the film—Streisand has little more to play than the sympathetic healer. Further, Tom Wingo is a challenge: a mercurial character at once depressed and vital, polite and touchy, charming and belligerent. Is Nolte up to all that? He gives a restless and noisy performance, mixing a lot of shallow "indicating" with more naturalistic moments. Still, he is most often so mobile and obvious that it's exhausting to witness. One starts to miss Robert Redford's expertly cynical walk-through in *The Way We Were*, the aura he gives off of being too ethical for Hollywood, too smart for the movies he writes, too Redford to live. He's mysterious, which is fascinating: what is he hiding? Nolte is so transparent he's like a shelter dog desperate to get adopted.

But Nolte is good when Doctor Streisand leads him into confronting a ghastly memory: those three prison escapees raped his mother, sister, and himself. We actually see the event in one of those flashbacks, and there is the young Luke as the family savior, shooting the crooks, though his gun jams and that redoubtable mother steps in to finish the job, catching the one surviving convict with a knife in the back.

As Nolte recounts the incident, he seems to become the little towhead who plays him in the memory scenes: almost unable to speak, eyes wide and head shaking in that typical trap of the psychoanalyzed, the exquisite despair that total recollection brings. Nolte sinks into the doctor's arms in tears, and Streisand weeps as well, though her reaction is just an appendix, as she has thrown the entire scene to Nolte.

Which leads us to Streisand the director, on her second such outing. *The Prince Of Tides* is not as satisfyingly picturesque as *Yentl*, but it's a far more difficult proposition, with a diffuse plot and many principals. *Yentl* has but one very colorful secret, the heroine's gender, but *The Prince Of Tides* is overloaded with them, like an analyst's most difficult patient, evasive and helplessly dishonest. What really happened? And why? And who are the Wingos, in the end?

The movie won respect, getting an Oscar nomination for Best Picture (which it lost to *The Silence Of the Lambs*). Streisand herself, having earlier won (actually shared, both times with a co-recipient) two Oscars, for acting and songwriting, was not mentioned as Best Director, giving rise to a Hollywood joke that *The Prince Of Tides* must have directed itself.

And the movie is indeed well made. One could quibble, as with Nolte's insistent address of Streisand as "Lowenstein" rather than as "Doctor" or "Susan." It becomes irritating after a while, as a meme determined to delight us with Tom's frisky informality. "Lowenstein, you're incorrigible," he declares at one point, as if voicing the praise of Streisand fans the world over, so intimate and festive. And Streisand shows off her French accent in a swank restaurant, suavely ordering for Nolte and herself like a bonne vivante. The scene is in the novel, set at Lutèce, though Conroy doesn't specify the ordering of dinner. He does make it clear Susan is fluent in French and well known to Chef André Soltner and his wife, Simone.[73]

Nevertheless, strong directorial touches outweigh any little vexations, as when, in Streisand's office, Nolte playfully tosses a football at Streisand and, when she throws it back to him, her son—in a completely different view, in the park—catches it. The idea is to show how close Doctor Lowenstein is to the boy, when her husband is so fiercely distant: "Quasimodo in a football uniform" is how Woodruff describes his son's athletic ambitions.

The underlying tension between Streisand and Krabbé comes through beautifully in the aforementioned dinner party, when, in some indefinable yet blatant way, the entire movie becomes a battle of looks. Folks are so plain in the south, so swank in the city, Krabbé a full-throttle beauty, with his floppy dark hair of some imperious Nordic brown and Streisand the lavish sophisticate. It affirms one of the most ancient rules of the movies, going back to D. W. Griffith's Biograph shorts: the way you look is what you are.

Director Streisand makes this dinner sequence the climax of the story— which, to repeat, is more about Tom and Dr. Lowenstein than, as in the novel, about Tom and his past. Thus, a woman guest at the laden table d'hôte tells Streisand, "I can't believe you'd let [your son] play a game that might hurt his hands." At which Streisand takes her best shot with a robust exercise in oneupmanship stichomythia:

DR. LOWENSTEIN: And I can't believe you'd come to my house when everyone knows you've been fucking my husband.

It's not quite the shocker that "Who's Frank McVeigh?" would have been in *The Way We Were* if Sydney Pollack hadn't spilled all the juice out of the political throughline in his panicky last-minute editing. But the dinner-party sequence, with Woodruff's taunting of Tom and then Dr. Lowenstein's outing of her husband's adulterous amour, is good old-fashioned moviemaking: exciting plot quirks that also illuminate character.

What Streisand has made of Pat Conroy's novel is a look at how endlessly haunting a rough upbringing can be. Yes, it's in Conroy in the first place. Still, in cutting away much of Conroy's tale (including, to repeat, Tom's touching hero-worship of his older brother), Streisand re-centered the narrative. The movie is not really about the simple culture (of Tom's south) versus the imperious culture (of Dr. Lowenstein's New York). It's about bad parenting, about how poorly adjusted the Wingos and Woodruffs are. Tolstoy's "Happy families are all alike" is a useless observation, because there are no happy families, not in art.

Let's quote a line from Streisand's current favorite Broadway songwriter, Stephen Sondheim: "Children you destroy together." That's what Streisand's *Prince Of Tides* is about, making it a bold and difficult film. And just as people find it hard to see Marilyn Monroe as a superb actress because, they think, her talent was her looks, people find it hard to see Streisand as a superb director, because she is a singer of songs.

It suggests that at least some folks don't know what to admire in art and base their judgments on preconceptions unrelated to the work. This is why we cherish our Originals: they reinstruct preconceptions.

Unfortunately, *The Prince Of Tides* was the last Streisand film of substance, though four titles remain in this travelogue. It is not clear why her movie career petered out, or why she ended up directing only three times, or why she would always choose a movie directed by a journeyman over one by a High Maestro. Streisand has said that she was not only in transatlantic conversation with Ingmar Bergman over his plan to film *The Merry Widow* with her, but actually went to Sweden to discuss the undertaking.

And then, as I've said, Streisand demanded script changes, and seemed surprised when Bergman dropped the project without another word.

Lady, even an American national treasure doesn't attempt to control Ingmar Bergman. No one's that big.

The Mirror Has Two Faces (1996) is Hollywood fluff about a platonic marriage that ends as a mad love affair. Streisand directed Richard LaGravenese's script, and she and Jeff Bridges play college professors in need of company. Streisand is the "youth" teacher, lecturing to doting students who just absolutely dig her because she's so utterly with it, you know? Streisand's oh so contempo rap and the gestures and cries of "Right on!" from the peanut gallery are risibly artificial, especially because in so many other ways Streisand is characterized as being helpless in even the most basic practices of lifecraft.

Meanwhile, if Professor Streisand is jazzy, Professor Bridges is a dud. He talks of "prime numbers" and "the twin-prime conjective," and the students, so energized by Streisand's lectures, find his tedious. Two co-eds wonder about his sexuality, but one says, "He's too boring to be gay."

Yet he's enterprising enough to create a couples ad. Streisand doesn't answer it, but somebody else does *for* her, and she and Bridges end up courting, to the thrill of Streisand's mother, Lauren Bacall, as acerbic as ever.

Bridges is cute, too, and Streisand—so the movie keeps telling us—isn't. It dresses her in dowdy clothes and woebegone hair. And of course Streisand's sister (Mimi Rogers) is a knockout, because that's how these movies work. And note that Streisand is so clueless about fashion, grooming, and the rest of the home beautician's arts that even when she tries she fails:

ROGERS (to Streisand): Why don't you ever wear some makeup?
STREISAND: I am wearing makeup.

Also of course, Bacall is a former looker and still has that je ne sais quoi, upstaging Rogers at her wedding:

ROGERS (to Bacall): You're the mother of the bride, not the opening act!

Everyone is good-looking in this story (again, except Streisand...at first). The sister's new husband is Pierce Brosnan, not only fit and handsome but an actor who epitomizes *zow!* just by having black hair and gala teeth. Even Brenda Vaccaro, Streisand's sidekick, who's supposed to be another wallflower, still looks cute (if plump).

So we're all set to go, in a romantic comedy of the "discordant couple" type—but the script lacks wit. *The Mirror Has Two Faces* should have been made in the 1930s: and it was, many times, written by smarties who were experts in the banter trade. LaGravenese does write some sharp lines, especially for Bacall, who lives with Streisand and is therefore always handy for a scene. One of the most arresting moments in the screenplay arrives when

Streisand has Bridges over for dinner and Bacall starts to get intrusive. Streisand fears her mother will scare Bridges off, so she urges Bacall to Go Into the Kitchen and Make the Coffee:

BACALL (sternly): I raised two daughters, I buried my husband. . . . I've *made* my coffee.

Most of the dialogue, however, is little more than functional, commonplace talk to keep the plot moving. Worse, the plot suddenly stops moving just when it has begun to get amusingly plotty—after Streisand and Bridges marry and it turns out he's "not interested in sex" and she is. This is director Streisand's fault: the pacing sags, and in a flash we understand why a ninety-minute running time was the rule in the old days. That was when moving pictures moved. This one waddles.

We have to question as well how Streisand the movie star fits into all this. As a talent star, in musicals, she delivers uniquely. *Funny Girl* is a classic and *Hello, Dolly!*, despite understandable misgivings about its roadshow grandezza, nevertheless gives the diva the music and comic lines ("It's no use arguing, I've made your mind up. Here, let me cut your wings") that enthrall us. Further, the Golden Age was filled with fifty-year-old Hamlets and Juliets, so who cares if Streisand was too young for Dolly? And even *Funny Lady*, despite a meandering and turgid second half, is a Wonderful Date With Barbra.

But the movie-star Streisand is in a more vulnerable position, because in straight dramatic films she can't pack music in her go bag. In titles such as *Up the Sandbox* or *The Way We Were* or *The Main Event* or *Nuts*, she is more dependent on the other people on the trip, especially the writers. Streisand in *Yentl*, an unusual and artistic film, is really dependent on herself, because she was its auteur in the most thorough sense. However, in a movie-star pastry like *The Mirror Has Two Faces*—a comedy short on humor—she's just going to waste.

One of the most insulting (but arguably accurate) things ever said about Streisand was Larry Kramer's accusation (cited in this volume in Streisand's Chronology) that she was neglecting the filming of his AIDS play *The Normal Heart* in favor of . . . okay, yes, a pastry. Streisand was so offended that she withdrew from the Kramer project forever. Anyway, to Streisand it wasn't a pastry. It was What Movie Stars Are Supposed To Do.

Still, this was not a good trade. A Streisand *Normal Heart*, under her direction (and there's a good role for her in the dramatis personae), could have been riveting, a kind of gay *Nuts* as another tale of the nonconformist versus the rule of fathers. Yet *The Mirror* does give us one very strong scene in which the movie's obsession about looks as the meaning of a person's worth comes into intense discussion.

It occurs late in the action, when Streisand confronts mother Bacall with When I was a baby, did you tell me I was pretty? So here comes a dodge:

BACALL: All babies are pretty.

No, your daughter is asking, Was *I* pretty? And now director Streisand has actor Streisand turn to Bacall looking leftward on the screen, so that we get her in perfect profile.

Because Streisand wants us to stare at her nose, her supposed "looks" flaw famous from the day of her national emergence and still a talking point even after decades of success as not just a talent star but a glamour star as well.

Will you like me as I am? Is this pretty? Does it matter? Streisand demands an answer, and Bacall has one:

BACALL: What's "pretty," anyway?

Well, whatever it is, Bacall was unreliable on the issue:

STREISAND: You made me feel unpretty.

Oh, and by the way, mother, how did being beautiful feel?

BACALL (after a bit of thought): It was wonderful.

Some thirty-five years after she burst forth in show business, Streisand needs us to know how hurtful it is to be categorized by not talent (or intelligence or creativity or other such qualities) but *whether or not we can be movie stars*. Yet that turning of her profile to the audience—it's not belligerent but rather self-accepting—is an oxymoron. *Now* you want us to sympathize, after you have run the biggest career in show-biz history? In your prime, no one was bigger. Yet in this scene you want us to understand that one's looks are not the key to one's soul but simply the wrong door that people love to open?

Even worse, you walk it all back when Bacall hands you an old Kodak of a very young girl. A cute kid, obviously Streisand's sister, the one who always got the compliments:

STREISAND (examining the photo): She was so pretty....Look at those eyes.

But it's not her sister. It's Barbra.

STREISAND (incredulous): I was pretty?

And Bacall confirms that she was. So looks *do* matter, after all? Movie, which side are you on?

Especially when the plot takes a very conventional turn. The unnoticed secretary (Loretta Young) removes her glasses and the handsome boss (Errol Flynn), who heretofore has treated her as an automaton instead of a woman, now cries, "Miss Johnson!...Clarice...Why, you're...you're..."

Assuming a confident, sexy pose in a black sheath with her hair in some cockeyed but no doubt trendy do while the camera eyes her from toe to top. Jeff Bridges much smitten. Streisand's students open-mouthed in awe. Pierce Brosnan (whom Streisand had secretly crushed on) eager to make her acquaintance.

Nevertheless, she ends up with the now amazed Bridges, and they reconcile outside in the street while the soundtrack gives us Luciano Pavarotti in what has become the single most popular vocal bit in all opera, "Nessun dorma" from Puccini's *Turandot*. Only it's not the soundtrack, we discover: it's a neighbor playing the recording and lip-synching to it, a cute touch.

It's almost a cute movie, and it seems all the more so when compared with its source, a French film of 1958 with what deceptively appears to bear the same title, *Le Miroir à Deux Faces*. In fact, this doesn't mean *The Mirror Has Two Faces* (which would correctly be *Le Miroir a Deux Faces*, without the *accent grave*) but rather *The Two-Sided Mirror*, referring to the heroine, Michèle Morgan.

Unlike Streisand, who starts her version of this tale looking just a little ungroomed, Morgan begins in "ugly" makeup, to be transformed into her usual beauty by a plastic surgeon. Her husband, played by the mononymous comedian Bourvil in a serious role, is no Jeff Bridges. And the film generally is talky and creepy despite a side trip for location shooting in Venice. Bourvil eventually murders the plastic surgeon, and Morgan ends with not a newly enamored spouse but an embittered and suspicious one, for Bourvil knows that every man will want her and she is thus forever out of his control.

What attracted Streisand to this drastic story is, presumably, its emphasis on physical appearance, for Streisand's career has been—in effect—a conversation with the American public on whether one should change one's looks (as Michèle Morgan does in *Le Miroir*) or simply pop them up a little (as Streisand does in *The Mirror*). This sixteenth Streisand movie, then, might have been a conclusive act in her output but for the way the full-frontal honesty of the "You made me feel unpretty" scene is overwhelmed by Hollywood's traditional solution: Clarice takes off her glasses. A snappy, quotable line helps, too. It was wonderful. There's no place like home. Print the legend.

This is instant art, by-the-numbers philosophy, a serious regression after *Yentl* and *The Prince Of Tides*. Worse, what comes after is what, in Hollywood, is categorized by a very precise generical description.

Dreck.

In *Meet the Fockers* (2004), Ben Stiller's fiancée (Terri Polo) and strait-laced parents (Robert De Niro, Blythe Danner) encounter Stiller's bohemian parents (Dustin Hoffman, Streisand) in a classic farcical premise, one perhaps best served in George S. Kaufman and Moss Hart's stage comedy *You Can't Take It With You* (1936). It's a very American idea: people vastly unlike one another can establish terms of agreement democratically.

The above are all at dinner, along with an infant in a crib who is related to the De Niro side of things. In the kitchen is Isabel (Alanna Ubach), a kind of family retainer, attractive and full-figured but directed and filmed with brash fascination by a man who has apparently never seen a woman's breasts before. His camera drools over her, apparently with comic intentions, the way an unenlightened stand-up comic of the 1950s would tell bimbo jokes. Hoffman, delighted to humiliate his son Stiller, merrily tells the party that, in his youth, Stiller would be "doing a little baziga to her passport photo," adding in the indicated gesture in case someone doesn't know what *baziga* denotes.

Rising above this, Stiller says Isabel looks great, and she reveals she has had a "boob job," which causes the baby to point at her. Yes, apparently the baby knows what a boob job is, and Isabel, keeping the level of wit high, acknowledges him with:

ISABEL: He's a *handsome* little Focker!

We already got the pun in the title, director. And now the baby makes grasping gestures with his fingers and runs his tongue over his lips so the director can cut to a close-up of Isabel's huge chest.

This is worked for laughs by everyone for quite some time, and by then a movie that was never going to be anything but stale farce has turned into such revolting trash that we wonder why Streisand, Hoffman, De Niro, and Danner, who have at various times distinguished themselves in cinema, wanted to participate in this project.

And could this be counted as a new kind of "doormat role" for Streisand? Instead of the woman who adores unappreciative men—roles she swore off long before this—she is now the actress who takes part in exploitative garbage comparable to *Whatever Happened To Baby Jane?*. It's not the love object that uses her, but Hollywood itself: Streisand and her co-stars become doormats for the industry (though of course they're well paid for their trouble).

I have said that *What's Up, Doc?* is witless and puerile, but at least it set out to revive a clever old Hollywood genre, screwball comedy. (And many feel it succeeded.) *Meet the Fockers* has no such defense; neither does the sequel, also with Streisand, **Little Fockers** (2010). These were hit films, though the critics scoffed, and, as with *For Pete's Sake*, they need not detain us further.

This leads us to Streisand's last film to date, **The Guilt Trip** (2012), about a mother and her unmarried son driving across the country to California. Thus the punning title, referring to not only the journey but also the way the mother (Streisand) uses emotional blackmail to manipulate her son (Seth Rogen).

In fact, she's a relentless nag, reminding, needling, controlling. It's weaponized natter. The son more or less puts up with it, trying to stop her but, when she resists, surrendering. True, at one point he explodes:

ROGEN: Just shut up! Just shut up!

but she blithely goes on hectoring him.

On a personal note: when I was very young, there was a movie starring Susan Hayward in which she was tried, convicted, and executed for murder. The poster showed her strapped into the electric chair with the title *I Want To Live!*. I always imagined my mother, in an alternate version, strapped into the electric chair with the title *I Want To Nag!*.

Guilt Trip is more or less unbearable for that reason: Streisand's mother is hateful without meaning to be. Anne Fletcher, *Guilt Trip*'s director, may have thought this was a comedy, but it is more of a horror film. Then, too, Seth Rogen is one of the most charmless performers in Hollywood today, and a mumbler as well. Someone trim and cute might have stabilized the son with youthful energy, especially as he spends most of the action feebly pitching his Sci-o-clean concoction—a household washing agent with organic ingredients—to uninterested business people.

Really, it's a loser's role. So it needs someone who at least looks as if he has something to offer—because near the film's end he suddenly shifts his entire approach and gets vital. He cracks a joke that is actually funny, and, having got everyone's amused attention, he runs with it by drinking his product: because it truly is *clean*. It's all the better that he gets to play this scene with Nora Dunn as a TV hostess, one of those suave experts at keeping a show moving with ad libs ("I'm impressed. I am"), good cheer, and the engaged curiosity of a professional housewife surrogate, who does this so we don't have to.

The film wakes up wonderfully at that point, but, in the long run, it's a drag. Yet, once again, Streisand is fine in an awful part. She seems to know what makes this woman so insanely irritating, and does it entirely without shtick. Referencing *Up the Sandbox*, forty years before, Streisand says, "I'm a grown woman, and the most exciting place I've ever been is ... Florida." Yet in the end she calls this cross-country trek "the best week of my life."

And that's where this chronicle ends, without the *Gypsy* that, twenty years before now, would have given Streisand a fine last entry in her surprisingly varied rota of roles. What other career counts Fanny Brice and Yentl, McCarthyism and screwball comedy, *Hello, Dolly!* and *Nuts*?

In fact, Streisand's recordings are more consistently satisfying than her films, even given a few duds and blunders along the way—the tentative approximation of contemporary pop in *What About Today?*, the incorrect *Classical Barbra*, the notion of giving the one-off *Guilty* a sequel. At that, it's really the First and Second Period and the beginning of the Third Period when Streisand is at her best, as her strangely finicky attitude toward recording led her eventually to avoid singing live with an orchestra and duet partners in the studio with her and to toy endlessly with the tapes till much of the vitality and flow have been edited away in favor of a "tighter" phrase, a "perfect" note.

This is why *Release Me*, Streisand's aforementioned CD of previously vaulted tracks from her past, seemed such a revelation. When it appeared, in 2012, these mostly youthful cuts reminded us of the avid, reckless singer Streisand had been, not the one who revises the heart out of her session tapes. This is one reason the public was so energized when she took up concert touring again: it was a chance to hear her singing *freely* for a change, Streisand herself rather than the digital version of herself drawn from so many different source tapes that she sounded like Frankenbarbra.

When Streisand recorded "Memory" (Andrew Lloyd Webber's Pucciniesque *Cats* anthem, released on the *Memories* compilation disc), she had Lloyd Webber himself producing the cut, along with an eighty-piece orchestra. As Lloyd Webber recalls in his 2018 memoirs, *Unmasked*, he believes "Memory" calls for "real emotion" instead of "technical perfection," and he was able to cajole Streisand into trying out a take live in the same room as the band. He thought her reading was a wee bit unsure in the first measures but utterly brilliant overall, and the players gave her a tremendous hand at the end.[74]

It would have been very special as it was. But, again, Streisand sometimes trades *live* for *processed*. Hearing the final version that she signed off on after revoicing bits here and there, Lloyd Webber was disappointed:

"Technically," he writes, "it was flawless," which is Lloyd Webber's way of saying that the very soul of the performance had been neutralized.[75]

It's all the more mystifying, then, that Streisand's last few films have been so unworthy of her talent. What perfectionism led her to the *Fockers* franchise—especially after she asserted herself in her rise from performer to director on the unique *Yentl*? It's not unusual for actors to direct in Hollywood, but it's not common, either. In fact, back in the very early days of the silent era, most directors started as actors, as "film director" was not yet a profession with a talent pool to draw on. It was, literally, an odd job.

As time went on, however, directing became specialized—but women directors in the talkie era have been rare. As rare, one might say, as a singer in the early 1960s updating the Songbook with passionate readings that listeners had never heard before. And to maintain a lifelong career doing the unusual is rarer yet.

It's still rarer when one looks unusual—only Streisand didn't. Again, it was her self-presentation, a combination of offbeat and confident. And in this culture, the offbeat aren't supposed—or allowed?—to be confident. Nevertheless, Streisand deals with the looks thing in many of her pictures—not just hers, everyone's. Robert Redford wasn't in *The Way We Were* to showcase his fine art of reserve, and even *The Prince Of Tides*, with all its complex views of human nature, still seems to settle on being about who deserves to be happy, and—as Hollywood has long told us—it isn't the character people.

No, they're sidekicks, employees, the Ritz Brothers. The movies are about It, the twenties term coined (by professional Hollywood Witch of Endor Elinor Glyn) to mean "charisma" but which everyone took to mean "sex appeal." Because who needs a synonym for charisma?

With all this working for her, Streisand should have closed out her movie career in something comparable to *The Misfits* (1961), a powerful tale that gives Clark Gable and Marilyn Monroe roles that show what ample imitators of life they really were rather than letting them give "movie star" walkthroughs. It reminds us, too, that one doesn't need talent to aspire in Hollywood. Gable and Monroe at first had only mystique to offer: he was as masculine as war and she improbably wondrous. Only at length, through seasoning, did they develop and then sharpen thespian skills.

Streisand, on the other hand, had talent. But, as we know, she didn't want to be a talent star. She hoped to get what Gable and Monroe had. As *Gypsy's* Madam Rose puts it, "Just wanted to be noticed."

It's that American notion that stardom is absolution without repentance, heaven the easy way: you get regarded as special just by being what you are. Streisand didn't want to have to carry a musical to be special. She wanted to be Streisand to be special. Hubbell, it's Katie.

NOTES

1. René Jordan, *The Greatest Star* (New York: G. P. Putnam's Sons, 1975), 68; William J. Mann, *Hello, Gorgeous* (Boston: Houghton Mifflin Harcourt, 2012), 176; Anne Edwards, *Streisand* (Boston: Little, Brown, 1997), 118.
2. Rex Reed, *Do You Sleep in the Nude?* (New York: Signet Books, 1969), 24.
3. James Spada, *Streisand* (New York: Crown, 1995), 174.
4. Ibid., 229.
5. Ibid., 269.
6. Tom Santopietro, *The Importance of Being Barbra* (New York: St. Martin's, 2006), 92.
7. Christopher Andersen, *Barbra* (New York: William Morrow, 2006), 327.
8. Ibid.
9. TriStar roundtable interview with twenty-four reporters at Four Seasons Hotel, Beverly Hills, October 29, 1996. Retrieved on barbra-archives.com.
10. Spada, 82.
11. Ibid., 70.
12. Jordan, 66.
13. Ibid.
14. *Just For the Record* (Columbia Records, unnumbered CD set), Disc One, Track Three.
15. Ibid.
16. Whitney Balliett, *American Singers* (New York: Oxford University Press, 1988), 149.
17. Spada, 108.
18. Mann, 224.
19. Randall Riese, *Her Name Is Barbra* (n.p.: Birch Lane Press, 1993), 148.
20. Edwards, 223.
21. Andersen, 116.
22. Ibid., 123.
23. Kevin Kelly, *One Singular Sensation* (New York: Doubleday, 1990), 168.
24. Jake Rossen, *Superman Vs. Hollywood* (Chicago: Chicago Review Press, 2008), 217.
25. Nikki Finke, "It Should Be Called 'Dickhead': Why Jon Peters' Proposal Sets New Low" (deadline.com, May 21, 2009).
26. Lewis Funke in the *New York Times*, October 23, 1961.
27. Jordan, 106; Andersen, 71.
28. Riese, 106; Andersen, 71.
29. Spada, 96.
30. Edwards, 122.

31. Harold Rome and Jerome Weidman, *I Can Get It For You Wholesale* (New York: Random House, 1962), 82.
32. Riese, 156.
33. Ibid., 161.
34. Ibid.
35. Ibid.
36. Jule Styne, Bob Merrill, and Isobel Lennart, *Funny Girl* (New York: Random House, 1964), 3.
37. Ibid., 7.
38. Ibid., 9.
39. barbra-archives.com/live/60s/funny-girl-broadway.
40. Spada, 155–56.
41. Personal interview with author, 1975.
42. Spada, 162.
43. *Coronet*, December, 1967. Retrieved on barbra-archives.com.
44. Spada, 500; Edwards, 494.
45. *The Second Barbra Streisand Album*, Columbia Records CK 57378.
46. Ibid.
47. *Streisand Live–1963*, Bel Canto 5001, Side Two, Band Three.
48. Ibid.
49. Ibid., Side Two, Band Five.
50. Ibid., Side One, Band One.
51. Helen Sheehy, *Eva Le Gallienne* (New York: Alfred A. Knopf, 1996), 369.
52. *Diana Ross and the Supremes Sing and Perform "Funny Girl,"* Motown MS672, Side Two, Band One.
53. Lisa Torem, Jimmy Webb Interview, pennyblackmusic.co.uk.
54. *Playboy*, September, 1976, The Playboy Interview (au. anonymous).
55. Streisand: *Release Me*, Columbia Records 88725 45855 2, Band One.
56. Andersen, 142.
57. Edwards, 250; Spada, 210.
58. Andersen, 149; Spada, 211.
59. Spada, 210.
60. Riese, 249–50.
61. Spada, 283.
62. Riese, 352.
63. Spada, 332.
64. Frank Pierson, "I Look at Barbra. She's Not Listening." Retrieved on afflictor.com, December 19, 2014.
65. Frank Pierson, "My Battles With Barbra and Jon," *New West*, November 22, 1976, retrieved on web.archive.org.
66. Spada, 354.
67. International Movie Database, *King Kong* trivia; *Saturday Night Live*, Season Two, Episode Twelve, Tom Snyder sketch. Retrieved on snltranscripts.jt.org/76/76/tomorrow.phtml.
68. " 'Yentl,' A Drama With Barbra Streisand," *New York Times*, November 17, 1983.
69. barbra-archives.com/films/nut.
70. Ibid.
71. Ibid.

72. Pat Conroy, *The Prince Of Tides* (Boston: Houghton Mifflin, 1986), 214.
73. Ibid., 383.
74. Andrew Lloyd Webber, *Unmasked* (New York: Harper, 2018), 371.
75. Ibid.
76. Margaret Styne, barbra-archives.com/live/60s/funny_girl_broadway.
77. Ibid.

BIBLIOGRAPHY

René Jordan's *The Greatest Star* (Putnam, 1975) was written so long ago that it seems fresh, like the first telling: which it in fact was. As the author had only just heard the stories from Barry Dennen, Bob Schulenberg, Arthur Laurents, Harold Rome, John Patrick, Jule Styne, and Mike Wallace, much of the Streisand lore dates back to Jordan's interviews.

He's especially good on *Funny Girl*, though he is inclined to honor Garson Kanin's martyred version of what happened, and Jordan suggests that *Up the Sandbox* would have benefited if the fantasies had been disintegrated from the narrative and turned into comic episodes. Thus, the expensive location shooting in Africa "would have been ten times funnier in a fake Marx Brothers–style jungle of papier-mâché and tatterdemalion lianas." Yes, but the point is that Margaret is desperate. The fantasies are her escape, not her playtime.

"She wasn't kooky," says one of Streisand's childhood friends in Randall Riese's *Her Name Is Barbra* (Birch Lane, 1993). "There was [*sic*] no purple eyebrows or green teeth." Riese's version of the young Streisand suggests that the very nonconformist young woman of her first professional days—the "too special" artist who made traditional impresarios such as Goddard Lieberson uneasy—was Streisand's calculated show-biz ploy, an invention designed to turn the world into one big audition.

Three times as long as René Jordan's book, Riese's was the first major biography, very well researched and fast-moving, with a strong knowledge of how Hollywood works. This allows him to explain at length how Streisand could fail to be Oscar-nominated for directing the Oscar-winning *Prince Of Tides*—and note that (as Riese reminds us) other directors of Best Pictures who failed to get nominated themselves include Steven Spielberg.

Riese gives also a sound treatment of Allan Miller's coaching of Streisand on the stage *Funny Girl*. One cannot be too emphatic about that show's importance in the forging of Streisand's future in acting; there were times during the Boston tryout (that is, before Jerome Robbins was brought in to doctor the show, in Philadelphia) when it seemed as though the suffering production might have to be put out of its misery before the New York premiere. To headline a show that implodes in tryout can destroy a tender career. True, Mary Martin overcame it.* But many do not.

---

* Martin's disaster was *Dancing In the Streets*, in her first starring role on Broadway, after her flashy emergence singing "My Heart Belongs To Daddy" in *Leave It To Me!* (1938). The new show even had a "Daddy" knockoff, "Got a Bran' New Daddy," though this time Daddy was not a rich protégeur but an equal match. "No sables I own," Martin explained, "it's love alone." While we're pausing, it's worth noting that, in all Streisand's

Given Streisand's talent and determination, she would have recovered in some way, and she already had her recording outlet, generally separated from her acting (except in show albums and movie soundtracks). Still, if *The Way We Were* remains Streisand's ultimate movie-star credential, *Funny Girl* was the passport to her entire career. It is impossible to imagine the Streisand we know without it.

James Spada gives us two Streisand books, the pictures-and-text *Streisand: The Woman and the Legend* (Dolphin, 1981) and the more substantial *Streisand: Her Life* (Crown, 1995). Spada is a fan in the best sense, knowledgeable about not only the hard data but also the folklore, and he seems to be right where no one else is in the always useful quoting of a Streisand collaborator. Thus, we hear Jerome Robbins on how, amid all the changes that *Funny Girl* went through in its protracted tryout, Streisand would absorb new material instantly and tear through lines and numbers tossed in that afternoon without an error at the evening's performance: "During the rehearsal, in her untidy, exploratory, meteoric fashion, she [is] never afraid [to] try anything.... That night onstage...a sorceress sails through every change without hesitation."

So Spada takes us into the auditorium with the *I Can Get It For You Wholesale* team when Streisand gives the famous audition that put her on Broadway; and when a CBS executive can't fasten his thinking around Streisand's intention to present her television specials without guest stars, warning that without Dick Van Dyke or Andy Griffith kibitzing, *My Name Is Barbra* will do "daytime ratings"; and even when Streisand makes her New York stage debut, at sixteen, in the aforementioned *Driftwood*. And there's the playwright, Maurice Tei Dunn, recalling Streisand as "sinister" and "mysterious." Even then, he says, "she seemed to have a history, a past."

This is very different from Streisand's reputation as a kook, that now nearly forgotten word that comes up repeatedly in the early chapters of every Streisand biography. But to be a kook is to carry baggage. In the Golden Age, it was the rule that a performer who punches out as an oddball would have to go on playing oddball roles thereafter. As usual making her own rules, Streisand played two such parts on Broadway but underwent a transition in her films, getting progressively less odd.

Thus, Fanny Brice is odd only when on stage; Dolly is less odd than impishly manipulative; and Daisy is odd but Melinda isn't. And after those three assumptions, Streisand moved out of the odd category. Even in *What's Up, Doc?*, in which she's supposedly a screwball, she turns it on and off at will, just as Streisand herself did when starting out.

Jordan, Riese, and Spada were working within a grasp of Streisand's artistic milieu, but Anne Edwards' *Streisand: A Biography* (Little, Brown, 1997) is of the now prevalent genre in which the biographer lacks familiarity with the subject, compiling data without discerning the cultural substructure that contextualizes events.

Not surprisingly, Edwards fumbles many names and titles, and often more than once, so these aren't typos: "Lisl" in *The Sound Of Music* (it's Liesl); "I Am Sixteen Going on Seventeen" (there's no "I Am" in the title, and this is in any case the second verse, with different lyrics from the first); the Jan Hus Theatre placed in New York's "Yorkville" (it's in a neighborhood to the south of Yorkville); *The New Yorker*'s "Roger Whitaker" (it's Rogers E. M. Whitaker); Sydney Chaplin's wife as "Noelle Adams" (it's Adam); Katharine Hepburn's drag role placed in *Christopher Strong* (it's in *Sylvia Scarlett*);

---

tour through the Songbook, she tended to avoid the novelty numbers like these "Daddy" pieces (especially after her early "Who's Afraid Of the Big Bad Wolf" era), preferring ballads, anthems, situation numbers of the Sondheim kind, and character songs such as "Adelaide's Lament."

"Butterfly" (it's *ButterFly*); the original *Yentl* screenwriter "Ted Allen" (it's Allan); and so on. Granted, these are small errors, but this many of them points to a meager grounding in this field. Edwards is also sympathetic to Jon Peters, which makes her unique among writers on the doings of Hollywood.

Christopher Andersen's *Barbra: The Way She Is* (William Morrow, 2006), like Edwards' book, is not partisan. He looks on, critically, entirely from the outside. Nevertheless, he has done his research, and, while his volume is shorter than Spada's and Riese's, he touches the known points in the Streisand dossier.

All the classic quotations and stories are here, along with details unique to his report, as when Katharine Hepburn recalls how "sophisticated" the real Fanny Brice was. "Absolutely regal," Hepburn calls her—and who would know better than Hepburn, who often seemed like Hollywood's personal Queen Of the Lot? She says Streisand's Brice was far from the real thing, "but who the hell cares?" As I've said, *Funny Girl* isn't a documentary study of Brice's life and love, and, as far as Hollywood (by way of Broadway, of course) bios go, the film has a certain "truthiness."

Hepburn is linked to Streisand if only because they shared the single Best Actress Oscar Streisand ever won, in the famous tie for which Hepburn was busy elsewhere and Streisand showed up in that see-through Arnold Scaasi pantsuit, which looked especially outré next to presenter Ingrid Bergman's stunning Old World evening gown. It was a moment when Streisand's refusal to play by others' rules caught her being not just nonconformist but, next to the radiant Bergman, incorrectly prepared.

Hepburn did tell Andersen of another link with Streisand, however: "We are [both] monsters of our own creation." And that could be one definition of a movie star, whether in the glamour, talent, or acting categories. The monsters play in a style past realism— Joan Crawford, Jack Nicholson, Brad Pitt. They're monsters not only in richness of personality but in their ability to expand their fascination by holding something back, encouraging the public to seek them out again and again, trying to collect that missing piece. Few who lack that quality ever break through to real fame; they might as well be Andrea Leeds.

But does Streisand work that way? One reason she talks her co-stars and director to death on how to play every scene is that she doesn't want to leave out a single nuance. And yet, as Robert Redford noticed on *The Way We Were* (quoted in Andersen), "She'd talk and talk and talk, we'd get down to doing it and she'd do just what she was going to do from the beginning."

William J. Mann's *Hello, Gorgeous* (Houghton Mifflin Harcourt, 2012) covers only the first years of Streisand's career, ending in spring 1964, during the New York run of *Funny Girl*. Admitting that he came to the Streisand saga as a "novice," knowing little about her, Mann even so uncovered a great deal more than had previously been published. This includes, for instance, material on Streisand's relationships with her first managers and PR people, all of whom dropped out or were pushed out, to be replaced by the ever faithful Martin Erlichman. Mann quotes one of the casualties, Ted Rozar, who found Streisand insatiably intent on being the focus of attention beyond anyone else in his life. As Mann writes it, Rozar was alienated by "the furious narcissism that blazed within her, fueled by...insecurities." Streisand wanted her own personal witch doctor, "who would travel with her wherever she went...to hold her hand, fight her battles, tell her she was wonderful, and be her slave."

Mann's approach is somewhat revisionist, especially about the colossal comings and goings of the participants in the *Funny Girl* saga, and he notes that Garson Kanin's "latter-day self-embellishments" to the effect that he had to convince Ray Stark to cast Streisand as Fanny are sheer fantasy: Stark "was her ardent champion right from the start." In all, Mann is very good at characterizing the figures in Streisand's life, with a novelist's precision in catching quirks of personality.

All the books described to this point are biographies. Tom Santopietro's *The Importance Of Being Barbra* (St. Martin's, 2006), on the other hand, is an analysis of Streisand as person and artist, with chapters on "Recordings," "Film," "Concerts," and such, but also one on "Politics." Its epigraph reads, in a statement Streisand made in 1996, "I'm a feminist, Jewish, opinionated, liberal woman. I push a lot of buttons."

Santopietro is refreshingly independent in his own opinions, and he brings much unusual material into discussion. For example, we take it for granted that Streisand's recitals are huge moneymakers. But Santopietro points out that *Je M'Appelle Barbra* and the following *Simply Streisand* didn't go gold (that is, selling half a million units) till thirty-five years after their release. Too, he notes that those really rather empty encomiums written by Songbook composers on her earliest albums were on one level a matter of their self-interest, as Arlen, Styne, and Rodgers were not only artists but "businessmen with publishing interests...in a musical world increasingly dominated by rock music." Streisand's success was their success.

Santopietro is especially good on what's wrong with *A Star Is Born*, such as the ridiculous scene in which Streisand shows her contempt for a gig singing an advertising jingle for cat food by laughing till she—and the other two Oreos—lose the job. As Santopietro points out, the three of them seem amused to give up the paycheck simply because their lead singer is too grand for commercial ditties, or cat food, or even cats.

Such nonsense in a supposedly realistic story is why the critics found the movie's storytelling so flimsy. Still, above this, Santopietro sees the vilifying of Streisand's movie (and it was hers, all the way along) as the continued assault on "a woman mocked and misunderstood...and daring to crash through the barriers in her way." It's Streisand as Cinderella, the author says, using that name and myth, explaining why "audiences forgave all, even when the critics forgave nothing."

And, yes, Streisand has always been more than Streisand the singer and actress: she is Streisand the Streisand, a personality quite aside from the artistic achievements. As she says, she pushes buttons—and yet I say again that she is not a Warholian figure, celebrated for what she represents, because no one can know her without having seen and heard what she does. Daffy Duck and the Kardashians are Warholian. Streisand, rather, is a collection of very various performances.

Neal Gabler's *Barbra Streisand: Redefining Beauty, Femininity, and Power* (Yale, 2016) is also an analysis, one ruled on every page by the notion of Streisand as an above all Jewish figure. As I prefer to write post-racially and -ethnically wherever possible, I am not in sympathy with this approach. Also, I don't see how Streisand's family background sheds any light on her art. Is there such a thing as Jewish singing of the Songbook or of "Stoney End"? Is someone ready to define Jewish acting? There are Jewish holidays, Jewish recipes, and Jewish novels. Streisand even filmed a Jewish story, as we know, in *Yentl*. But what on earth would a Jewish *performance* be? Gabler's book is part of a series called Jewish Lives, so apparently there is a call for this approach, at least at Yale University Press. I don't find it at all enlightening.

Now we move to fiction, for Garson Kanin's revenge on the *Funny Girl* he was fired from, in *Smash* (Viking, 1980). It's a backstager, about a musical based on the life of Nora Bayes, a contemporary of Fanny Brice and very much like her, though Bayes worked in plain show-biz English rather than a Jewish accent. *Shine On, Harvest Moon*—Kanin's imaginary show—is also very much like *Funny Girl*, as Kanin supplies versions of Jule Styne, Ray Stark, Carol Haney, John Patrick, and possibly many others of the company that he headed until he didn't.

Perhaps for legal reasons, the leading woman—referred to only as Star—is both like Streisand and unlike her, and makes very few appearances. She is said to be relatively new to the stage, as Streisand was, and an enthusiastic rehearser, which was true of Streisand on that production. And at one point, when the director tells her, "You get better all the time, and it's because you're learning," Star replies, "Don't butter me up, buster. I'm not a piece of toast." Is that Streisand, in that impatient tone, cutting through the show-biz flattery?

To cover himself, Kanin carefully has the Styne-like figure actually bring up *Funny Girl* and Streisand by name, when he is arguing with both producer and director over whether or not to interpolate some of Bayes' actual numbers into *Shine On, Harvest Moon*. Of course, the real Styne had the same argument during *Funny Girl* over Fanny Brice's actual numbers. And Styne no doubt also said, as Kanin's songwriter does, that they can "put in any goddamn thing you want" when they make the film, because "Who gives a shit what's in a movie, anyhow?" So *Shine On, Harvest Moon* is *Funny Girl* in effect but not, so to say, biographically.

What makes *Smash* so fascinating is its authentic look at what happens during the making of a big Broadway musical, with a ton of skullduggery, illicit sex (a chorus boy befriends the stage manager to get the key understudy job), and terrific disappointments for some. It's especially interesting to watch the development of a number called "Big Town," for a pair of minor players while Star makes a costume change. Bit by bit, the two "live" themselves into the song until it stops the show during the Philadelphia tryout. This infuriates Star, so the number is cut.

But it's too good to lose: so now the male player is doing it with Star and the female player is denied her big chance. More: Star begins to oversing in order to steal the number, and her partner (the male player), trying to keep up with her, bursts a blood vessel, leaving Star to take over the scene as her solo. Finally, Ray Stark (or whoever Kanin had in mind) sneaks into the orchestra pit before a performance, confiscates all the charts for the song, and disposes of them without telling the conductor or his band. They don't find out till they reach "Big Town" during an actual performance and suddenly realize they have no music to play from.

I've taken extra time with *Smash* because there are few books, whether non-fiction or yarns like this one, that are so imbued with genuine theatrical atmosphere. Kanin may not have been a great director of musicals, but he was steeped in Broadway lore and used all of it here. It reminds me of the middle-aged former chorus boys and stage managers I knew when I first came to New York, mentors teaching young gaylings about the show-biz past. No one knows a production like its stage manager, and these fellows gave me so many stories that after thirty-odd books I haven't used them all. In fact, one of the tales they told, about how Gertrude Lawrence was able to finish the first dream in *Lady In the Dark* decked out for fashion and then, after two seconds of blackout reappear in the psychiatrist's office in street clothes (to the audience's excited wonder), is recounted as well by Kanin in *Smash*.

Last, for research purposes, we should take note of Matt Howe's self-described "unofficial" site, *Barbra Streisand Archives*, very elaborate yet easy to navigate, with a tremendous amount of data, anecdotes, unused recording-cover art, quotations from Streisand career participants, and so on. Just for instance, the *Funny Girl* pages include a load of information about the tryout in both Boston and Philadelphia, not least of all the songlists from the playbills that prove how much in flux the score was. It's almost amusing, too, to see the show's New York ads, with the top ticket price of $8.80 ($5.50 at matinees).

Howe's *Funny Girl* pages give us as well an interesting new view of how Fran Stark (Fanny Brice's daughter, we recall) felt about Streisand's playing her mother. Of course, the standard telling is that Madame Stark hated Streisand but had to accept her in the face of unanimous enthusiasm by the creatives, including her husband, who was producing the show to get a hit movie version out of it, not to placate his wife's hauteur.

But Jule Styne's then wife, Margaret, is on the *Archives* site recalling Fran saying, "That girl play my mother? I wouldn't have her as my maid"[76]—and never veering from that view even after the show proved a hit and a star was born. It reminds us that Streisand has been so thorough an artist and personality that she was bound to set off controversies even aside from her statement about the obvious ways in which she, as she said, "pushes a lot of buttons."

"I've since realized," Margaret Styne concludes, "that the world is split into those who love Barbra and those who don't."[77]

INDEX